THE
WALL STREET
JOURNAL
on
MANAGING

ADDING VALUE THROUGH SYNERGY

THE
WALL STREET
JOURNAL
on
MANAGING

David Asman

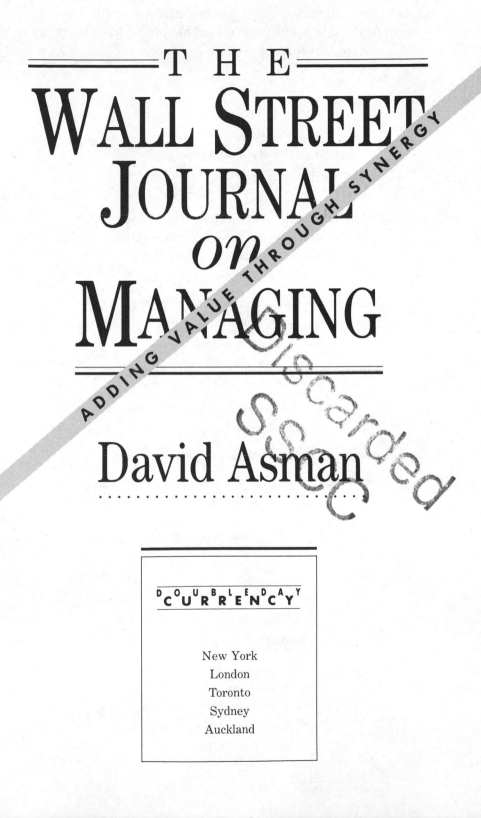

DOUBLEDAY
CURRENCY

New York
London
Toronto
Sydney
Auckland

Dedicated to Barbara Phillips: the unsung hero, who copy editing behind the scenes, has added the polish (and more than a little substance) to the pieces collected herein.

—D.A.

PUBLISHED BY DOUBLEDAY

a division of Bantam Doubleday Dell
Publishing Group, Inc., 666 Fifth Avenue,
New York, New York 10103

DOUBLEDAY and the portrayal of an anchor
with a dolphin are trademarks of Doubleday,
a division of Bantam Doubleday Dell
Publishing Group, Inc.

Doubleday/Currency offers new ideas on business. For more
information, please write:

Doubleday/Currency
666 Fifth Avenue
New York, NY 10103

The Wall Street Journal is a registered trademark of
Dow Jones & Company, Inc.

Library of Congress Cataloging-in-Publication Data

The Wall Street Journal on managing: adding value through
synergy/edited by David Asman. — 1st ed.
  p. cm.
  1. Management. I. Asman, David. II. Wall Street journal.
HD31.W245 1990
658.4—dc20   89-27635
                                                   CIP

ISBN 0-385-26492-5

DESIGNED BY CHRIS WELCH
April 1990
FIRST EDITION
RRH

Contents

SYNERGY WITH YOUR EMPLOYEES   65

SYNERGY IN THE WORLD MARKET 185
· ·

As the roaring 1980s ground to a close, their spirit of enterprise and almost limitless expansion was replaced by the beginnings of retrenchment and a nagging suspicion that disaster was just around the corner. Like the new millionaire who has risen too far, too fast, we have become fearful of our success: We're afraid of losing what we thought we could never attain.

However, we mustn't allow our tendency to romanticize the past cloud our vision of the future. Yes, the 1980s was an era of expansion. But it was also a decade fraught with fear—fear of takeovers, fear of the deficit, fear of foreign competition, fear of a "rusting" industrial sector, fear of the "hollow corporation." We experienced a severe recession in the beginning of the period and a frightening stock market crash toward the end.

And we came through it all.

That's the real lesson of the 1980s: Despite all the very genuine fears and the dire warnings, we generally pulled through far better than anyone dreamed we would.

Of course, as always, the business landscape was peppered with the unfortunate few who ended the decade worse off than they were at its beginning. But the exciting lesson from which both winners and losers can learn is that there was a common link to the successful strategies of the 1980s. That link can be summed up in one word: synergy. By combining seemingly incompatible elements, managers discovered new ways to solve old problems. And they did so with courage; rather than fighting those things that scared them, successful managers found ways to work with the objects of their fears to create a superior product or service.

In 1980, business journals and magazines were filled with talk of foreigners squeezing out American business interests. Today, most of the talk is about how to do business in Japan or prepare for Europe 1992.

In 1980, the cost of labor in the United States was threatening our international competitiveness, and no one saw a way out. But the decline of a union voting bloc, combined with inventive new strategies like employee stock ownership plans, softened the barriers between labor and management; both sides realized if they didn't find synergy between their own goals, they would be out of work.

In 1980, investors were counting out the U.S. industrial sector. Scarce capital was instead being channeled into the more competitive and more inventive service economy. But by adopting service sector management techniques, and employing state-of-the-art technology, the "rust belt" found synergy with the modern age and is now keeping pace with—and occasionally surpassing—the service sector.

In 1980, manufacturers viewed the consumer marketplace as a fixed pie chart: "I can only get a bigger slice by taking some of yours." But as the market became flooded with electronic items that consumers gobbled up, manufacturers learned that the marketplace was more like a rubber band than a pie, able to accommodate practically any product or service that stood out for its efficiency or innovativeness. Think back to when Hollywood executives wanted to burn all video rental stores, thinking the video craze would severely cut into their movie-theater market. Then they discovered that the synergy between the two products led to an exponential growth in both markets.

Finding synergies in the eighties became the hallmark of success.

This book will explore the synergies that keep managers from giving in to their fears. Through carefully documented case studies, many times told by the participants themselves, this collection brings together selections from one of the most popular regular columns in *The Wall Street Journal*, the "Manager's Journal."

Throughout the eighties, this column tracked a huge variety of business strategies. But in preparing this collection, the editor has gathered those articles in which managers have wrestled with the concept of synergy in their own fields. The book has been completely updated. The editor and the authors reviewed the articles and, where appropriate, have added new examples and developments to make the pieces even more timely.

The book is divided into four sections. Each section combines practical advice with the larger economic issues that shape our business environment.

- In "Synergy Within Your Marketplace," the authors focus on challenges presented by the three major elements that define the marketplace within which you operate: your product, your customers, and your competitors. Managers describe their strategies for success as well as their encounters with disaster.
- After refining your product and defining your market, you must address yourself to that activity that defines your role in the workplace: structuring the time and activity of others. "Synergy with Your Employees" shows how best to motivate your work force at the lowest cost.
- Now you're ready for strategy. "Synergy with the Market" looks at the larger economic issues about which we so often feel helpless. Practical advice is offered about how best to weather the barometric swings of a most unpredictable market. Special attention is given on how to better understand and survive the world of mergers and acquisitions.
- How to develop a "Synergy with the Global Market" is no longer a question that concerns just the corporate giants. And it's no wonder. Since the technological revolution has shrunk the size of the global marketplace, even the smallest enterprise can feel the pressures of (and the opportunities within) markets far from home. This section demystifies foreign markets—particularly the Japanese

market—and places specific emphasis on how to break into them.

When preparing the crisp, focused articles that make up this collection, great care was taken to make sure the material is easily understood and jargon-free. The reader is presented with practical advice based on the experience of those managers who have grappled with the subjects about which they are expert:

The founder of a chain of restaurants describes how he had to develop a better synergy between his employees and his customers before he lost everything.

A top investment analyst explains how to spot synergy between your company and the stock market BEFORE your company becomes the object of a takeover.

A manufacturing plant manager shows how to "retool" your work force to adapt to new, modern machinery.

A chief executive explains how to keep employee medical costs down without alienating your workers.

These stories are described from the front line, not from the sidelines.

There is something for everyone in this collection, whether the authors are describing synergies with foreign markets, synergies within the industrial marketplace, synergies between service providers and customers, or synergies between employees and employers.

The world of synergies in business is not as complicated as it might seem. But managers in the 1990s need to be aware of those synergies that kept businesses roaring through the 1980s.

It may well be true that tough times lie before us. But it's important to remember that the road we have just traveled so successfully had just as many potential hazards as the road ahead. Applying the proper synergies helped many managers smooth over what could have been a much bumpier ride. *The Wall Street Journal* on Management is a perfect road map to make sure tomorrow's managers don't get stuck along the way.

THE
WALL STREET
JOURNAL
on
MANAGING

ADDING VALUE THROUGH SYNERGY

SYNERGY WITHIN YOUR MARKETPLACE

T his chapter explores the three primary elements that fashion your company's marketplace: (1) your product; (2) your customers; and (3) your competitors. Developing a proper synergy between these three elements can result in a turnaround even in the most hopeless case.

One such reversal took place in the smokestack industries, despite the most dire predictions of analysts.

In March 1986, *BusinessWeek* featured a collection of articles under the heading "The Hollow Corporation." According to *BusinessWeek*, foreign products had so overpowered those produced by American manufacturers that a new kind of American company had evolved: "Manufacturers that do little or no manufacturing and are increasingly becoming service-oriented. They may perform a host of profit-making functions—from design to distribution—but lack their own production base. In contrast to traditional manufacturers, they are hollow corporations."

While the growth of our service sector was impressive, it would never pay out as much as hard industry and would do little to improve the nation's GNP. We had, in effect, emasculated our country's productive base by focusing precious capital on the razzle-dazzle of the service sector at the expense of our industrial muscle.

This neat theory turned out to be dead wrong. A June 1989 Morgan Stanley study by Stephen S. Roach reports that "a stunning turnaround has occurred in Smokestack America—

evidenced by a rebound in profitability, a restoration of trend productivity, and the first inklings of improvement on the foreign trade front." In fact, the question the author of this study now finds worthy of including in the title of his report is: "Can Services Learn from Manufacturing?"

What the experts missed was the Herculean commitment American manufacturers made to improving product quality, process design, and customer relations. Pioneering managers invested enormous amounts of time, energy, and resources integrating technology into what had been purely mechanical methods of production. And management techniques geared toward these changes were also put in place. A synergy had been developed that led to higher productivity and, for many companies, survival.

Owners and managers of service companies likewise invested throughout the 1980s in information technologies. Of course, sometimes in their emphasis on technology, service organizations lost sight of the human element; relations with customers suffered. Service providers—who had led the way in technological integration—were forced to rethink (and reinvent) their commitment to their customers.

These exciting developments are documented in this chapter by many of the pioneers themselves. Their discoveries and techniques proved the experts wrong. No one knows the U.S. marketplace like our own managers. And in this section, they tell their own stories.

A GOOD COMPETITOR IS NOT ALWAYS A DEAD COMPETITOR

by Michael E. Porter

"**M**y *competitors make* my life miserable. I would like to gain share against all of them, particularly the competitor with the strategy closest to mine." Right? Wrong.

Good competitors can improve a firm's position in a variety of ways. For example, they can make it easier for a company to differentiate its product. International Business Machines Corporation had difficulty securing premium prices for its management information system software until several "Big Eight" accounting firms entered the business and charged high prices for their version of similar software.

Competitors can also serve unattractive segments of the market. General Electric Company's profits in turbine generators have benefited from the fact that Westinghouse Electric Corporation serves the price-sensitive, smaller electric utilities.

On a macro level, competitors can help to stimulate the overall growth of particular industries. How? Competitors share the cost of market development; they help fight against substitute products; they frequently help standardize or legitimize a new technology; and they can lend credibility to an industry and raise its overall image, as Century 21 Real Estate Corporation has done for real estate brokerage.

Competitors' strategies may also work to reinforce desirable changes in industry structure, such as reducing the price sensitivity of buyers or raising entry barriers. In soft drinks, for example, Coke and Pepsi both have competed historically through heavy consumer advertising and new product introductions. They both have prospered, but their competition has made it difficult for smaller competitors to enter the market and grow.

The presence of good competitors can also deter from entering other competitors that are more dangerous in the long run. Good competitors block logical entry paths and crowd distribution channels. Rivals can also serve as the first line of defense against newcomers who do enter, absorbing the cost of battling with them.

A final benefit of competitors is the role they serve as motivators. A viable competitor can be an important impetus for reduction of costs, improvement of products, and keeping pace with technological developments. American Telephone and Telegraph Company, for example, is showing signs of benefiting from the emergence of serious competitors in the U.S. market.

Good strategists use competitors as motivators, highlighting them as targets for the entire organization. Squibb thinks about Merck this way in pharmaceuticals, for example, as does Komatsu about Caterpillar in construction equipment. Conversely, industry histories are littered with examples of firms with no viable competitors who were ultimately destroyed by their own complacency or failure to adapt to changing market conditions.

A good competitor has a strategy that does not attack you head-on. In the copier field, Eastman Kodak Company is a good competitor for Xerox Corporation. Kodak concentrates on the high-volume segment and emphasizes image quality and productivity-enhancing features such as collators and sorters, while Xerox competes with a full line for a broader range of users. And Kodak does not view copiers as part of an office automation strategy that would justify accepting low profits in pursuit of market share, unlike other copier companies.

Contrast this with oil companies' entrance into the fertilizer and chemical markets. Oil companies had goals that were incompatible with companies that viewed fertilizer and chemicals as their core business. Flush with cash and desiring revenues substantial enough to show up on their financial statements, oil companies made massive investments in new capacity that exacerbated industry capacity-utilization problems. They competed on price rather than research and development and customer service, accelerating the commoditization of the industry they entered.

Managing your competitors requires you to:

Know your good competitors. Many companies do not recognize which of their rivals are good competitors and which are not, leading them to pursue across-the-board moves, or worse yet, to attack good competitors while ignoring bad ones. In the process, industry structure can be severely damaged.

Protect the viability of good competitors. Even a good competitor can undermine your position, or even the attractiveness of the whole industry, if driven to desperation. Desperate competitors have a tendency to resort to desperate actions, like departing from established pricing structures. They also look for salvation by being acquired, and new ownership sometimes transforms them into bad competitors. Bausch and Lomb was too successful against its good competitors, for example, and one by one they sold out to larger companies anxious to crack the growing soft-contact-lens market.

Maintain industry balance. This requires continual attention and effort even if you face good competitors. Time has a way of changing competitors' goals and circumstances. Having occupied for years a relatively profitable Number Two position, for example, a competitor may forget the reasons that it did not try to become Number One. Periodic competitive moves and quick retaliation to errant competitor behavior are crucial for maintaining industry stability.

Select whom you compete with. There are a variety of ways you can influence the array of competitors you face. You can retaliate selectively against new entries or companies trying to reposition themselves. Or, if some entry is inevitable, you can license your technology to a firm with the characteristics of a good competitor.

Competitors are both a blessing and a curse. Seeing them as only a curse runs the risk of eroding not only a firm's competitive advantage but also the industry's structure as a whole. A firm must compete aggressively but not indiscriminately.

Mr. Porter is a professor at the Harvard Business School. His most recent book on strategy is The Competitive Advantage of Nations *(The Free Press, 1988).*

CUTTING YOUR COMPETITOR TO THE QUICK

·····································

by Gary Reiner

A *senior manager* at Xerox in 1990 could easily reflect on the value of quick product development. From 1978 to 1982, the company's worldwide market share in copiers dropped to 45 percent from 80 percent. Thus, in the early 1980s, Xerox initiated a sweeping set of changes in the way it approached new-product development. By 1984, the time required to bring a product to market was reduced from roughly six years to three. Wayland Hicks, president of Xerox's reprographics business group at the time, commented: "We cut in half the resources and the time we used to require to develop comparable products. . . . [This] will keep Xerox's customers from going to someone else." Indeed, Xerox management saw a growth in share to almost 60 percent by 1987, improved product quality, lower product costs, and higher employee morale.

Why has faster product development become so critical? For one thing, product life cycles have shrunk and therefore, to keep up with market needs, new products must be developed more quickly. Product life cycles have shortened thanks in part to improved design technologies (e.g., computer-aided design and computer-aided manufacturing), which speed up the development process. More flexible components, such as semi-custom microprocessors, have also contributed to the trend. And aggressive, mostly Asian competitors have stepped up the pace by adopting powerful approaches to new-product development.

Compaq Computer Corporation (the company that took only four years to go from start-up to Fortune 500 status) attributes its success to rapid new-product development—six to nine months, far ahead of the industry's typical twelve to eighteen months. Compaq was the first to introduce a transportable PC following IBM's desktop PC introduction. After staying roughly even with IBM on introductions of 286 machines, Compaq leaped ahead of IBM with a PC based on Intel's more powerful 386 microprocessor. Compaq worked closely with Intel to ensure compatibility of the 386 chip with existing PC software; once Intel finished redesigning the chip, it took Compaq only one and a half months to introduce the DeskPro 386.

What are the benefits of faster new-product development? They are straightforward, yet so many businesses seem not to focus as much on speed as they should. Some of the key external benefits include: (1) freedom to charge more, because prices typically decline for a given feature set—such as the old two-head VCR—once a more innovative feature set—such as the four-head VCR—comes on line; (2) the ability to incorporate the latest available technology into a product; (3) more accurate market forecasts, because time horizons are shorter; and (4) increased market share, resulting from filling a vacuum in customer needs and from the brand advantage associated with being first.

Internal benefits are equally important: (1) since faster development times allow a greater number of product development experiences in a given time period, production developers become proficient more quickly; (2) since faster development times are impossible without more open information flows in the organization, employees develop more trust and loyalty across functions and vertically in the organization; (3) the classic "vicious cycle" of product development is avoided—if the development process is slow, frequent changes in the market force the management to constantly rework the design, slowing the process further.

Faster developers continually gain on slower developers as their experience improves—the gap increases. Honda, for example, can design a new car in two years, compared with GM's five to six years. In ten years, Honda's employees will have been through the new-product-development process five times, GM's, only twice.

There are a number of principles that fast new-product-development companies seem to abide by. Clearly each company has its own personality and culture and, therefore, implements these principles somewhat differently. But the common elements appear to dwarf the distinct ones. The following are some of the key common elements:

- Time is the key variable. Cost and quality goals are, of course, important, but the clock or calendar is the dictator.
- Each new-product-development project is managed by a small, focused, decision-oriented, and empowered team. In many cases this team consists of one member from each of the relevant functions—marketing, developing, and, particularly, manufacturing.
- The team takes the development effort through four steps: definition, design, manufacture ramp-up (the time it takes to work the bugs out of the manufacturing process and gear up for high-volume manufacturing), and improvement (a step that enables either cost reduction or feature enhancement).
- The team members are all in the same location and, in fact, often work in the same room at important times during the project.
- Design specifications for the product do not change after the new product or innovation has been defined by the team.
- Internal capabilities necessary to speed up the product development (i.e., market research, design libraries, new technologies, cost-estimating models, and competitor tracking) are anticipated, invested in, and updated actively so that they never slow down the process.
- Senior management layers are few. The role of senior management is to ensure that the product teams have the

appropriate resources, incentives, and environment to be fast.

Fast new-product development has risks, basically similar to those encountered with just-in-time manufacturing: Moving at breakneck speeds emphasizes organizational deficiencies. But it is better to identify and correct these deficiencies than to allow competitors to enhance market positions that will be increasingly difficult to win back. Improved market share, increased internal expertise, and the brand enhancement associated with new-product development will be your reward.

Mr. Reiner specializes in new-product-development programs as a vice president of Boston Consulting Group.

BUSINESS IS ENOUGH OF A TRIAL; WHY GO TO COURT?
. . . .
by James F. Henry

I*f you were* in the middle of an important lawsuit and your attorney suggested a way to avoid a lengthy trial, reduce your large legal costs, and achieve a satisfactory settlement, would you want to know more? The executive at BP Alaska Exploration did. In lieu of protracted litigation, they agreed to use a private alternative to litigation, known as a minitrial, to resolve a multimillion dollar dispute. Five days after the minitrial began, the dispute was resolved.

When Xerox was sued in a breach of contract dispute by a Uruguayan distributor of its products, the companies used a minitrial that resulted in a settlement on the second day. Robert Banks, then general counsel of Xerox, said the minitrial avoided a six-week trial, saving his company at least four hundred thousand dollars in legal expenses and weeks of top management time.

Dramatic savings in litigation costs are prompting legal departments from a growing number of major corporations to use the minitrial and other methods of avoiding litigation. These savings are evidenced in a survey conducted by the Center for Public Resources Legal Program, a national effort of leading corporate counsel and major law firms to develop alternatives to the high costs of litigation. The CPR survey found that the sixty-one member corporations and government agencies that practiced alternative dispute resolution (ADR) estimated savings in legal expenses in 1987 and 1988 at $49 million. Kaiser Aluminum and Chemical Corporation general counsel David Perry reported in 1988 in the *San Francisco Recorder* that his company saved "well in excess of $5 million on outside litigation by using ADR."

But savings in legal costs are just part of the story. Litigation avoidance can eliminate other significant costs. These include the loss of important business relationships, diversion of management time and energies, unwanted publicity, and the delay and uncertainty of judicial decisions. Although it is difficult to quantify such costs, it is not difficult to assess their impact.

After learning that an engineer spent a hundred and sixteen hours on litigation support in a single month, Mack Trucks CEO John B. Curcio noted in the October 1988 issue of CPR's newsletter *Alternatives*: "That time would have been much more productively spent the way Japanese engineers spend their time—developing new products."

How can the minitrial—perhaps the most successful means of avoiding litigation—help to avoid these costs? In essence, this nonbinding settlement process is designed to turn a lawsuit back into a business problem. In a minitrial, lawyers focus on the central issues and present their abbreviated case, not to a judge or jury, but to top executives of the disputing companies, who have full authority to settle. Following these presentations, the executives meet without their lawyers to negotiate. After hearing arguments from both sides, these executives are able to appreciate, usually for the first time, the merits and downside risks of their cases. It is this balanced perspective that leads to speedy, economical settlements.

The minitrial has been used in diverse disputes facing corporations, including commercial, employment, product liability, and antitrust matters, and disputes with the government. Results are often quick. They are confidential. And in regard to balancing the considerations of both parties, minitrials are invariably better than the results of litigation. Since clients know their business objectives and operations, they can entertain options for resolution that their lawyers—and certainly judges—cannot. A minitrial can preserve business relationships that are usually destroyed in the acrimony of litigation.

A minitrial between Atlantic Richfield and Standard Oil Company illustrates the dynamics of the process. Their dispute centered on the interpretation of a sales agreement reached twenty years before. Instead of filing complaints, noticing depositions, and serving interrogatories, resulting in the production of countless documents, inside counsel conducted a minitrial.

Executives met in a Dallas hotel and heard three hours of presentations by both lawyers. Technical experts for each side also participated. Following a "team lunch" the executives met alone to discuss the dispute. Before dinner they reached an agreement. How did it happen?

The attorneys zeroed in on the essentials of the dispute, enabling the executives to focus on the basic business interests involved and to gain a clear understanding of the strengths and weaknesses of their cases. The dispute was over an issue common to the industry. Thus, the executives' expertise was more productive in reaching a solution than the lawyers could have been.

Since these executives had the power to settle, they were able to reach a firm agreement in one day. Arco's senior attorney, Albert D. Hoppe, reported in the January 1987 issue of *Alternatives*: "A substantial amount of money was involved, and there might have been some second-guessing if more junior officials were used."

Minitrials can, but do not always, include the participation of a "neutral"—a retired judge, technical authority or distinguished lawyer—agreed upon by the parties. Depending upon the parties' needs, the neutral can do one of three things: preside over the process, provide a nonbinding advisory opinion to assist settlement negotiations, or mediate. In the minitrial involving BP Alaska Exploration, for instance, the mediating role of Lester E. Olson, a retired California judge, was key to success.

Minitrials are demonstrably successful. An American Bar Association survey of minitrials showed an 85 percent success rate. Speed, economy, and flexibility were cited as recurrent benefits. Even when the negotiators failed to settle immediately, the minitrial process invariably led to settlement eventually.

The minitrial and other forms of ADR—such as binding forms of arbitration—offer U.S. businesses a more pragmatic, cost-effective way of resolving disputes than lawsuits, which too often take on lives of their own. Recognizing that "there has to be a better way," the CEOs and counsel of several hundred major corporations have signed a corporate policy statement, put together by CPR, agreeing to explore nonlitigatory settlement in any dispute with another signatory before resorting to full-scale litigation. Seventy-six percent of signatories responding to a CPR survey used the policy.

Yet too often management reacts to a business conflict with a message to counsel to "sue the bastards." In this competitive era, sound management is well advised to instruct counsel to explore all of the alternatives for dispute resolution—of which litigation is but one.

Mr. Henry is president of the New York-based Center for Public Resources, Inc.

FINDING THE RIGHT COMPETITIVE NICHE

· ·

by Michael Nevens and Evan Dudik

In 1986, *Gimbels*—one of New York's landmark department stores—closed its two Manhattan outlets and most of its suburban operations, having been caught between higher-priced stores such as Bloomingdale's and Macy's and aggressive discounters such as Marshalls and Zayre. Asked about the closing, National Retail Institute president Richard Hersch commented, "The worst place to be today is in the middle—people either want a bargain or quality goods with service for which they will pay."

Today's competitors caught in between face drastic alternatives. They can try to compete head-on with industry leviathans or focus on niches. But here they often encounter new companies spawned by deregulation or based on new technology. That leaves them between a rock and a hard place. McLean Trucking Company, the country's fifth largest trucker with $550 million in 1985 revenue, filed for bankruptcy law protection in January. Three industry giants, each at least three times larger, had muscled into McLean's southwestern U.S. market with new equipment, terminals, and routes. At the same time, smaller nonunion start-ups were aggressively picking up business with twin trailers. McLean was squeezed into Chapter 11.

This story is going to be repeated many times over the next few years in many different sectors of the service economy. Over three thousand of fourteen thousand commercial banks in the United States incurred losses last year—most of them smaller, regional institutions—for the same reason McLean had to file. At the same time, the industry giants reported strong profits.

Is there a way out of this problem for medium-size service companies? In many markets there is, but the answer is not a high-priced niche or a low-cost commodity. A carefully considered middle-of-the-road strategy still has winning potential in certain markets.

The hotel industry provides an example. Luxury high rises dominate most U.S. business-center markets, offering rooms at $150 a night and up. Quieter, and not too far from downtown, are all-suite hotels at $95. The trade-off: convenience, services, and amenities versus more space, quieter surroundings, fewer services, and a lower price.

The skyrocketing cost of business-district hotel construction forced the big chains to raise prices, which they justified by providing highly visible amenities (e.g., lounges, restaurants, limousines, health spas). This left the business traveler who wanted a reasonably priced room with no option except a downmarket motel.

A "midlevel" service strategy worked in the hotel business because it zeroed in on a very specific customer segment: the upscale traveler who is price-sensitive and does not want extra services. Operators of luxury hotels can respond by building hotels under new names (so as not to tarnish their images), but this takes time and allows the new players to become entrenched.

On the other hand, U.S. airlines operate in a market where a middle-of-the-road strategy backfires. At first glance there appears to be plenty of room for it to work. No-frills airlines are available at rock-bottom prices and with few amenities. At the high end there are first-class services on major airlines that often include helicopter and limousine transfers from the customer's office or hotel.

Is there a middle-ground strategy for airlines? Probably not, as witnesses the demise of People Express. Unlike the big hotels, the big airlines can respond in kind to lower prices; the variable cost of filling an empty seat on a plane is almost zero. The result has been numerous price wars, complicated fare schemes, and plenty of options for the traveler—but no distinct midlevel market that can be won and owned.

The air-freight business is different. Customer needs are distinct enough that a defensible midlevel niche can be carved out. If a package must be at its destination early the next morning, customers will pay top dollar to one of the express companies that own their own planes and trucks and guarantee delivery. However, if the afternoon of the next day or the following morning is acceptable, customers can have a freight forwarder (who buys space from the airlines and contracts with local truckers) send the package at a fraction of the price. The high cost of operating an early-morning delivery system created an opportunity for competitors to set up a completely different business system serving customers that are sensitive to price as well as time of delivery.

There are three things service companies caught between premium-price giants and low-cost niche players need to do. The first is to find a midvalue market that is defensible from entry by bigger competitors—where, for example, market image or their current deployment of assets prevents them from moving downward.

The second is to confirm the existence of a midvalue market. Current buying criteria and market perceptions are often changed by the entrance of the premium-service giants. Customers may have redefined acceptable service, features, and prices. The dynamics can be troublesome, but create opportunities to discover needs not satisfied by the premium marketers or to provide extremely good service on selected features. For example, the rush of financial services firms to capture wealthy individuals with premium services has left room for products targeted at middle-class consumers who require more than basic banking services. Agile firms are beginning to explore this; witness Sears's Discover card and American Express's Optima Card.

Be wary if prices seem to rise in lockstep with service levels.

That may mean that there is no distinct midlevel market or that it already has been found.

Finally, it's important to analyze the economic viability of a new strategy. There has to be some leeway between a mid-value price and premium products. Can lower costs be obtained, for example, by greater utilization of assets? Yes, but companies also have to guard against a tendency to cut costs and shave service levels too much. People Express's initial success depended on full planes and long lines at ticket counters to keep clerks and terminals utilized. This approach necessitated low service levels. There is a minimum service level one should not cross; otherwise the market may see you as just another low-service competitor. Midlevel doesn't mean second class. The strategy is to sail against the wind a bit by deleting and perhaps adding services in order to offer a simpler, less costly package to discerning buyers.

Mr. Nevens is a partner and Mr. Dudik is an associate in McKinsey's Los Angeles office.

WHEN BRANCHING OUT, REMEMBER YOUR ROOTS
. . . .

by Sir Michael Sandberg

One of my predecessors as chairman of Hongkong and Shanghai Banking Corporation was at his desk one day when there was a knock at his door. In came an elderly lady; she produced a tiny stack of cash and said she had come to see him about opening an account.

Showing no surprise that she had bypassed the counters and found her way to his own office, he politely invited her to sit down and called for the necessary forms, which he signed personally. He then escorted her to the banking hall and explained that the next time she had a deposit or withdrawal to make, it might save her the trouble of climbing the stairs to his office if she spoke to one of the staff there. Exit one happy new customer.

The only remarkable feature of this story is that it occurred in a big organization. In a small business, it's natural for the top man to take a personal interest in each of his customers.

The problem for banks today is that they have to try to be big and small at the same time. On the one hand, they need to be able to offer their clients a variety of financial services in almost every part of the world. The process of deregulation and the increasingly international nature of financial markets have made this a prerequisite for successful banking. Bigness has other advantages, too. It brings greater security for depositors and shareholders and enables banks to achieve economies of scale and make the huge investments required in new technology. For all that new technology, however, banking remains a highly personal business that must cater to the individual requirements of customers.

Judged by size alone, Hongkong and Shanghai Bank can compete with any of the world's major banks. It currently ranks among the world's top banking groups, having risen almost a hundred places since 1976.

The challenge that faced the group during the past quarter century of very rapid growth was to avoid the problems that can afflict many large organizations: indifferent, impersonal service to customers; a loss of a sense of belonging, and the loyalty and dedication that go with it, on the part of employees; and bureaucratization of procedures.

At Hongkong and Shanghai we met this problem in a way that, while it is by no means original, is unusual for a bank. Rather than create a unitary organization that almost inevitably would have begun to result in the classic "big organization" syndrome, we have created a federation of banks and financial institutions.

Most of these were acquisitions. Each of these major group companies has preserved its own highly distinctive culture, staff, traditions, corporate identity, and expertise. Each group company has the freedom to make its own commercial decisions immediately—without referring back to the head office—on matters that affect clients. In this way the entrepreneurial spirit that made each company successful in the first place does not come under the deadening influence of some vast bureaucratic apparatus. The role of the head office is to set broad policy guidelines and operational objectives, and to have the final say on major strategic decisions.

So strongly do we believe in the principles of federation and decentralization that they are applied even within the parent bank. Branch and area managers enjoy considerable freedom within their personal lending limits. Even when authorization is required, telexes to the head office must be answered within twenty-four hours.

Above all, however, the highly autonomous structure of the group brings special advantages for the customers. Locally they are able to enjoy a level of specialized personal services normally associated with a small organization while at the same time having access to the resources of a very large one.

In retrospect, the structure of the group and its basic business principles have been key factors in the bank's growth. They have helped it become one of only a few Asia-based banks so far to emerge as an international financial-services institution of global stature.

I would not claim that Hongkong and Shanghai Bank's answer to the problem of size is the only solution. Nevertheless, the drift toward standardization is one of the problems of an emerging free-market economy. In all spheres of business activity, successful innovations are quickly imitated by competitors who waste as little time as possible in launching their own comparable products and services. The result is all too often the emergence of anonymous monoliths, and the loss of the individual style and customer orientation that brought success in the first place.

Sir Michael recently retired after thirty-six years with Hongkong and Shanghai Bank, the last nine as chairman.

CUSTOMERS GO OUT THE DOOR WHEN SUCCESS GOES TO YOUR HEAD

. . . .

by Daniel R. Scoggin

I*t was a* successful manager's worst nightmare come true. We opened seven restaurants in 1975 and business was good. So good, in fact, that customers were lined up outside the doors. And then—BOOM!—sales plummeted 50 percent in less than six months.

What happened? I was convinced it was more than a matter of increased competition or the fickle nature of diners. So I toured the country looking for answers, visiting not only our own restaurants but many others as well. I studied young restaurants just starting to build their clientele, established restaurants at the height of their popularity, restaurants whose appeal was fading.

Then the nightmare became clear to me. We had come face-to-face with the Success Syndrome.

The Success Syndrome is the point at which a successful business begins to rest on its laurels. It is the ugly hybrid of confidence and complacency. Its symptoms are sliding standards, indifference to customers, and the naive belief that one can do no wrong.

The syndrome can afflict any service business, not just restaurants. The typical pattern goes something like this:

Stage One: You open for business. You and your employees are a little nervous about the whole thing: "What if we're not a success? I've got kids to feed and rent to pay." When the first customers walk in, you turn cartwheels in your effort to please. No request is impossible, no detail too small.

Stage Two: Business has been steady and strong for months. You're more confident, less nervous. You even think at times you've got more business than you can handle. "I guess I was a little short with that customer, but so what? Time is money. I've got a business to run, and there are more where she came from." Suddenly there's no time for those little details anymore. Your employees start to slack off, too, because they know you don't have time to notice.

A restaurant I visited in Minneapolis during my cross-country tour showed all these classic symptoms. A major news magazine had billed it as "the most successful singles' bar in the universe," and the place was packin' 'em in.

I walked up to the bar and waited while the bartender made time with one of his more vivacious customers. Finally he turned, flipped a coaster at me, and barked, "What'll ya have?" as the coaster came spinning to a stop.

I found that hotshot attitude among the waiters and waitresses as well. Gone were the days when those employees felt serving customers was a privilege. Now the customer was privileged to be served.

Stage Three: You've let your service and your standards slip, and you're the last to know that your slip is showing. Your customers have been seeing it for a long time, and many of them aren't coming back. You think they must have forgotten you. So you launch sales specials and maybe even rent a portable sign that flashes "Now Open" to passing cars.

Meanwhile, you try to save a little money by laying off a few employees and scrimping on the services or products you provide. A restaurant, for example, tries to get by with fewer waiters and busboys and cuts back on the portions it serves. Again, you naively think the customer won't notice. Your specials may lure a few customers back, but they find that it's as bad as ever—and maybe worse. This stage carries a high mortality rate.

I like to think that none of our restaurants had sunk that low when we diagnosed the problem. We fought back, and in six months sales had recovered. The good news for any business afflicted with the Success Syndrome is that there is a cure.

The first step is recognizing the problem. When sales start to slump, don't look for excuses outside of your business. Are your employees helpful and friendly? Is your workplace clean and presentable? Chances are declining standards are the source of customer dissatisfaction.

In the decade since we identified the syndrome, it has struck every restaurant we've ever opened. Whenever a manager tells us sales are down because of competition or the local economy or other outside factors, we take a hard look inside. We draw up a checklist of problems that need correcting inside the restaurant—everything from a waiter's bad attitude to a burned-out light bulb. By the time the manager gets to the end of the list, sales have rebounded.

The only way to know how customers see your business is to look at it through their eyes. We insist that our managers sit periodically in every seat in the restaurant. How else will you know if there's ketchup on the chair or an annoying draft from the air conditioner?

You must insist on the same level of excellence from your employees. Because the success or failure of any service business rests at the point of contact between employee and customer, rudeness cannot be tolerated. That's why we spend almost 75 percent of our training time on one subject: being nice.

A few years ago we opened a restaurant in Atlanta that quickly became the local hot spot. One of our bartenders decided that he was what made the spot hot. Fortunately, an alert manager noticed the syndrome taking hold and quickly recommended some changes. But when the bartender's attitude didn't improve, we fired him. We may have lost a good bartender, but it's a small price compared with the customers he might have cost us.

The Success Syndrome can afflict your business at any time. You may not notice its symptoms at first, but you'll certainly notice its effects. Remember, the syndrome doesn't attack from outside—it is a threat from within. But it is curable.

Mr. Scoggin was president and chief executive officer of TGI Friday's Inc. at the time this article was published.

CUSTOMERS MAY BE YOUR BEST COLLABORATORS

by Michael Schrage

If *you really* want to create successful innovations, forget about "listening" to your customers and trying to be "sensitive" to their needs. That's lazy and paternalistic. Clever companies should take an aggressively collaborative approach to the design of new products and services.

Top software houses count on their sharpest customers— their "beta sites"—to both track down bugs and suggest new features for their products. High-tech-systems companies like IBM and Hewlett-Packard increasingly depend on their "user groups" to identify and create new technical opportunities. Even an office furniture company—Steelcase, the nation's largest—has concluded that its customers should become partners in design.

This shift in emphasis is tremendous: design becomes something that should be done *with* customers, not for them. "Most designers are elitists," says John Rheinfrank, a senior vice president with FitchRichardsonSmith, a design-consulting firm, "but, fortunately, the day of the hero/genius designer seems to be fading pretty quickly." Instead of playing genius or market-research games with customers and then going "back to the old drawing board" to design a product, industrial designers are now taking customers back to the old drawing board with them.

That means companies are foolish to rely on traditional methods of market research. "I think the current notion of market research is going to be completely overturned in the next ten years," says Mr. Rheinfrank—who has worked with clients from Steelcase to Dutch electronics giant N. V. Philips—because it doesn't address the role of customer as collaborator.

"In principle, things like focus groups do what they're supposed to do," says Donald Norman, author of *The Psychology of Everyday Things*, a popular book (Basic Books, 1988) that explores examples of successful and failed designs. "In practice, however, they don't work that way—they're more focused on salability than usability," he says.

According to David Kelley, a Palo Alto, California, new-products designer who has worked with clients from Apple Computer to Procter and Gamble to Minolta, "The end user is usually so adaptive in getting around the problems of the product that they can't really tell you what they want; they've adapted around the inefficiencies. . . . They have no real opinions until you actually show them some alternatives."

The trick is to go beyond market research data and into models and prototypes. Instead of relying on what people say, have designers encourage customers to build a conceptual model of the innovation and diagram how they want to use it. Then harden those images into prototypes that customers can see and feel.

Rapid prototyping—the ability to quickly build a computer simulation, a mechanical model, or a cardboard mock-up of the innovation—is key to evoking customer collaboration. The prototype becomes the vocabulary of the innovation and each successive prototype enlarges that vocabulary and deepens both designer and customer understanding. In effect, says Mr. Rheinfrank, the conceptual models and prototypes become the "clay" that customers help mold into the final product.

Rapid prototyping isn't a one-shot effort—it's a collaborative learning and design process. "The number of prototype cycles you do is directly proportional to the ultimate quality of the product," says Mr. Kelley, who notes that he can now get some of his clients to develop four or five rapid prototypes in a year compared with only one or two cycles just three years ago. "Unfortunately, in the back of people's minds, they think that doing it five times is going to take longer and cost more. It really costs more to have the product debugged in the field."

One big benefit of designing with the customer is that it's a great way of managing expectations about what a product can or can't do. The chances of an unpleasant surprise shrink significantly. Conversely, the new-product-development team is forced to consider how customers perceive the value of proposed design changes.

Bill Verplank, a designer of the technically brilliant but sales-poor Xerox Star computer system, recalls, "We weren't focused on the user—we were focused on getting the most out of the technology." Now a designer at San Francisco's ID-TWO firm, Mr. Verplank relies on slides, videos, papers, maps, scripts, and other techniques to get customers to be as explicit as possible about their concerns and behavior.

Marketing people in companies may view this kind of customer intimacy as a threat to their powers: "You're invading their turf," acknowledges Mr. Kelley. Nevertheless, smart managers who want to encourage the flow of successful innovations should be at least as concerned with good design as with office politics.

Indeed, it's possible that picking the right customers to design innovations with may be one of the most important strategic decisions a company can make. The right customer can be a springboard to the entire marketplace.

Of course, one shouldn't get carried away by the notion of designing with the customer. Like all successful professional relationships, a certain amount of distance is undoubtedly necessary. But the traditional perception of a customer as someone you study and then sell to is dangerously out of date. Designing with the user can be a profitable symbiotic relationship.

Mr. Schrage, a visiting scholar at MIT's Media Lab in Cambridge, Massachusetts, is completing a book on collaboration.

LESSONS OF THE GREAT CRANBERRY CRISIS
· ·

by Harold Thorkilsen

A*ll too often*, successful companies can fall victim to a by-product of their own success: complacency.

It is when products are moving well, customers are happy, and profits are high that complacency, like an undetected virus, can move in on a firm. The effects can sometimes be devastating, in terms of lost markets, plummeting sales, job layoffs, plant closings, and even takeovers or company closedowns.

A classic example is Detroit's experience in the 1950s and 1960s, when automakers with full order books believed their hold on the U.S. market was secure forever. Not until the public began buying the new, high-quality imports did Detroit realize it might have been taking its customers for granted. It took years of attention to workmanship, quality standards, and production costs before a significant turnaround began. Carmakers, in their complacency, had failed to keep abreast of their clients' changing needs.

Similarly, companies with bestselling products that overlook subtle changes in consumer tastes are susceptible to the complacency bug. Back in the days of the so-called energy crisis, my organization started looking around for ways to package our products that would be more cost-efficient and less energy-dependent. Nowhere in the United States could we find anything suitable. But by looking abroad we discovered the new technology of aseptic "paper bottles," which we promptly introduced. American container makers, it seemed, had been perfectly happy with their existing product line. Their complacency lost them a lucrative new market.

Sometimes it can take a near catastrophe to reveal the extent of corporate complacency. At Ocean Spray, we learned the hard way after a crisis situation years ago that almost put our cranberry growers' cooperative out of business.

In those days, consumption of the fruit was almost entirely confined to the serving of cranberry sauce at Thanksgiving and Christmas dinners. We were quite content, at the time, with this single-purpose, single-season usage of our product. We were complacent.

Then disaster struck. Just before one Thanksgiving holiday, federal authorities reported that a pesticide used by some West Coast growers had caused cancer in laboratory rats. Although this widely publicized scare turned out later to be erroneous, preholiday TV coverage of "the Great Cranberry Crisis" cut sales drastically and came close to ruining our growers and their cooperative.

In the aftermath of this catastrophe, we were forced to rethink our entire marketing philosophy and management style. We acknowledged, first, that self-satisfaction, short-term thinking, and ignorance of consumer needs were the reasons we had never developed a year-round product line. Then, after an extensive R&D effort, we embarked on a continuing program to diversify and create a year-round market by producing cranberry-based juice drinks and other products. By marketing our new beverages as "good for you"—just when consumers were starting to demand natural, healthier products—our organization was fortunate enough to save itself.

Our experience showed us several ways in which managers can spot early signs of "the complacency factor" and take corrective steps. One way is to institute a regular corporate review and self-examination process. This can work in any organization, but seems particularly apt for old, established companies, where the risks of status quo thinking and entrenched working methods may be high.

At Ocean Spray (founded in 1930) a small management committee monitors every aspect of our operation on a biweekly basis. We examine and question, for instance, the breadth of our product line and consumer outlets, new products and packaging under development, our manufacturing and distribution methods, customer comments and complaints received, salesmen's reports, results of ongoing market research, our company policies, and actions by competitors. In particular, we watch closely any product, packaging, or working system that has remained unchanged for three years or longer. In some cases, we appoint a study group to examine a specific product whose performance might be improved.

As part of the corporate culture, we also let employees know that we encourage a spirit of innovation, entrepreneurism, risk taking, questioning of orthodox methods and "thinking the unthinkable." Through such measures, and by staying vigilant, it is possible for a company to keep smugness and complacency at bay.

Other effective countercomplacency steps can include:

- *Staying in close touch with consumers, trade factors, and suppliers to get an honest reading of how outsiders view the company's products and marketing methods.* This process has helped us to quickly spot our occasional product failures, such as a cranberry-prune juice drink and a vegetable juice cocktail that consumers flatly rejected. It has shown us shortcomings in package sizing or design. It has also led us to capitalize on successful new ideas such as a tropical drink using Hawaiian guava fruit and the blending of a pink-grapefruit-juice cocktail.
- *Encouraging the free exchange of ideas and suggestions, however far-fetched, at every employee level.* In our case,

this "bottom up" approach has been responsible for innovations such as the first ultraviolet cranberry sorter, better methods of crop harvesting, lighter shipping cartons, a cost-saving revision of our truck delivery system, more effective quality control with fewer inspectors, and an improved way of moving bottles down a line, suggested by a new employee.

Openness to new ideas, closeness to consumers, and constant watchfulness are among the most potent weapons an organization can use to guard against the dangers of self-satisfaction and complacency.

Mr. Thorkilsen is president of Ocean Spray Cranberries, based in Plymouth, Massachusetts.

KEEPING YOUR INTERNAL CUSTOMERS SATISFIED

by George H. Labovitz

I*n the ideal* organization, every employee would have direct contact with paying customers and be effective in meeting their needs. But the reality in large companies is that most employees are shielded from customers, either by organizational layers or lack of proximity. The shop foreman in a Detroit auto factory, for example, may never speak with the Texas housewife who buys and depends on his product.

However, the foreman and other employees who lack direct contact still have opportunities to contribute to customer satisfaction. Every employee is part of a chain of internal "customers" and "suppliers" that ultimately extends to the external customer. The manager's job is to process work through the internal customer-supplier chain, helping employees play their parts in ensuring that the end product or service fully satisfies the end user.

At IBM, the notion of internal customers dates back to the "Basic Beliefs" articulated by founder Thomas Watson. "It has always been implied in our culture," says William Eggleston, vice president of quality. "And since the late 1970s, it has been explicitly stated in our management guidelines. The objective is to meet the needs of your customer, and your 'customer' is whomever your work moves to next," he says.

Jean Bernard, Bell Canada's vice president of personnel, says her company is actively building an "internal customer orientation" into its management style. "The terminology is becoming commonplace here," she says.

More than ten thousand Shell Oil employees have participated in a quality-improvement training program, part of which focuses on working together in customer-supplier relationships. "Shell's emphasis on the internal customer is paying off," says Vic Figurelli, manager of quality improvement. "It has already provided a common language that engineers, craftsmen, clerical staff, and business managers can all share to get work done."

The formula for successful internal customer-supplier relationships varies. But it always begins with people asking their internal customers three basic questions: (1) "What do you need from me?" (2) "What do you do with my output?" (3) "Are there any gaps between what you need and what you get?"

Mr. Eggleston observes: "Throughout IBM you find people setting 'contracts' at the internal-customer interface. Each contract contains explicit statements of what the internal customer expects and clear criteria for measuring success in meeting those expectations. We manage directly to the goals established in these contracts."

At Bell Canada, the assignment group processes service orders and assigns telephone equipment installers to specific customers. "Assignment group staff rarely have direct contact with our paying customers, but our 10 percent error rate in assigning and scheduling installers had a direct and negative impact on customer satisfaction," notes Ms. Bernard.

Assignment-group managers met with their counterparts responsible for installations and service orders to address the 10 percent error rate. "First they tackled critical issues that could be solved or alleviated in the short term," Ms. Bernard says. "Then they looked ahead to explore all the aspects of their interdependent roles in satisfying our customers."

One activity required managers from different functions to work together to create "service maps" illustrating barriers to customer satisfaction, thereby suggesting specific changes likely to improve customer service. "The assignment group has since documented a tenfold decrease in their error rate, from 10 percent down to 1 percent," Ms. Bernard reports.

Mr. Eggleston stresses that the successful internal customer-supplier relationship is a two-way street: "Accounting is a good example. Virtually all departments supply accounting with data and in turn depend on accounting to process that data into useful information."

At one point, 3 to 5 percent of all of the accounting department entries were miscoded at IBM. "That may not sound too bad. But because we make millions of entries each year, this miscode rate translated into more than thirty thousand separate errors," Mr. Eggleston says. "Good management sense demanded that we take steps to reduce this figure."

IBM attacked the problem in terms of customers and suppliers, even though no paying customers were directly involved. "Accounting managers worked out a series of agreements with internal suppliers of the data their people enter. They did the same with the internal customers who depend on accurate information from the accounting department. Often, the supplier and customer were the same person," Mr. Eggleston notes.

Specifically, managers from the accounting department had three objectives in regard to their internal customers. First, they negotiated acceptable levels of accuracy for information coming into and going out of accounting. Second, they identified and developed the tools required to meet their accuracy commitments. For example, accounting provided a personal computer software program that helped internal customers screen their own data for errors before submitting them to accounting. Third, they established feedback mechanisms by which accounting and its internal customers could identify and return erroneous information to each other and offer suggestions on how to prevent the errors from reoccurring.

"Managers in other parts of the company were a little surprised to have their data supply errors pointed out by accounting," Mr. Eggleston recalls. "But they quickly saw that this was the first step in a whole new process designed to help accounting provide more accurate information." The result? "We have reduced the miscoding rate to less than 1 percent."

Management is a key to reaping the benefits of an internal-customer orientation. "You begin with executive commitment to the idea, but it quickly comes down to the skill and commitment of individual managers," Mr. Eggleston says. Ms. Bernard agrees: "We have concentrated on middle managers to bring about this change. Senior executives set the strategy and tone, but the deeds and actions of middle managers show employees that we truly intend to move in this direction."

Mr. Labovitz, professor of management at Boston University, is also president of Organizational Dynamics Inc., Burlington, Massachusetts, a management consulting and training company.

REACHING OUT TO YOUR CUSTOMERS
THROUGH THE EVENING NEWS
. . . .

by Michael M. Klepper

C BS News, *long* recognized as a pacesetter in network cost distribution, was ordered in 1987 to trim $50 million from its annual operating budget. With less money available to produce network and local news, news directors, especially in smaller markets, are increasingly willing to accept—and many are actively seeking—reliable video footage from the companies, trade groups, and organizations they cover. Correspondingly, more and more of these organizations are recognizing the immense value of supplying TV news outlets with something relatively new—the video news release.

A video news release is an alternate source of programming for network and local television stations. For example, NASA-produced video footage is often used by networks to illustrate space-related stories. Medical reporters frequently add meaning and clarity to complex technical stories with the aid of visuals—animation, charts, and graphics—provided by drug companies and health care agencies. One of the Big Three networks combined an interview it conducted with a company executive with background footage produced and supplied by that company.

There are good reasons why news organizations use outside-produced video material: Sometimes local stations simply can't obtain the material to help tell a story; they find it easier and less expensive to use outside information; or they lack the personnel and resources of network news departments and often use video releases to help program larger news blocks.

The only way a video news release will be used is if it contains news. If a news director perceives your material as a commercial, it will end up in the circular file. There's already a glut of self-serving video material in the marketplace, all of it unacceptable to news programmers. So don't oversell. Don't rely on slick packaging to make up for a lack of newsworthiness. When you send video material to a TV station, keep it simple. An unpretentious box will do. The news content should sell the story.

Slant your piece to a news trend. One of the most successful video news releases was produced to gain mass exposure for a new talking doll. But rather than extoll the virtues of the product, the company made a video describing the history of artificial voice synthesis. The doll was featured as an example of how that technology is incorporated into everyday life. The video aired across the country. News directors got timely, interesting news. The doll maker got valuable nationwide exposure.

Consider producing a video news release when:

- *Your corporation/organization is involved in a legitimate medical, health, or scientific breakthrough.*
- *Your visuals can be used as background footage while the reporter or news anchor discusses pertinent news copy.*
- *You can provide unusual visuals television stations can't obtain on their own.*
- *You have an interview segment that television stations can't get for themselves.*

Television stations—no matter how large or small—will use outside-produced video footage only if it meets their own standards. Similarly, news directors, editors, and reporters will better welcome outside material if it's easy to use. Formatting, writing, and producing are best entrusted to top professionals familiar with the ins and outs of TV news. The more familiar the professionals you hire are with how news organizations work, the better the chance your material will be aired.

Ideally, a video news release should run about ninety seconds per segment—two minutes at most. If you need more time to tell your story, consider a multipart series. It might be a series with two, three, four, or five parts, with each segment running ninety seconds. Multipart series, with a different segment airing each day, can dramatically increase audience size. But the hard reality of television news is that once the footage is in the station's hands, the station will do with it what it wants. While a station might be happy to air one segment, a five-part video release is a tough sell. Some news directors consider them too self-serving for a news program, especially if a company's name, products, or services are mentioned so often that the series becomes nothing more than a multipart advertisement.

Third-party endorsements are one of the most effective methods of positioning a product or service in a video news release. Endorsements are especially useful if the third party is a recognized expert, specialist, public figure, or sports personality. For example, the well-known publisher of a business magazine appeared in a video news segment produced to highlight trade relations between the United States and Canada.

It's a good idea to include one minute of background footage, a "B-roll," providing stations with extra visuals to use with their own on-air personalities. Animation footage, graphics, and third-party spokesmen enhance the presentation and heighten the credibility of your video story.

A video news release can be distributed to newsrooms via satellite feed or by direct mail. Direct mail is usually best because it provides stations with a tape in hand that can be used at the station's convenience. The tape is mailed directly to the appropriate person at each station—the news, science, business, or health editor, for example. Once mailed, a few phone calls will determine usage.

However, if you're sending out a hard news story or a late-breaking one, a satellite feed is faster. But for a station to be able to record and air the piece, it must have personnel and a satellite downlink available at the precise time of the feed. When using a satellite feed, you trade speed for control; stations may or may not be ready to receive your material when you send it.

A high-quality, single-segment feature costs twenty thousand to thirty thousand dollars to professionally produce and distribute. Costs vary according to the number of locations, travel, special effects, and the number of stations targeted. A multipart series of five segments can run to forty thousand dollars, considerably lowering the cost per segment.

Cost-effectiveness of a well-executed video news release is enhanced even more if it's applied far beyond television distribution. The cost per exposure drops dramatically when pro-rated across a variety of other uses—annual meetings, marketing and sales presentations, as part of a speech, or as background material when representatives of your organization appear on television interview programs.

Of course, it's not uncommon that a video release accepted for broadcast will be bumped to make room for a breaking news story. The station might hold the material for airing at a later date, but sometimes it's lost forever. The ball is always in the news director's court.

Mr. Klepper is chairman of a New York marketing communications company.

REFUTING HOLLOW ARGUMENTS ABOUT MANUFACTURING

by Peter L. Scott

Magazines and newspapers are flooded these days with articles suggesting that our manufacturing base is destined to become little more than a collection of "hollow corporations," dinosaur smokestack industries doomed to choke on their own polluted fumes. In addition, our current problems in manufacturing are blamed on generally poor economic conditions, or unfair trade practices, or taxes, or inflation, or huge national deficits, or Japan Inc.

In my view, the people responsible for these articles are deficient in both perception and understanding. There seems to be a broad-based failure of interpretation of what is really going on in manufacturing. Part of this is a by-product of an inability, or an unwillingness, to face reality.

Our problems basically stem from management's myopia

about technology and its fear of taking intelligent risks and diversifying. We managers are comfortable—too comfortable—in the sanctuary of the status quo. For two decades after World War II, we took our nation's industrial growth for granted. In our cozy maturity we looked at our remarkable manufacturing accomplishments and thought we saw, reflected, the whole course of our future. A guaranteed future.

We were wrong. Dead wrong! We did not see, nor even sense, the colossal impact of technological progress. We could not accept the reality that our domestic markets were no longer "safe havens." We were not perceptive enough to recognize that technology had so altered manufacturing that for the first time, excellence in manufacturing through technology added at least as much competitive value as marketing, promotion, and distribution. We didn't properly diagnose the structural weakness of a manufacturing sector committed to sequential production in an era when the market dynamics called for product variety, short runs, and change—the very antithesis of our much-revered "mass production" psychology.

Some of us panicked. We rushed off-shore to take advantage of cheap labor. But we are finding we have created a Trojan Horse of our own design. What we have done, naively but with the best intentions, is teach the developing countries our manufacturing techniques and processes. In essence, we gave them out industrial birthright. And they're proving to be fast learners. They don't need us any longer.

Our predictable knee-jerk response to the invasion of the Japanese, the Koreans, and the Taiwanese was to call for legislation, erect trade barriers, and impose quotas. Like a swimmer who's ventured out too far, we looked for the lifeline of an "industrial policy" to rescue us from our misjudgments and our own complacency.

The answer to our problems does not lie in legislatures; no amount of legislative help—or tax bailouts—will resuscitate manufacturing anywhere in this nation. Competitiveness cannot be legislated. We have to become more competitive by changing our fundamental thinking.

Threaten a company competitively, and its managers will flail away with time-honored cost-cutting measures to become more "efficient." This is what they have been taught to do in times of crisis, and this is what they are comfortable with and good at doing. But there is a finite point to such pencil sharpening. It will take you only so far before you're liquidating your company. Harvard's Wickham Skinner wrote in his excellent book *Manufacturing: The Formidable Competitive Weapon*: "In a new competitive world, the mindset that says worker productivity is the key to manufacturing success is just as obsolete as a counting house mentality would be in today's corporate finance."

What is needed is a new attitude: a new, more flexible methodology to manufacturing, and a fresh approach to the management of technology and people.

This means making the long-term capital investments required. Instead, what do we do? We overreact to our problems, pull in our horns. On a nationwide basis many companies are actually proposing to reduce their investments in modernization of plants and processes.

This reflects, I regret to say, the virulence of the short-term mentality that got us in this mess in the first place. I can assure you that I know all about the tyranny of the quarterly results—artificially imposed on us. However, at Emhart we spent some $76 million for capital improvements in 1986—further automation, etc.—and we invested about $45 million in technology. Some 23 percent of this was directed toward advanced research activities. Though figures are up somewhat, we have not reduced our level of spending in these two pivotal areas of growth for several years.

But checkbooks alone won't do it. We must cultivate innovation. We must create an environment in our plants and among our people that accepts and encompasses all the relevant technologies—from microelectronics and superconductors to exotic metals, electron beams, and computerized engineering, design and manufacturing.

Now we come to the real guts of the matter: people. We need manufacturing engineers who aren't seduced away by the glitter of the semiconductor and electronics world. We need fresh, uninhibited talent that is turned on by the bustle and pace of life on the factory floor—young people who thrive on solving practical problems. We need skilled employees capable of original thinking, of systems planning, and of leadership.

To achieve this we must make a major investment in our human capital. The primary purpose of American higher education, says former manufacturing engineer Frank Newman in a new Carnegie Foundation report, is not to prepare graduates for specific jobs. The goal is to develop the knowledge, the intellectual capabilities, the motivation, and the values that build the confidence young people need to take advantage of opportunities. And that fosters an entrepreneurial attitude. Unless we understand this, I have to wonder where we will get managers capable of independent thought and action, and the nonconformists who are the catalysts of change.

Now, some of you are no doubt saying to yourselves, isn't Scott aware of the near-disastrous shortage of engineers in this country? Liberal arts are fine, you might say, but let's get our priorities straight! We have more immediate needs at hand. Or so the conventional wisdom suggests.

Well, for one thing, we're not facing anything like a technical manpower Armageddon. In fact, the number of engineering and computer science graduates is at an all-time high. The real problem is whether these graduates will have the capacities needed beyond technical expertise.

Such capacities lead to a society that not only preserves tradition and culture, but also places a premium on new ideas and self-confidence, rather than on passivity and submissiveness, and fosters optimism rather than cynicism.

Not only must we rediscover our childhood standard of the

"three Rs" we must supplement it with the "three Is"—namely, individualism, innovation, and initiative.

Mr. Scott was chairman and chief executive officer of Emhart Corporation at the time this was written. On May 18, 1989, Mr. Scott was named chairman of Black and Decker, after Black and Decker completed a successful tender offer for Emhart.

AMERICA'S ENGINEERING GAP
······························

by Leif Soderberg

A *nother advisory group* has recommended that the U.S. government "coordinate" research—this time in super-conductors—so that the United States doesn't fall behind in an important new technology. If only we had an advisory panel that worried about something less glamorous: *engineering*.

Most of the people in Washington making noises about "competition" don't know much about how a new product is invented, developed, and made. If they did, they would realize that in many cases our products are uncompetitive because they are badly engineered, not because we lag in a new technology or can't make them as well or as cheaply as the Koreans. We have an engineering gap in the United States and that's where we have to catch up.

A car door for a U.S. automobile costs twice as much as one with the same performance and durability produced by a Japanese manufacturer. Almost 75 percent is the result of differences in design. Most of this is engineered scrap—the waste generated in the blanking and stamping process. In this case, half of the incoming material is designed to leave the plant as scrap. The remainder of the gap stems from differences in the number and complexity of components, the type of material specified, and unneeded performance margins. All that is an engineering, not a manufacturing or technology, problem.

Engineering is not the only reason U.S. companies fall behind, but it's one of the main reasons they fail to catch up. One company, facing a 30 percent cost disadvantage to an Asian manufacturer, put a big push on to improve plant operations and reduce labor. It ended up 40 percent behind. While it was making improvements in the factory, its Asian competitor was making changes in product design, most of which should have been foreseeable.

Our problem is not a shortage of engineers. The United States appears to have the same number of engineers relative to gross national product as West Germany and perhaps just 15 percent fewer than Japan. And U.S. auto companies devote almost twice as many product-engineering resources to a vehicle program as their Japanese competitors. But they wouldn't need to if U.S. engineers spent more than 15 percent to 25 percent of their time actually engineering products.

Typically, our engineers develop concepts, designers finalize the designs, draftsmen put them on paper, and checkers follow up the drawing details. Japanese engineers perform a much broader spectrum of tasks (lay out their own designs, do their own drafting and detailing). Sound familiar? At a time when many U.S. companies are eliminating specialists on the plant floor through work-rule changes, they are letting them thrive in the drafting room.

More time spent actually designing parts is a self-reinforcing mechanism. Greater familiarity with the parts being developed lets an engineer know where minor changes may arise (i.e., where sheet-metal changes should be anticipated for packaging considerations), and the engineer can communicate the uncertainty downstream. This saves time for everyone—by cutting down on reviewing time in meetings, eliminating paperwork and administrative tasks, and lowering reworking costs. The freed-up resources can be channeled back to the primary task of designing good parts.

This problem will sound familiar too: Most U.S. engineers don't get the opportunity to feel responsible for the product they work on. They're usually organized by function and work anonymously on any product that reaches the top of somebody's priority list. A United States destroyer requiring a major hull repair pulled into a Japanese shipyard. A repair team of engineers, supervisors, and ship workers swarmed all over the damaged ship. Drawings were prepared twenty yards from the hull while damaged sections were removed. No review or signature by higher levels in the engineering department, no bids processed by purchasing—just a team totally dedicated to the ship. The repairs made, the captain could only speculate why a typical sixty-day job had taken only three.

Rx: Organize engineers around products or customers, and reduce reporting levels to three. That may take some retraining, but it's doable for most companies and won't increase head counts.

Unlike most Japanese engineers, who spend considerable time in the field, most American engineers don't have a business perspective. They're there to design products, not deliver them profitably to satisfied customers. This became very clear when McKinsey was asked to find out why the manufacturing costs of a U.S. office-products company were nearly three times those of a Japanese competitor. A supplier of electrical components described to us the purchasing processes of the American and Japanese companies: "Your client gives us very detailed plans and specifications for a proprietary subassembly. We bid seventy-five dollars and won with about a 12 percent margin, not too attractive, and we'll have to bid again next year."

The supplier told McKinsey a very different story about the subassembly methods used by our client's Japanese competitor: "They asked us to put our best people on it, showed us what the subassembly has to accomplish. Two of our engineers suggested they modify another part of their circuitry to make it possible for us to use catalog parts. We cut their costs to twenty-five dollars on which we make a 40 percent margin—we negotiate prices. Next year we'll take it down to twenty dollars. We make money, so do they."

Developing engineers to make these kinds of design-or-buy trade-offs has to become part of the agenda. The focus should be on engineers, not on trying to factor in a business perspective: It will be easier to teach an engineer basic business skills than to train MBAs to design products.

We also have to reduce the number of design changes we tend to make and "freeze" the design early on, the way foreign competitors do. McKinsey has worked with U.S. companies where 45 percent of the time engineers spend on design work is consumed by engineering changes. Parts are, on average, designed twice: once as an initial release and once as a changed design. The changes usually snowball, yet most—two thirds in a case McKinsey recently analyzed—are unnecessary.

It's dangerous to generalize about commercialization. Developing a new jumbo jet is a little different from inventing a new coffee pot, but this much can be said: Today's competitive environment has fundamentally changed what it takes to meet the demands of the commercialization process. What really counts is being faster to market with products based on new technologies, more externally focused on alternative sources of technology, and quicker to upgrade and modify products after their initial release. Not long ago, being good at innovation meant being successful with this or that product. Now it means building and maintaining an organization's systemic capability to bring a flow of new products continually to market.

The United States has spent a decade catching up in manufacturing, and we are still pre-eminent in research and technology. But in the middle ground of engineering and developing we are losing ground. We're not being outproduced, but outdesigned. Many of our companies need to regain and sustain their competitiveness by closing the engineering gap.

That has to be their priority, and there's not much Washington can do to help them.

Mr. Soderberg is a principal in the Cleveland office of McKinsey and Company.

PUSH YOUR INNOVATIONS
BEFORE SOMEONE ELSE DOES
....

by Rick Whitaker

I*n the world* of songbirds, the cuckoo is a major threat to reproduction. The cuckoo is not adept at nesting or incubating activities. Rather, it seeks out the nest of an unsuspecting songbird where it places its egg. If the songbird does not detect the interloper, in a few weeks it finds its nest occupied by one large, ugly, and very aggressive cuckoo chick, while its own offspring litter the ground below. In many ways, this is the situation that U.S. managers in innovative, high-tech companies face today.

Historically, basic research in large corporations, universities, or the government has acted as the flash point for high-tech companies. Entrepreneurs develop a product idea from that research, break away to form a company with a prototype, introduce the product, develop some sustainable advantage as a company, and, finally, make a long-term business out of it. When the company or industry becomes large enough, it begins to spin off new businesses from its basic research. There is also a capital cycle which parallels, and is rewarded from, this product cycle. Of course, products and companies can and do fail at every step in this process. But enough succeed, and capital and research are generated to renew the cycle.

The major change in the last few years has been the

entrance of "cuckoos"—usually large, well-financed, and well-managed companies that may not have the interest or ability to develop technical innovations, but excel at driving a new product into a long-term business. These activities have accelerated and compressed the reproductive cycle tremendously. As an example, the integrated circuit industry developed for fifteen or twenty years before there was significant foreign competition; the PC industry was allowed only five. The final regulatory hurdles giving birth to the mobile telephone business were cleared only five years ago; today there is fierce price competition. And it is not just foreign companies: firms like Digital Equipment Corporation in office automation and Lotus in microsoftware have jumped on product ideas originally thought of by others, and pushed their product to domination.

The results of waking up and finding a big, ugly cuckoo in your nest are painful, and are reflected in today's headlines. Companies like Gavilan and Applied Information Memories lost $30 million each before folding. Storage Technologies and Victor Technologies have visited Chapter 11. Commodore and Corvus Systems have shrunk drastically. Fortune Systems, Computervision, and others are experiencing traumatic layoffs. And worse, the reproductive cycle is being broken; investors in early innovators—either venture capitalists or public equity holders—are not receiving the rewards they expected, and are pulling back from the entire industry.

The good news is that significant progress toward correction can be made from practical and achievable changes in innovator-company management strategy. The first change, and probably the most difficult, is one of attitude. Management must understand that from "day one" their technical breakthroughs, no matter how stunning, are worthless unless they can be shaped to meet customer needs, and delivered in a way superior to competition.

Compaq Computer Corporation is a very positive example to follow here. Rather than being dazzled by the fact it could make a smaller, faster version of the IBM PC, the company immediately started identifying its customers' needs, building a quality distribution network, and working on next-generation responses to competition.

Other necessary and achievable changes include:

- *Grabbing enough information on customers and competitors to become market-driven.* One can start this process by asking simple questions and taking small steps. Develop a hypothesis on "why would anyone buy this product," and then test it with ten phone calls. Set up a program of talking to a customer every day, and taking an industry contact to lunch every week. An afternoon spent in a public or university library can yield enormous amounts of information on market trends and competing products. And make sure that the scope of this effort is wide enough. The semiconductor equipment manufacturer who missed a directly competing product entry because it had been publicized in a business journal rather than in engineering journals is an example of the pitfalls of too narrow a field of view.

- *Narrowing your focus.* New companies usually can do only one thing well. Choose that one value-added step, and purchase everything else. A now-defunct computerized publishing system company spread itself too thin by trying to develop both proprietary software and hardware. Software was its real distinction, while adequate hardware was available on the market. The same goes for choosing customers. A PC printer manufacturer had the opportunity to serve both corporate and individual PC owners but found they had different purchase criteria and distribution channels. By choosing to concentrate on individuals, the company avoided diffusing its limited resources.

- *Pushing a product into the market quickly.* Generating revenue is a great method of shifting focus to the outside world. Even if it is not the final form of the product, it will be an invaluable learning experience. The market-busting product which is never quite ready to be introduced, and ends up being stillborn, is an all too common story. Symbolics, which was able to deliver a commercialized artificial intelligence software product to the market after only one and a half years of existence (and eventually three products in three and a half years), is an example to follow.

• *Understanding that outsiders can be valuable friends, rather than foes or impediments.* One inexpensive means of obtaining some outside expertise is to include a person knowledgeable in the market or industry on a company's board. A company in educational software would probably do well to include an educator on its board, rather than the usual composition of three venture capitalists and a lawyer. And finally, hire professionals in marketing and sales as soon as it can be afforded. The situation of a research engineer continuing to fill the VP of sales position because he was one of the founders and liked the opportunity of traveling to Europe occasionally is more common than one would like to admit.

There are potentially huge high-tech industries still waiting to be shaped: biotech, robotics, artificial intelligence, telecommunications, and others. But the only innovators who will find success in them are those who know the cuckoos are out there, are able to recognize an intruding egg when they see one, and boot it out of the nest before it's too late.

Mr. Whitaker heads Booz Allen and Hamilton's Southeast Asia operation from its Singapore office.

PROCESS DESIGN IS AS IMPORTANT
AS PRODUCT DESIGN
. . . .
by John Mayo

"*J apan Does Away* with Quality Control." An article with this provocative title appeared in an Asian business journal a while back, and must have come as quite a shock to those impressed by Japan's traditional concern with and commitment to manufacturing quality.

Has Japan decided that quality is no longer a priority? Hardly. What it has decided is that traditional quality control techniques are no longer sufficient, and that something beyond these traditional approaches is needed. A similar realization has taken place at certain companies in the United States, AT&T among them.

Traditional quality control programs in the United States and elsewhere have relied on a combination of inspections and statistical quality control methods such as control charts. The emphasis has been on tightly controlling manufacturing processes. But about ten years ago, when many products—and their associated manufacturing processes—began to assume then-unheard-of degrees of complexity, managers and engineers were forced to redesign their approach to quality control.

The number of manufacturing steps involved in many of today's products is tremendous. For example, it is not unusual in the making of a state-of-the-art integrated circuit to have two hundred manufacturing steps. As the control of these complex processes becomes an unwieldy task, the emphasis at some companies has shifted to reducing the influence that variations in manufacturing processes would have on the final products. At AT&T we have come to realize that high quality can be achieved in complex products only by starting at the front end of the product cycle, with the design of both the product and its manufacturing process.

A new and somewhat revolutionary approach to quality control has thus been developed: "design quality," or what some call "off-line" quality control. Broadly stated, off-line quality control includes all quality engineering activities carried out before a product goes into full-scale production. It is not enough to come up with a product that works well when manufactured exactly according to the design specifications; the product must also be easy to manufacture and insensitive to variability on the factory floor.

An example may help clarify how these principles can be applied. Many AT&T products contain hundreds or even thousands of circuit packs. (A circuit pack is a collection of electronic components mounted on a printed circuit board.) A critical step in circuit-pack fabrication is the mass soldering of up to several hundred components to a printed circuit board. This mass soldering process can be cumbersome to control, since the optimum soldering machine settings depend on many factors, such as the physical layout of the printed circuit board, the type of components and their orientation, and the total number of components.

Rather than continually striving to control this process, we designed a soldering technique that was much less sensitive to the variations in the manufacturing process. A new flux (a chemical that prepares the surface for soldering) was developed to increase the effectiveness of the mass soldering process without requiring a change in the soldering machine settings. The key idea is that it is cheaper to reduce the influence of manufacturing-line variability than to try to control it.

The same principles can be applied to product design. For example, AT&T recently developed an integrated circuit that could be used in many products to amplify voice signals. As originally designed, the circuit had to be manufactured very precisely to avoid variations in the strength of the signal. Such a circuit would have been costly to make because of stringent quality controls needed during the manufacturing process. But our engineers, after testing and analyzing the design, realized that if the resistance of the circuit were reduced—a minor change with no associated costs—the circuit would be far less sensitive to manufacturing variations. The result was a 40 percent improvement in quality.

Unfortunately, many industries are still stranded in the old "inspect and fix" mode. One American laboratory I know of was testing a new product design for durability. Components that failed during the tests were simply replaced by better-quality (and more expensive) counterparts. No attempt was made to redesign the product around the less expensive components. The final design released for manufacture therefore exceeded the original budgeted cost. This story is all too common in America.

The Japanese, on the other hand, have excelled in redesigning for quality, largely because, in the past, they built an economy around improving products designed elsewhere. One Japanese watchmaker found that it isn't necessary to use an expensive quartz crystal to achieve high accuracy in a wristwatch. An inexpensive capacitor could compensate for variations in a cheaper crystal without sacrificing overall accuracy.

If American industry embraces design quality it will realize not only improved products, but lower costs as well.

Mr. Mayo is executive vice president, network systems, at AT&T Bell Laboratories.

R&D JUST AIN'T WHAT IT USED TO BE
. . . .
by Michael Schrage

A*fter more than a decade of* double-digit increases, the growth rate of America's research and development spending has dropped. The "competitiveness" pundits are already gnashing their teeth over what a headline in *Business-Week* described as this "perilous cutback in research spending."

But realists know that these aggregate R&D numbers are as meaningless as gross sales figures without a hint as to cash flow or profitability; you know there's a business there—you just don't know if it's making any money. "What people are hoping is that R&D spending is some measure of competitiveness when, in fact, it's only an input measure," asserts McKinsey and Company's Richard Foster, who oversees the consulting firm's extensive technology practice. "The whole notion of inferring competitiveness out of lump sums is flawed."

Yet that is precisely what most companies do. Top managements and their research staffs describe their solemn commitment to innovation with phrases such as "R&D as a percentage of sales" and "R&D spending per employee." A top executive of one semiconductor firm boasted at a meeting a few years ago that R&D expenditures as a percentage of sales at his company continued to rise in the teeth of an industry recession. Of course they did: The company's sales had plummeted!

More relevant than any precise accounting for R&D expenditures are the following questions: What does research and development really mean to the enterprise, regardless of the dollars invested? How are the organization's priorities reflected in its innovation infrastructure? What signal, if any, does the investment in that innovation infrastructure send to the rest of the organization?

The notion of research and development as an assembly line that delivers spanking new product ideas and innovations suitable for manufacture and marketing is outmoded and dangerous. And in disciplines ranging from biotechnology to computer software to financial technology, the line between theoretical and applied research is vanishing: A clever differential equation can quickly become the soul of a new security; the discovery of a new enzyme can lead to the creation of a new diagnostic tool. Some organizations have historically done basic research without development—Bell Labs is a classic example—and others develop products and services without research—MCI, for one.

Kleiner, Perkins, Caufield and Byers venture capitalist John Doerr—whose capital played a large part in the hyperfast growth of such companies as Compaq Computer and Sun Microsystems—says that output is the best way to measure the effectiveness of research and development expenditure. In this bottom-line context, output doesn't mean patents or published papers; it means products. "New items on the price list is the crispest way to go," says Mr. Doerr. "What percent of sales revenues come from products less than 'x-months' old." 3M, for example, is well known for insisting that new products account for a significant percentage of divisional sales.

But, like measuring R&D as a percent of sales, there's more to organizational innovation than a clutch of new products. "There may be a new role for corporate research," says John Seely Brown, who oversees Xerox's large and diverse research portfolio. "Research and development has to start looking inward and figure out how it can help the organization better cope with accelerating change." In the last two years, says Mr. Brown, the research portfolio of Xerox's influential Palo Alto Research Center has changed more than 50 percent. "We're getting out of things that can be done elsewhere," Mr. Brown says.

Instead, Xerox is now reorienting along lines of "sustaining" research and development for its ongoing product lines (such as photocopiers), and "pioneering" research and development (as in fields such as computational linguistics, which would let computers process language in more effective ways). These new demarcation lines between sustaining and pioneering research send a signal to the organization about Xerox's priorities and its focus—signals that otherwise would be ignored in the crush of everyday crises.

Similarly, Xerox and other technology companies are growing much more sensitive about the distinction between "new-product research" and "process research." The need for new-product research is obvious: unless the company believes that imitations are the surest form of profitability, it can't afford to diminish the search for new products. But too few realize the importance of process research, designed to give the company a new set of tools and techniques to improve its internal processes.* To invest in new products without investing in new processes will hollow out the organization.

The lump-sum agglutinations of the traditional R&D budget obscure these fundamental differences in emphasis. However, organizations are becoming more aware of the need to link process R&D with new-product R&D. That's the only way companies will be able to maintain a technical edge within practical economics.

"We've gone to tremendous lengths to make that link," says Ralph Gomory, vice president of research and advanced technology for IBM. "It's not a spontaneously occurring thing—[in this respect] mechanisms are more important than measures."

In recent years, IBM has created some eighteen special groups throughout the company that link researchers with developers. Mr. Gomory has been particularly pleased with the groups working on silicon chip fabrication and packaging. These aren't "skunkworkers" intended to produce a new product. They're special teams working at the cutting edge of technology designed to produce workable and demonstrable prototypes. "Instead of doing pieces of technology," Mr. Gomory says, "we produce a coherent whole."

Science and technology have changed along with the process and meaning of innovation. Organizations need to customize their definition of research and development to meet their needs. "Product" versus "process" research, "sustained" versus "pioneering" research, and new mechanisms to link innovators are but a few examples of the dimensions along which R&D priorities should be evaluated. The "creative struggle," as Xerox's Mr. Brown puts it, isn't just about innovating for the

*University of Pennsylvania economist Edwin Mansfield has done research indicating that successful Japanese firms spend fully two thirds of their R&D budgets on process R&D—significantly more than their American counterparts.

marketplace—it's innovating a new understanding of what research and development should mean to the organization.

Mr. Schrage, a visiting scholar at MIT's Media Lab in Cambridge, Massachusetts, is completing a book on collaboration.

SEPARATING SLUDGE FROM GOLD IN YOUR INVENTORY

· · · · · · · · · · · · · · · · · ·

by Doug White and Mike Graff

U S. *companies have* been cutting inventory to reduce costs. That makes sense. The trouble is, the wrong products have been cut. In many cases companies actually have reduced the availability of their bestselling products and let other slower-moving products stack up.

For example, an auto dealership has an inventory of fifty model X cars and fifty model Y cars. Model X cars are selling well and generate most of the profit. Model Y cars, on the other hand, are not selling well and are generating little profit. The owner of the dealership sees the need to reduce inventory from a hundred units to fifty units and so directs the purchasing manager, who stops ordering new cars. A month later there are fifty cars on the lot, but only three model X cars and forty-seven model Y cars.

This method of inventory reduction squeezes out the quick-moving inventory while allowing "sludge" to build rapidly as a percentage of the total. The result is very poor service levels, as customers are seldom able to find the car they want in stock.

Until recently, most American managers have not had to manage inventory levels, because maintaining service standards was the top priority for warehouse managers. Lost sales due to stockouts were a rarity because managers were not expected to turn over their inventory of finished products more than a couple of times a year.

Over the past several years, however, as slower growth and foreign competition have squeezed margins and reduced working capital, U.S. managers have been pressed to speed up inventory turnover while holding the line on service. During that time the proportion of inactive or slow-moving products has moved upward. Even at the old turnover standard of twice a year, stockouts have thus become a major worry.

To understand how this happens, think of inventory as a pond with three layers and an incoming and outgoing stream. The water, or inventory, in the top layer is a fresh stream because it stays in the pond only a short period of time. This inventory turns over very quickly, but stockouts are high and service levels are low. The middle layer of water moves more slowly. It is out of the main flow, but close enough so that some portion of it is pulled out with the fresh stream. The sediment in the bottom of the pond moves even more slowly or not at all. Think of it as sludge inventory that sits around for years, creating high holding costs but adding no value.

No matter how well they manage inventory, most companies create some sludge. That is not a big problem as long as sales and, consequently, inventories are growing rapidly, because the sludge component will remain a relatively small percentage of the total. But when sales growth slows and/or prices fall, total inventory will grow more slowly, and sludge, which is still being generated, will increase as a percentage of total inventory. That's what has happened to many American companies.

To reduce inventory levels, most managers are ordering less new stock for inventory than is being sold. This has the effect of further reducing the fresh-stream inventory but not the sludge—as was the case with the auto dealership.

The answer to this problem is not just-in-time inventory, or some other Japanese technique. In fact, many U.S. companies run what is, in effect, a just-in-time inventory system, but for only a small percentage of their products—the ones that sell. The rest of their sales come from large inventories that turn very slowly. As a result, they can't compete in either price or service.

The solution, of course, is to remove inventories of slow-moving products crowding the country's warehouses. The auto dealership would have been able to provide far better service to its customers if it had chosen to reduce inventories by running a sale on the slow-moving model Y cars and adding more X cars.

But managers don't like to reduce prices or, worse, scrap products. To them, that means lost revenue and profits. But it costs money to hold a product in inventory—sometimes more than the costs of marking it down or writing it off. The best approach is to figure out how long an item could be held until the cumulative holding cost equals the cost of the most attractive alternative. This period of time establishes the cutoff point between sludge and middle inventory. If any product's current inventory would last beyond the cutoff point, it is considered sludge, and steps should be taken to eliminate it.

For example, at one integrated steel producer, the most financially attractive alternative for a sludge product is usually to sell it for a similar product of lower quality that is moving more rapidly. Of course, the lower-quality product will sell at a lower price, often about 25 percent less. That means that any time the cumulative holding cost from the present until the expected sales date exceeds 25 percent, the product is sludge and should be downgraded and sold.

This kind of analysis will show large amounts of sludge clogging our warehouses. It's not uncommon to see an otherwise well-managed company where sludge represents 50 percent of the inventory value, but accounts for only about 10 percent of the sales. What is worse is that after carrying charges are subtracted, these sales produce no profit at all.

After companies have identified which products they should get rid of and how to do it, they can test their new approaches in some representative warehouses. But then changes in the systems that control inventory will usually be necessary to keep the level of sludge inventory low. Both total inventory and sludge levels need to be tracked.

Regardless of real growth, most American companies have experienced declining sales growth due to slowed inflation. Even companies that have seen the price of their products grow steadily may thus have a large layer of slow-moving goods in their factories and warehouses. The important message is this: By reducing inventories to free up cash and cut costs, many U.S. companies are destroying service levels and driving off the very customers they are trying to retain. Inventories can be reduced but not indiscriminately. What management needs to do in many cases is decrease the amount of sludge and invest some of the savings in fast-moving inventory at the top of the pond to improve, not destroy, service.

Mr. White is an associate and Mr. Graff a partner in McKinsey's New York office.

LESSONS FROM THE FACTORY FLOOR

by Harvey Gittler

As today's business school students are winding down their summer internships, they are faced with two objectives: graduating next June and getting a job. Chances are that very few are thinking of entering the manufacturing industry. They prefer the cleaner fields of marketing, finance, banking, or consulting. And they are correct when they complain that factories are not sophisticated places and that manufacturing does not pay as well as the service fields.

But before these future managers—or their advisers—are thoroughly seduced by the glamour and pay of, say, a manufacturing consultant, they should be introduced to the many seductive qualities of the real thing: running a factory itself.

First of all, for those with an artistic bent, the smells, sounds, and sights of a factory at full steam are invigorating. The pungent odors of degreasing vapors, or the sweet smell of wood being formed, tickle the nostrils. The thump, thump, thump of a punch press produces a dance rhythm. The interrupted whirring of sewing machines as operators position material mimes the rock 'n' roll off beat. The swishing of air escaping from a plastic molding machine, as it opens its jaws and ejects a part, is music to the trained ear. The flashing of red lights and the clanging of bells as a bucket of molten iron moves overhead from the furnace to a pouring area brings a feeling of electricity, as does the splashing of cutting oil against a plastic shield as parts being formed at high speeds eventually take shape.

For those majoring in math or accounting, any factory making and assembling parts is a great exercise in logistics and a constant challenge. There is the almost insurmountable task of getting the right parts to the right place at the right time in the right quantity every day—or more likely, every hour. In some factories, where thousands of parts are involved, this task is as complex as organizing a trip to the moon. And whereas in most service industries you can often allow for a 10 percent margin of error, assembly lines do not run with just 90 percent of the parts. Either all the parts are on hand or the lines do not run.

If you are fascinated by human behavior, you will soon realize that factory workers are a breed apart. They may lack the sophistication and education required by other segments of the business, but they are artists in what they do. And actually their standards, ethics, and morality differ from the office force only in style: One guzzles beer, the other sips martinis; one "borrows" parts or tools, the other pads expense accounts; one vents frustration or anger by punching a hole in a vacuum line, the other by selling company secrets. Factory workers are no less and no more moral than their counterparts up front.

Tempers are often short in a factory, but recovery is quick. Calls in the middle of the night, when a line or machine go down, could be considered a great bother—or, to those born to the trade, a challenge that adds to the excitement. Working around the clock to fix a machine so people can go to work the next day is exhilarating—and exhausting. A factory is one damn crisis after another.

The operations of a factory, although complex, are dynamic and measured daily. Today's output, today's cost, today's efficiency, today's variances, are all measured, reported, and dealt with. Every day is a new ball game with a new score.

The end-of-the-month crunch, to ship everything in sight in order to hit the shipping target, is a cause for continual griping. But like the soldier who continually gripes, everyone seems to rise to the occasion. During the month when a customer calls with an emergency, it is truly remarkable to see a product that normally takes two weeks to move through a factory arrive on the shipping dock in two days—or maybe less; factory workers and managers have great respect for their ultimate boss, the customer.

Work never ends in a factory. Controlling and reducing costs are constant objectives. There are more projects in every factory than employees, supervisors, and engineers could ever complete. A factory that is not improving is a dying factory.

A walk through a factory that is not running, with only the hissing of steam leaks or air escaping from a pipe, gives one an eerie feeling. To walk through a factory that has shut down permanently is akin to walking through a cemetery where friends and family are buried.

Papers, magazines, and journals are filled with stories about robots. There probably are fully automated factories, but they are the exception. There is little to fear about robots. There will always be factories with people in them; if nothing else, someone has to make the robots. Robots are just new friends that may be a little more animated than a punch press.

One doesn't have to be an economics major to understand

that in any community the homes, the gardens, and the museums are important, but it is the factories and what is made in the community that are the town's raison d'être. And while the wealth of a nation lies in its factories, its strength rests in the dynamism of its youth. Our factories need new ideas and added vigor that enterprising graduates eagerly supply. These young entrepreneurs must be introduced to the challenges, excitement, and satisfactions of factory management, lest we become a nation of shopkeepers and service people. We need a renewal of our basic industries to survive.

Mr. Gittler was a materials manager in a factory manufacturing heating and air-conditioning equipment before he retired. He now writes lectures from his Oberlin, Ohio, home.

DON'T AUTOMATE—ELIMINATE!

by Ray Howard

I t is 1930 and you are sitting in on a board meeting of a major grocery chain. These are the days before the automated supermarkets—the days when the cheerful grocery clerk personally takes from the shelves the items you request. Concerned with increasing payroll costs, management has made a study that suggests that enormous cost savings would accrue if robots were substituted for grocery clerks. "We could eliminate almost all payroll costs attendant to waiting on the customer," boasts one senior vice president.

Fortunately, the computer and robots did not exist commercially sixty years ago and we were spared the spectacle of grocery stores manned by robots toppling oatmeal drums off twelve-foot-high shelves. Instead, entrepreneurs operating local and regional chains wrestled with payroll problems on a more fundamental basis: They conceived the idea of letting consumers serve themselves. Massive service costs were transferred from the paid labor force to the "free" consumer force.

Today, computers and robots do exist, as do the means for automating communications. As a result, managers are skipping over fundamental ideas for cost reduction in favor of the complex, costly, and often less reliable means of automation.

A major automaker is now setting up a communications network to increase efficiency. When a customer orders a car, the dealer "inputs" the network with all relevant information on make, style, color, options, price, etc. The automated network then inputs the sales department, orders the appropriate parts from suppliers, schedules production at the assembly plant, and far-forward orders the appropriate replacement and crash parts. All this to reduce the more than $2,500-per-car cost gap between Detroit and Tokyo.

The plan seems logical until you go back to fundamentals. A major internal study done by General Motors suggests that the bulk of the cost gap is directly attributable to systems complexity. There is an enormous complexity gap between Detroit and Tokyo in overall marketing-manufacturing systems. Japanese cars are "packaged" with few options available. American cars are almost custom-built with myriad options and thousands of combinations available. For example, the Honda Accord can be purchased in one of thirty-two possible combinations. There are American models with over forty thousand combinations! Detroit's incredible systems complexity results in overmanning, excessive capital demand, bloated inventories, slow cycle times, and poor quality.

Instead of building an automated network to institutionalize the current business system, the company should sharply reduce the number of options, eliminate overlapping models, and more sharply pinpoint consumer segments with compatible product and pricing strategies. These steps would eliminate massive quantities of labor, capital, machinery, real estate, and inventory.

The automation disease can spread quickly down through an organization. The sub-bosses jump on board with two major thrusts: "make-work" and "make-thing." One major automotive company in Detroit, unconcerned about a twenty-nine-day supply of sheet metal per warehouse, attempted to automate its inventory process to reduce labor costs. While Detroit's engineers were adding "make-things" to the warehouses, Tokyo was transferring to its suppliers the costs of sheet-metal inventory above a nineteen-hour supply. While Detroit automated, Tokyo eliminated.

There is real trouble when the automation bug hits the sub-sub-bosses and lower-level engineers. In a different division of the same Detroit company mentioned above, the multidrill press station in the rough machining area frequently broke off drill bits, which then became imbedded in the casting's machine holes. This meant that a casting would flow down through the line until caught in assembly. It was then trundled over to the repair shop, repaired, and sent back up the line—obviously a costly procedure. The engineers solved the problem with an automated make-thing that probed the machine holes for broken drill bits. Soon probes and plugged machine holes were merrily colliding—resulting in broken probes. Now there were broken drill bits, plugged machine holes, broken probe ends, and bad castings all flowing through the system.

The solution? Automated electronic sensors that would tell whether the probes were broken! How much simpler it would have been to improve the quality of castings and implement a tool-change program for the drill press. Unfortunately, the automated factory has a tendency to institutionalize both the basic process and the wide array of make-things built into the system later. While labor costs may be reduced, the automated factory tends to artificially increase capital demands and cycle time. It is far more rewarding to eliminate costs or transfer them somewhere else.

One example of how to eliminate costs through product

transfer can be seen any weekend. Look around at all the folks wearing peak-billed caps. Originally produced in six to eight different sizes, the caps you see now are made in only one size; the plastic tab in the rear adjusts the cap to any head size. The producer benefits in sharply reduced costs of material, space, cycle time, machinery, labor, and inventory. The customer benefits in lower costs and greater product availability.

Chrysler has ingeniously transferred the "one size fits most" concept to automobile platforms—the wheels and axles, drivetrain, and braking system of a car. By putting the Caravan-Voyager on the already-paid-for K-Car platform, Chrysler incurred program costs of $700 million. In contrast, Ford Motor designed its new Taurus/Sable program from the ground up at a cost of $2.9 billion.

Many ingenious companies have generated megasavings by transferring work to the consumer. A nation raised on Erector Sets and Lincoln Logs is capable of doing all kinds of finished production work. Today, consumers are providing final assembly on an incredible array of products, ranging from Weber grills and furniture to automobiles (car kits) and houses. Even the company making webbed sports belts makes us cut the ends to fit our waist sizes. The majority of consumers have more time than money, and are willing to trade work time for lower prices. Twenty years ago, who would have believed that most of us would be willing to pump our own gas to save a few pennies a gallon?

You can also transfer a large quantity of work (and rework) to your suppliers. A food-oil processor found it could eliminate the need for an additional production unit by buying oil of a more consistent molecular density. New York movie houses have transferred their lobbies (people warehouses) to the supplier of sidewalks—the city of New York. With retail space costing $380 per square foot in Manhattan, the average movie theater has transferred about ten thousand dollars a year in space costs to the city. There are about a thousand Korean greengrocers in New York. The average fifteen-foot shop front has "added" another five feet of sidewalk display space. At $150 per square foot, this tiny industry has transferred more than $11 million in space costs to the city.

Before you automate, try to eliminate. Or transfer the work to someone else. You will save on everything—not simply labor.

Mr. Howard is president of Howard International, a West-port, Connecticut-based management consulting company.

SYNERGY
WITH YOUR
EMPLOYEES

Developing a synergy with your employees has become particularly difficult at a time when downsizing, frequent turnovers, the lure of cheap foreign labor, and the ever-increasing costs of employee benefits have strained the concept of loyalty in the workplace. This chapter will examine these growing tensions, how they affect your role as a manager, and what you can do to motivate your employees while cutting costs.

What makes these two seemingly contradictory goals compatible is the way in which successful managers have been able to exploit synergistic forces at work in employer-employee relations. For example:

The decline of union membership—down to about 16 percent of the entire labor force—has simplified labor negotiating, and all costs pertaining thereto;

The growth of employee and management stock ownership plans has led to a synergy between management and labor which is actually being used as a joint labor-management defense against takeovers;

Workers' increasing familiarity with electronic machinery and their enthusiasm to learn more have allowed many managers in both the manufacturing and service sectors to update their workplace with the most competitive equipment.

Long-term company loyalty on the part of both labor and management, which used to be a part of corporate America's landscape, is indeed becoming a thing of the past. However, this in turn allows for greater flexibility in what used to be a rigid set of rules guiding employer-employee relations. Ideas and strategies that can help you adapt to this new environment are found in the following section.

HOW INDUSTRIAL RECRUITERS
SELL THEMSELVES SHORT
. . . .

by Bob Luck

T*his should have* been the year that Smokestack America regained competitiveness in recruiting graduates of the nation's top MBA programs. Wall Street, which had siphoned off nearly one fourth of the graduates from top-ten schools in recent years, has lost much of its attractiveness since the 1987 stock market crash. Business schools have increased their emphasis on manufacturing and operations, and have modified their admissions policies to admit more students with industrial experience. In addition, there is a broad national consensus that our country needs more plant managers and fewer money managers. All of these factors should make industrial companies look more attractive to MBA graduates.

Don't bet on it. Although early placement statistics show that hiring by Wall Street has declined dramatically, students are not exactly flocking to the factory floor. At the Massachusetts Institute of Technology School of Management, for example, preliminary statistics show that hiring by investment banks has been cut in half, from 22 percent of graduates in 1987 to 11 percent in 1988. However, manufacturing companies have increased their share of graduates only slightly: 32 percent of 1988's class compared with 28 percent in 1987. The big winners in the recruiting sweepstakes in 1988 were management-consulting firms (26 percent of graduates compared with 18 percent in 1987) and computer-service companies (9 percent, nearly double the 5 percent hired in 1987).

Why do industrial companies continue to have such a hard time recruiting MBAs from the top business schools? The standard reason given by recruiters is money. Last year, the average starting salary for MIT MBA graduates was 12 percent higher at nonmanufacturing companies than at manufacturing companies. Students who chose consulting received 30 percent more than those who chose manufacturing.

There is no question that many MBAs are lured to nonindustrial careers by the promise of fatter paychecks. To suggest that MBAs are motivated only by money, however, is a dangerous simplification that ignores other problems industrial companies have in hiring talented managers.

One problem is that most industrial companies are being badly outrecruited by service companies. When I started school a year ago, I wasn't sure of the career path I intended to follow. But I was very interested in the idea of marketing some sort of industrial product: chemicals, telecommunications equipment, or maybe computer software. My plan for the year was to learn about as many industrial companies as possible, and try to get a summer job in marketing with a company like AT&T, General Electric, or Microsoft.

Recruiting activities started with fall-semester presentations for first-year students under the auspices of the MIT placement office. A moderate number of industrial companies sponsored presentations. These affairs usually were held during the lunch hour, an inconvenient time of day for most students. Participants were provided with cold sandwiches and soda, or encouraged to bring a bag lunch. The presenters were generally junior-level managers or personnel department staffers, and publicity for the events consisted of a few posters.

Several major consulting firms and investment banks, on the other hand, sent me personal invitations and scheduled their events in the late afternoon or evening when my schedule was more flexible. Given my lack of interest in these fields, I had intended to skip these gatherings. But I was so flattered by the attention, I went to presentations by several consulting firms.

These presentations typically included a talk by a senior officer of the firm, along with cocktails and/or dinner. Over drinks or dinner, I had a chance to mingle with consultants who were roughly my age and to learn much more about the consulting profession and the type of work I might be doing than I could have in a forty-five-minute lunch meeting. Along with their formal recruiting presentations, consulting firms made continuous efforts to stay in touch with MIT students, both in and out of the classroom.

Well-known consulting firms such as McKinsey, Bain, and the Boston Consulting Group each received applications for summer employment from over half of my class. However, many of the industrial companies that had given fall presentations weren't even planning to interview for summer positions. These companies apparently felt that the recruiting benefits of a summer program, combined with the amount of real work the students could do, wouldn't justify the cost of hiring students. Most large industrial firms recruiting on campus received applications from between 5 percent and 25 percent of my class.

Some of the industrial companies to which I applied rejected me based only on my resume; they were not interested in interviewing me to get a better idea of my skills and qualifications. The industrial firms that did interview me typically set up a thirty-minute meeting—hardly enough time to get acquainted, let alone to see whether a match could be found between the firm's needs and my interests. Many of the firms sent personnel managers to conduct the interviews; these people were very helpful in explaining salary structures and corporate hiring policies, but weren't much use in describing the work I would actually be doing.

The consulting firms interviewed virtually everyone who applied. First-round interviews were generally an hour in length, and were followed up by second- or third-round interviews to help assess especially promising candidates. Many of the interviews were conducted by senior people: During my

THIS WILL NOT BE USED

second round of interviews with one firm, I was interviewed by the chairman. He spent thirty minutes patiently answering all of my questions about the consulting profession in general and his firm in particular.

By the end of the interviewing process, I had been sold on working for a consulting firm. The consultants I had talked with convinced me that I would be working with interesting colleagues on important management problems. They took a personal interest in me and assured me that I would be a valuable member of the team. None of the industrial companies I interviewed with came close to the consulting firms in providing such an attractive picture of employment. As a result, I decided to work for a consulting firm this summer, and I intend to work in consulting after I graduate from MIT next year.

Companies that preach that "people are our most important asset" could do much more to cultivate MBA recruits than flying in twice a year for a quick presentation and a token summer job interview. Industrial corporations that emulated consultants' tactics in recruiting business school students might be surprised by their success in attracting top students.

Mr. Luck was a second-year MBA student at the MIT School of Management when this article was written.

POORLY SERVED EMPLOYEES
SERVE CUSTOMERS JUST AS POORLY

by Robert E. Kelley

Sears *recently advertised* a special sale on its new top-of-the-line vacuum cleaners. I called our local Sears to buy one. The salesclerk had never heard of the product and was unaware of the advertised sale. I asked to speak to the boss, who said that the product was not in stock nor did she anticipate receiving it. She suggested that I call around to other Sears stores to find one. I suggested that she do the calling for me, but she said she was too busy for that kind of service.

Undaunted, I asked for the customer service department. A representative there offered to order the vacuum cleaner but said I would have to drive to a distant Sears warehouse to pick it up. With my blood pressure rising, I asked to speak to the store manager. He said he would look into the situation and get back to me. Four days later, a salesclerk called, inquiring if my wife might be interested in buying a vacuum cleaner.

The U.S. "service economy" is in big trouble. The reason: The quality of much service today, like the quality of many manufactured goods fifteen years ago, stinks. When you do encounter the rare high-quality service, the experience stands in stark and lonely contrast to the undifferentiated mass of miserable service.

This poor service has been of minor importance in the past—mostly a customer irritant. However, the service sector now faces a double-barreled competitive threat. First, the White House Office of Consumer Affairs recently released some alarming statistics: 96 percent of dissatisfied customers do not complain about poor quality directly to the company. Instead, they simply never buy at that company again and broadcast their dissatisfaction to friends and acquaintances.

Second, in July 1987, Congress's Office of Technology Assessment warned of a coming onslaught of international competition in services that will challenge United States dominance. For example, foreign airlines are taking away market share from U.S. carriers, as witnessed by the rise of JAL and Swiss Air at the expense of Pan American. Given these realities, U.S. service providers must learn the lesson that was hammered into the manufacturing sector—either shape up or face three possibilities: (1) be replaced by a competitor, probably foreign; (2) get taken over; (3) go bankrupt.

Why is the quality of service so lousy? Executives blame the poor quality of people who are willing to work in lower-paying service jobs. But this argument does not explain why higher-paying manufacturing jobs turned out poor-quality goods for many years. High pay does not equal good service, and, as McDonald's has shown, low pay need not result in poor service.

These executives next blame deregulation and the ensuing competition. But a reasonable person would think that increased competition among banks or airlines would motivate higher-quality service. They also argue that they are providing services that are no worse than that of their competitors. That, at least, is truthful—but the standard hardly is worth aspiring to.

There are two explanations that are more compelling. First, too many providers do not understand the nature of a service. Most are intangible: You cannot see a lawyer's advice nor take home a waiter's behavior. Services are generally consumed when provided: Unlike a defective car that can be recalled, you cannot recall a blundered heart operation or a demeaning comment to a customer.

The second and more powerful explanation for poor service is management. Service providers treat customers similar to the way they, as employees, are treated by management. In many such organizations management treats employees as unvalued and unintelligent. The employees in turn convey the identical message to the customer. If management treats employees' concerns with indifference, then employees will not care about the customers' complaints. It is a rare employee who can rise above the effects of such poor management.

In poorly managed organizations, a pecking order exists. The boss gets the most respect and receives the widest degree of tolerance for less-than-social behavior. If the top executive treats a middle manager with rudeness and disrespect, then that manager mimics the executive by acting similarly toward his subordinate. This process continues until the last person in the organizational chain has no one to dump on. And that person is usually the airline ticket agent, the order taker at the fast-food chain, the bank teller, or the nurse's aide. Since he has no one to abuse inside the organization, he treats customers as if they were the ones on the next rung down.

If managers want to improve service quality they must treat employees the same way they want employees to treat customers. Managers are the servants of the employees, not just the bosses. They must provide services to the employees in a friendly, helpful, and efficient manner that will enable those employees to better serve the customers. Customers thus become the beneficiaries of high-quality service that mirrors the organization's inner working.

ServiceMaster Company, an Illinois-based provider of support services in housekeeping and food service, exemplifies this approach. Employee illiteracy in these jobs is high. ServiceMaster understands that illiteracy handicaps its employees' job performance and self-image, resulting in poorer-quality service to the clients. The company offers education programs; develops pictorial, color-coded instructional material to improve job productivity; and provides performance-based promotion opportunities to improve self-respect and upward mobility. The results: low turnover in these traditionally high-turnover jobs; productivity levels higher than industry averages; and an average 30 percent return on equity after taxes from 1973 to 1985. Most important, clients are pleased. A company with a billion dollars in annual revenue, ServiceMaster now exports its services—its customers include fifteen hospitals in Japan.

High-quality service depends on high-quality management. If U.S. providers fail to learn this lesson, they should not be surprised if Americans have accounts at Japanese banks, fly Singapore Airlines, or eat in French-owned restaurants.

Mr. Kelley teaches management at the Graduate School of Industrial Administration, Carnegie-Mellon University.

SLOWING THE SERVICE SECTOR'S
REVOLVING DOOR
. . . .

by *Kenneth B. Hamlet*

T*urnover rates in* service industries are appalling. The average annual turnover for full-service restaurants is 210 percent, meaning that every job slot must be filled twice a year. In fast food, annual turnover is 270 percent—the average jobholder lasts just four and a half months. The hospitality industry—with a turnover rate of "only" 104 percent—is slightly better off. But since it costs about $2,500 to replace each hotel worker, turnover still is enormously costly. These trends have worrisome implications for our national competitiveness.

High turnover is partly caused by the well-noted aging of the baby boom generation. The traditional entry level labor pool for the services industry—sixteen-to-twenty-four-year-olds—has already begun its decline to just two million by the year 2000, so the competition for these workers is becoming more intense. The decline of our education system is also to blame. Employees who are functionally illiterate (or for whom English is a poorly understood second language) often quit in discouragement and drift from job to job without hope of advancement.

Managers who have not adapted to demographic changes are yet another part of the problem. The work force is growing older, it is swelling with immigrants from south of the border, and more and more households have two wage earners. These changes present a whole new array of work-force issues to contend with.

At Holiday Inns, we realized some time ago that we had to begin to slow the revolving door by developing management programs aimed at attracting and retaining qualified applicants. These programs have had a major impact. At our one hundred and seventy company-owned or -managed hotels, we have reduced turnover from 100 percent to 65 percent—nearly forty percentage points better than the industry norm. As a result, the number of openings to be filled at a two hundred-employee hotel has dropped from two hundred to one hundred and thirty annually, our training costs have declined dramatically, and the quality of service has improved as well.

Our strategy isn't fancy, but it works. Here's what we'd suggest to managers facing similar challenges:

Let bonuses abound. Offering bonuses to every employee—as we began to do five years ago—is a powerful weapon in the fight against turnover. Every line employee of a centrally owned and operated Holiday Inn receives a fifty-dollar quarterly bonus and a hundred-dollar annual bonus if the hotel reaches 95 percent of its profit goals and the employee meets his or her own performance objectives. These bonuses are doubled if the hotel reaches 100 percent of its operating goals. For a worker who makes eleven thousand dollars annually, an additional five hundred to six hundred dollars a year gives good reason to perform well and to stay with the company.

The design of bonus packages is—within limits—developed by individual management teams. At many Holiday Inn Crowne Plaza hotels, for example, employees receive "crownes" for outstanding work. For accumulating ten crownes, the employee receives twenty-five dollars; for fifty crownes, a day off with pay.

To keep them, teach them. Employees have the highest degree of job satisfaction when they know exactly what is expected of them. Have all staff members participate in a video orientation when they start their jobs, and, if necessary, make it available in languages other than English.

Holiday Inn University, which began as a residential institution for management training, now provides field instruction for all levels of Holiday Inns personnel. Under our "Roads

Scholar" program, for example, trainers traveling in company vans—equipped with prototypes of our new computerized reservations systems—visited fourteen hundred U.S. hotels in 1988, training every Holiday Inn front-desk person.

Reveal a path, not a treadmill. Because many basic service jobs are maligned as dead-end positions, it's critical to provide advancement opportunities for all employees. Workers are more likely to stay with their jobs if they see a real career path before them. We make sure that opportunities for advancement are well known throughout our work force. All available supervisory positions throughout the company, from front-desk supervisor on up, are listed on the company's computerized communications system. Once a week, information on these openings—including salary, location, and contact—are printed out and posted on the employee bulletin board of each of our hotels.

As a result, scores of our employees who began in entry level jobs now hold positions of significant responsibility. For instance, the Holiday Inns executive who developed and oversees the Roads Scholar program began with us a decade ago as a desk clerk.

Nurture the entrepreneurs. Managers who are on the front lines of the turnover battle sometimes find creative, entrepreneurial remedies. Put their insights to good use. For instance, Victor Vongs, a native Thai who is the general manager of a Holiday Inn Crowne Plaza in White Plains, New York, has developed programs to aid employees who are new to the United States. He registers them in free English classes, helps them find apartments, and provides vital moral support. "Because many of our employees left their immediate families behind, they think of our hotel as a second home," he explains. By building employee loyalty, Mr. Vongs has turned a demographic "problem" (an increase in immigrant workers) into an advantage: In just two years, he has reduced turnover at his hotel from 82.5 percent to 10.5 percent.

Start at the beginning. Since half of those employees who

quit do so within the first thirty days, we train our managers in interviewing techniques so they can seek out the right attitudes, skills, and work habits in prospective employees. Recently, we developed a screening program that identifies those applicants most likely to excel. Under the program, answers to about twenty-five basic questions are correlated with the responses of our most successful current employees. With this comparison, we can begin to predict three key components of job performance: customer service, job attitude, and competence.

Rapid turnover is not an isolated problem, but the manifestation of a disaffected work force. Employees enjoying a high degree of job satisfaction will not only stay with the company longer, but work better as well. And while demographics may create unprecedented challenges for today's managers in the battle against rampant turnover, they need not dictate the success or failure of any business.

Mr. Hamlet is president and CEO of Holiday Inns.

RETOOLING YOUR WORKERS
ALONG WITH YOUR MACHINES
. . . .
by James L. Sheedy

A *worker in* my plant, a man I will call Joe Davis, recently earned his high school equivalency certificate. Not so unusual, you say; a lot of young people discover they can't get a good job without a diploma of some kind. That isn't the case with Mr. Davis. He has held a good job for more than twenty-five years. But he also couldn't read this article, or anything more complex than a comic book, before he returned to the classroom.

Mr. Davis is one of approximately twenty employees at

Ingersoll-Rand's Athens, Pennsylvania, plant who earned equivalency credit during the past year. They completed their high school work through a special program designed to help workers cope with plant modernization, a program that made stepping-stones of words and sums that once were stumbling blocks.

The program, operated by Penn State University's Institute for Research in Training and Development, began in 1987 after Ingersoll-Rand decided to modernize its Athens plant, the primary manufacturing location for the company's power tool division. Parts of the plant had been in operation for more than a hundred years, and it was in many respects typical of older factories found throughout the Northeast. Ingersoll-Rand made a commitment to the community and to employees by keeping the plant going, realizing at the same time that changes were necessary.

When we reviewed the alternatives, we decided that to keep our business competitive, we would have to upgrade our equipment. Our employees historically have operated conventional machine tools—cranks, dials, buttons, etc. Now, as a result of upgrading to numerically controlled machinery, they have to be capable of performing computer setups, interacting with the controls of this new technology, and integrating these abilities with their regular work teams.

Production methods went from the traditional assembly line system to cellular manufacturing. Workers are grouped in cells of twenty individuals, and each cell handles similar manufacturing functions, regardless of product. The operation is fully computerized.

Traditionally, companies in this position hire people with specific skills for specific jobs for a short term. If and when their skills are no longer needed, those people often are let go. However, that cut-and-dried approach fails to take into consideration intangibles such as pride of workmanship, loyalty, and good work habits.

Rather than hire new, already qualified workers, we decided

to retrain current employees. Most had long service with the company. They were familiar with our products, with customer complaints and compliments, and, most importantly, with the plant's long-established culture. These attributes cannot be instilled through a training seminar.

Having thus decided to commit ourselves to the retraining of current employees, we invited professors and graduate students from Penn State's University Park campus to visit the plant and test the skills of our hourly workers. This was the first step of a five-year program, cosponsored with the State of Pennsylvania's Ben Franklin Partnership.

The researchers concluded that training should take place on two levels: basic skills (reading, writing, and arithmetic), and floor skills—skills employees would need in the day-to-day operation of computerized equipment. Those enrolled in the program's small classes start with basic math before moving on to algebra. Reading assignments also increase in difficulty during the fifteen-to-twenty-four-month learning cycles. Employees like Joe Davis can go on to earn their graduate equivalency diplomas. Associate's degrees also are offered in the fields of electrical and mechanical technology.

The results have exceeded expectations. The Penn State program helped Ingersoll-Rand to profit from plant modernization, since computerization keeps costs down and products priced competitively. But it did so while giving veteran workers increased pride and a greater feeling of self-worth. We also have retained dedicated, proven employees.

The employees' response to the program is overwhelmingly favorable: 99 percent of those eligible volunteered to participate. And many don't stop with the basics. For example, some, having learned algebra, asked to move on to geometry. Since the inception of the retraining program, our employees have spent more than twenty-seven thousand hours in the classroom. The magnitude of this number certainly demonstrates the commitment our employees have made, because approximately 50 percent of those hours were on the employees' own time.

Gerald Chandler, who is a machine operator on our night shift, states, "I do not mind that the refresher training was on our time . . . I never had a chance to take algebra or advanced math in high school." Plant electrician David Shanks says, "I certainly had some misgivings . . . I had been out of school for over twenty years. [But] I have decided to take advantage of the program, as I do not wish to be left behind my peers. Advancement and merit should come to those who earn it, not those who are next in line."

The plant isn't the same place it was before the summer of 1987. Not only do the employees feel better about themselves, but the program has been an eye-opener for their supervisors as well. For example, not long ago management scheduled a plant open house. The workers basically told us, "It's our show. We'll handle it." They did—for the first time ever without managerial support—and made quite an impression on the several thousand people who attended.

Now other Ingersoll-Rand plant managers are looking at the Athens plant to see whether a similar program can help them. According to plant manager Mark Amlot, "If anybody's looking for particulars, he can always ask someone like Gerald Chandler or David Shanks."

Mr. Sheedy is manager of human resources at Ingersoll-Rand's Athens, Pennsylvania, plant.

ADAPTING TO A UNION-FREE ENVIRONMENT
. . . .

By Thomas J. Raleigh

As the recent overwhelming rejection of unionization by Nissan workers in Tennessee attests, the current government and business climate presents a unique opportunity for companies, both large and small, to develop and implement long-term strategic plans for conducting business in a union-free environment. For the first time in five decades (going back to the union organization drives of the 1930s), management has the opportunity to develop a productive relationship with employees without the intrusion of third-party agents.

This window of opportunity has been brought about by a series of events that have taken place over the past three to four years. These events include, but are not limited to:

- *A union movement torn by dissension, shrinking finances, and lack of direction and purpose.* In 1970, labor membership as a percentage of the overall labor force stood at 24.7 percent. In 1982, according to figures of the Bureau of National Affairs, union membership weighed in at 17.9 percent of the work force. By 1989, union membership had dipped to 16.7 percent.
- *The "laissez-faire" philosophy of the Labor Department in the field of labor-management relations.* There now is a marked tendency for the Labor Department not to get directly involved in major negotiations throughout the country.
- *Recent court decisions heavily weighed against the continuance of unionism in some bankruptcy, acquisition, and divestiture proceedings.* The Continental Airlines case is a classic example of this.
- *A distinctive shift in National Labor Relations Board philosophy from pro-union to a more evenhanded stance.* There is much evidence to support this, such as recent rulings that support an employee's right to resign from a union, and an employer's right *not* to bargain with a union over certain basic management decisions.

We do not see any major development in the immediate future that will reverse the strong tide moving in the direction of a pro-management, union-free working environment.

As history teaches, management had a similar opportunity in the years before the 1930s. But rather than capitalize on the situation, the short-term business thinkers of the day followed the precepts of worker exploitation and, hence, materially contributed to the very essence and substance of union organization in this nation.

Now, five decades later, we stand at the same threshold. The critical test in the nineties is whether management has the intellectual discipline and foresight to capitalize on this rare moment in our history, rather than fall victim to short-term expediency and repeat the errors of the 1920s and 1930s.

Within this context, and based on our client experience and contacts, we have developed the following principles that turn directly on the issue of developing and maintaining a union-free environment:

- *Management philosophy:* It should be realized there are no short cuts or free rides to successfully operate in a union-free environment. Management from the chief executive officer on down must be disciplined and totally committed to the demands and challenges of dealing directly and fairly with the employees. This means the organization must develop and consistently maintain a doctrine of fairness in all aspects of the employer-employee relationship. This applies to all dynamics of the relationship, whether pay, communication, policies, overall treatment, or equity between the parties.
- *Organization:* The stewardship on maintaining a healthy, union-free environment must be entrusted to the pro-active, strategic wing of the organization. This is not the arena for short-term, "corner-cutting" players who don't understand the bottom-line benefits and value of the union-free scenario.
- *Consistency:* The hallmark of organizations that successfully operate in a union-free environment is consistency. Notwithstanding the ever-changing cycles of business, a doctrine of fairness is consistently applied.
- *Discipline:* At the core of union-free management is the discipline to do the right thing rather than submit to short-term expediency. A classic example of this is the

case of a software manufacturer that moved to the Sun Belt seven years ago to avoid high union-mandated employment costs. Now, after seven years of substandard wage increases and cavalier treatment of its employees by the company, another union has moved in. In this case, the short-termers prevailed for six years in a row, and as a consequence must now bargain with an even stronger union over the same issues the company moved south to avoid. It takes discipline, conviction, and leadership to override the corner-cutting mentality that eventually leads to union organization.

Companies that fail to grasp the significance of the current opportunities in employee-employer relationships will simply continue to cope, put out fires, and lose competitive advantage. In such cases, expediency will prevail over taking the high road in human resources management. Those organizations that move quickly and take advantage of the current situation have the rare opportunity of upgrading the long-term destiny of the enterprise in terms of quality relations, growth, and profits.

Mr. Raleigh is a labor attorney and president of Raleigh and Company, a Dallas-based human resources consulting firm.

EFFECTIVE TURNAROUNDS
DO NOT REQUIRE EMPLOYEE TURNOVERS

by John O. Whitney

T*he current wave* of downsizing, restructuring, and reorganizing—often euphemisms for firing people—has an alternative, as was refreshingly demonstrated a few years ago by Hugo Mann, managing director of Deutscher Supermarkt Handels-GmbH, a West German food retailer. When

Deutscher acquired a marginally profitable food chain, Mr. Mann returned the chain to an acceptable return on investment without reducing personnel. At the outset he promised that no one would be fired if the employees helped him achieve a 5 percent sales increase by year-end.

This is the story Mr. Mann told at a European seminar I conducted in 1986. He had learned that the food chain might be for sale. Quietly, he visited all ninety of its stores, noting their strengths and weaknesses. His staff provided demographic data and competitive analysis. He hypothesized that the fundamentals were in place that would return the firm to profitability if he could achieve a modest sales increase. When financial data were provided, his hypothesis was confirmed: A 5 percent sales increase, augmented by other operating efficiencies, would restore profits with no reduction in personnel or pay. Granted, Mr. Mann operates in Germany, where custom, regulations, and union constraints make it more difficult to lay off or fire people than in the United States. In this instance, however, he had the option of firing people—he just chose not to do so.

Mr. Mann's reasoning was a model of clarity: "I can achieve the sales increase in the following ways: I can sell more per shopping trip to present customers through better in-store merchandising. I can improve my service so my customers will forsake the competition and shop with me more often. I can attract new customers. Or, I can achieve a combination of all three—and I can achieve it easier with an experienced, motivated, enthusiastic work force."

Immediately following the acquisition, Mr. Mann met with employees to present his proposition: "No layoffs if you will help me achieve a 5 percent increase in sales." The employees accepted the challenge enthusiastically. That was 1982. Today, the acquired chain is still profitable and growing steadily.

One of the keys to Mr. Mann's success was his willingness to make decisions based on analysis of data, rather than following the apparently obvious, but often obviously wrong, conclusion.

He did not fire people and close stores, then ask questions. Instead, he asked if the water was too high or the bridge too low. Too many turnaround experts mortgage the future of a company by indiscriminate firings and hasty divestitures.

True, Mr. Mann's experience may be the exception, not the rule. Many troubled companies can be returned to long-term profitability only after the removal of unproductive managers and employees along with ill-advised or outmoded ventures. But most terminations and divestitures are irreversible and should be decided only after careful thought and painstaking analysis.

In 1972, the Pathmark Division of Supermarkets General, operators of food stores on the U.S. Eastern seaboard, faced a price war initiated by A&P, which was trying to restore its former glory. Exacerbating Pathmark's problems was the recent acquisition by its parent company of several small department store chains whose inventory requirements soaked up more cash than the supermarkets could produce. An operating analysis showed Pathmark could not afford to meet A&P's prices across the board. Pathmark's war chest at the time was minuscule compared with A&P's. Further analysis demonstrated the impossibility of making sufficient personnel and other expense cuts to restore profitability.

Clearly, a marketing solution was required, and fortunately Pathmark had an energetic work force and management team that could rise to a marketing challenge. The decision was made to open all of Pathmark's stores twenty-four hours a day—a revolutionary decision at the time and one that produced an additional $170 million in sales, enabling Pathmark to break even in 1972 and to build a solid customer base for the future. Pathmark would have survived without the twenty-four-hour program, but the momentum created by the campaign shortened its recovery period by years.

Employing a marketing solution for a turnaround does not suggest one should use a sales increase to paper over operating inefficiencies and ineffective personnel; the fact that the firm is in trouble implies the need for intrinsic change. And even though early operating improvements can be achieved through heightened motivation and improved morale, a substantive reorganization nearly always will be necessary. Bureaucratic entrenchments need to be dismantled, and marginally useful work needs to be excised.

But Hugo Mann demonstrated that it is possible to make such changes—reorganize the company's structure and energize its management process—without closing stores or firing employees. Both the raiders and the corporate leaders whose backgrounds may direct them to divest or downsize rather than to manage should diagnose before they prescribe. In many instances a successful marketing effort will restore the company's fortunes . . . or buy the time required to make a proper evaluation of the company's problems and opportunities.

The Genghis Khan approach may sometimes be necessary, but it also may preempt the golden opportunity to maintain momentum while restoring profitability. A turnaround does not have to be either-or.

Mr. Whitney is a visiting professor at Columbia University's Graduate School of Business, and is author of Taking Charge: Management Guide to Troubled Companies and Turnarounds *(Dow Jones Irwin, 1987). He was president of Pathmark 1972–1977.*

STEPPING DOWN IN SIZE
BUT UP IN REWARDS
. . . .
by Elaine Goldman

As an executive recruiter, I see hundreds of resumes each week from highly qualified Fortune 500 managers. Many of these men and women have lost their jobs, or live with the anxiety that they soon will. National statistics tell the larger story: More than six hundred thousand middle-level managers last year fell victim to mergers and takeovers or belt-tightening caused by deflation and competition.

These casualties do not come just from manufacturing. High-tech companies also are undergoing massive restructuring. Recent upheavals at CBS and the other TV networks again emphasize that change is virtually across the board, and across the country.

My firm recruits corporate marketing, communications, and human resources professionals. These specialties are bellwethers of industry—barometers of what's happening now and what's likely to happen tomorrow in the job market. Corporate communications, for one, has always been vulnerable to the swings of economic favor. In good times it has been a fount of large staffs, generous salaries, and nearly unlimited expense budgets. In bad times, this area is hit hard—and often first—with staff and salary cuts, and tight budgets.

Corporate communicators are among the first to be let go—critics say—because they do not deal directly with moving the company's product. Not that the corporate communications function itself is without merit. But public relations executives have a hard time substantiating their own worth. Their personal qualities have often been lost in the image building of the company, its senior management, and its products. After a company's image has been developed, the chief executive may begin to question the need for those who do not directly contribute to the bottom line—especially if aggressive competition or takeovers are threatening the market.

These communications professionals must reevaluate where they fit into today's corporate landscape. They, and their peers in many staff functions in large corporations, must take a fresh look at their surroundings. As the sun sets on employment opportunities in many of the Fortune 500 companies, a new horizon can be seen in the rising "Inc. 1,000," and in even smaller new businesses.

This presents a dual challenge. For the displaced manager unable to find another job in the Fortune 500, these new, adventurous, high-growth firms are oddities. They are entrepreneurial—where stock options mean more than high salaries, and individual perks are frowned upon. Limos and spacious offices overlooking parklike settings are a thing of the past for them. They are everything that large corporate managers aren't accustomed to.

It's not surprising, then, that displaced managers often fail to realize, explore or accept this new challenge. I hear in many interviews this unrealistic career objective: "I want my next job to be pretty much like the last one—including the salary!" Such managers fail to realize the huge contribution they could make in a smaller pond: a bigger splash, and probably with increased respect from senior management. Increased autonomy and independence are the psychic rewards of operating in a smaller network.

Middle managers operating in smaller firms are held more personally accountable for their own job performance and for the success of the firm as a whole. And high-quality performance doesn't necessarily entail high salaries. Indeed, salaries may be lower than the managers previously commanded. But the availability of stock options, profit sharing, and the occasional bonus are the longer-term rewards, especially when an entrepreneurial firm succeeds. Who knows which company might become the next IBM?

Looking from the other side of the desk, owners and managers of the Inc. 1,000 companies often overlook the wealth of talent, experience, and contacts offered by the seasoned professionals who may be looking to step down in size but up in responsibility. Youth is too often put at a premium in the start-ups. And sometimes the smaller companies assume that they could never attract and keep executives accustomed to life in the fast lane. Little do managers of these smaller firms realize that an executive just dumped by a lumbering giant may find work at an unencumbered, inventive firm a great way to get a new start on life. And the growth prospectus of a fledgling company could be greatly enhanced by inheriting the hard-won and invested wisdom of the middle managers nurtured by a Fortune 500 firm. Displaced professionals are a real bargain.

What is desperately needed today is convergence. Both sides can capitalize on today's restructuring, if they open themselves to the possibilities. It's a time of great change, but change creates a combination of circumstances with room to grow, a chance to try something new, a look into a different world—an opportunity, in short, for those wise enough to use it. For those of us in executive search, we see some of this new wisdom both on the part of our client companies and in the upbeat attitudes of forward-looking candidates.

Ms. Goldman is president of Goldman, Gschwind and Company, a New York-based executive search and consulting firm.

HOW TO HANDLE PROFESSIONAL TURNOVERS
....

by Michael R. Cooper

Economic downturns, paradoxically, often act as apparent cures for existing problems. In the midst of the past recession, for example, few companies paid much attention to a management problem that was pervasive during the prerecession growth period: professional turnover.

With fewer jobs available in the sluggish 1981–83 period, the turnover flow was reduced to a trickle. Other employee-related concerns, such as pay-and-benefits control or productivity improvement, dominated management time and energy. Now, however, a new demand for engineers, computer scientists, and data-processing and systems professionals is beginning to put a renewed premium on their valuable services.

Let's not forget the hiring bonuses that lured geologists to jump ship during the oil crisis and produced a rash of job hopping in high-tech industries. In the case of Silicon Valley, such turnover began to reach a crisis phase until the recession intervened to halt it. Because prospects for internal advancement were limited or ill-defined, high-tech professionals commonly had their own job banks and other "external career paths." Such employees considered moving to other companies a better form of advancement than getting ahead in their own organization. Many companies that had invested substantial amounts in training people to be effective contributors to the organization incurred heavy losses when many of them left for other positions.

Alarmingly, many managers may still be unaware of the gravity of potential professional turnover. When we asked professional employees in two hundred organizations about their plans to remain with their companies as the recession was winding down, less than half responded favorably—fewer than in any other employee group, including clerical and hourly workers. Professional turnover is like a coiled spring ready to unwind and do damage to unwary managers and their organizations.

What, then, is the right reaction to this situation? Although managers cannot control the business cycle or the supply of professionals, they can manage their professional employees to their advantage. A significant part of this management must involve a recognition of the distinctive features of this employee group. Consider these two points:

- The values and perceptions of professionals differ from those of other employee groups—managers and clerical or hourly workers, for instance. While pay is a value common to all employee groups, professionals have a unique need to be confronted with challenge and given avenues of opportunity.

    Our Hay attitude data show that compared with managers or clerical employees or hourly workers, professionals have (1) the least understanding of how their performance is judged, (2) the poorest opinion (less than 30 percent favorable) of their opportunities to advance, and (3) the least favorable opinion of their companies, insistence on quality work.

The prevailing myth is that professionals turn over because they are more loyal to their professions than to their employers. Not so. The problem really is an absence of appropriate responsiveness to the unique values of this professional group.

• Another important difference between professional and other employee groups is that the critical period in a profession employee's job cycle is shorter. Data show a three-year period where companies either "win or lose" most employees. However, the professional employee's "commitment window" is only twelve months—and shortening.

With this understanding, more managers must realize that their goal is not necessarily to reduce turnover, but to be in a position to control turnover. Practices that try to keep everyone aboard are as devastating as policies that lead to a continually unstable professional work force. Certainly professionals will come and go. The challenge is to make sure that those whom you want will be encouraged to stay.

Management must try not just to make its company a conducive place for professionals to work, but specifically to make it almost an irresistible place for "standouts" to remain. As our data on professional values indicate, dollars—while always an important factor—are rarely the single most effective motivator for retaining better performers. Professionals actually are relatively satisfied with their pay and benefits.

How then can managers keep their best professional performers? The answer lies in an effective individual approach, not a formula:

• Identify whom you want. Distinguish those professional employees who are critical to your business success from

those who are only marginal performers. This obvious evaluation practice is seldom conducted in more than a cursory fashion.
- Identify what they value. Pinpoint those values most important to professional employees in your organization. In particular, note differences between marginal and star players.
- Provide it. Begin a deliberate program, in concern with business objectives, to satisfy those values.
- Get in touch early on. Open up channels of communication, especially for the outstanding professional performers. Are they receiving what they value?
- Stay in touch. Continue to monitor professional values. Are they shifting? Do your practices need to be changed or fine-tuned?

Above all, approach managing a special employee group as you would approach managing a special market. First get to know it well, then stay in touch, because it changes.

Mr. Cooper is the partner in charge of Hay Management Consultants' Worldwide Organizational Effectiveness Practice.

IN PRAISE OF THE MIDDLEMAN

. . . .

by Richard T. Clawson

I*n an effort* to become lean and mean, some companies have recently restructured by reducing the number of middle managers. The results, in many instances, have been disappointing. The middle line has been weeded out, structures have been flattened, head counts have been decreased. But the cost of doing business has not been appreciably reduced.

In some instances, including two companies for which I

worked, costs have actually increased due to middle-management trimming. The initial savings of such trimming must be balanced against whether it creates inefficiency that could send a corporation into a tailspin.

Most current middle managers were originally specialists whose positions grew up with the company's position in the market; when the business expanded, the rewards went to those who were the best at their specialties. As the companies continued to grow, new and sometimes higher levels of management evolved. Specialists became the managers of more and more groups of other specialists. And as the pyramid spiraled upward, it also expanded sideways.

Even though this scheme of promoting from within is as it should be, the nature of the horizontal expansion has created an organizational complex with a life of its own. It is a loosely connected set of specializations that cannot be easily recombined, particularly by the arbitrary elimination of the middle line.

In the large companies where I worked, broadly defined functional units such as "Electronic Engineering" or "Financial Analysis" no longer exist. There are only compartments of specializations. And the larger the company, the more narrow the specialization has become in each compartment. There are compartments of Digital Circuit Engineering, Packaging, Stress, Safety, Component, and Research and Development Engineering.

There are specializations of Budget Analysis, Profit Analysis, Capital Investment Analysis, Operations Accounting, General Accounting, and Cost Accounting. Purchasing has become a collection of experts that includes Material Analysis, Subcontracts, Electronic Components, Mechanical Components, General Supplies, Machinery and Plant Equipment, and Traffic and Transportation. Personnel has segmented into Human Resource Development and Communications, Salaried Administration, Recruiting and Placement, Organization and Personnel Planning, Safety and Fire Protection, Medical Services, and Security.

All these functions have managers who are experts; they are experts in managing the day-to-day operations of their specialization. They are functional managers for that very reason, not because they are long-range planners, or innovators, or because they can fine-tune their operations better than anyone else.

The next level consists of the middle managers—those who make broader decisions than do the functional managers. They may, for example, decide which supplier to buy a part from and whether that decision will suit the needs of all the functional managers (balancing the designer's need for the best material with the accountants' demand for the best price). In short, they are the ones who hold the loosely connected pockets of specialization together and move the company forward.

The elimination of the middle manager's position is a common method of restructuring; its result is to elevate the functional manager's reporting level one notch—to the manager who used to be known as the "boss's boss." These higher-level managers analyze the operation as a whole and determine how it will perform in the market. They have the heavy responsibility of allocating the company's limited resources.

Elevation to a higher reporting level brings new pressures that the average functional manager wasn't even aware of: He needs to know what his group will look like and be doing six months or a year from now; before, the concern was today, next week, or at most, next month. Budgeting becomes just as important as accomplishing the daily tasks (i.e., completing a design if you're an engineer, or getting specific parts on time if you're a purchasing agent). There are more meetings to attend, more questions to answer, more reports to write. There are decisions to be made: priority decisions, personnel decisions, resource-allocation decisions. Meanwhile, the fine tuning of the day-to-day operations is expected to continue as usual, without interruption.

Overnight the functional manager discovers that there is a vast difference between proposing a recommended course of action and actually making the risky decision. Just as suddenly, the "boss's boss" discovers that problems that had been handled completely by those below him have been brought to his office. Some of these problems he never knew existed. Since the "boss's boss" is further removed from the operations, that escalation requires more research, more meetings, more time.

In this scenario, cutting out the middle-man results in delays, lower-quality decisions, lower morale, increased frustration, and chaos. All of which adds to costs. A company may appear to be lean and mean for the short term, but the hidden costs of the restructuring technique can undermine the cost cutting.

To expect a functional manager to perform the middle manager's tasks may be unrealistic. The best specialist may not be the best manager when his duties expand beyond fine tuning the day-to-day operations of a particular specialization. And since the purpose of an organizational structure is to provide the smoothest possible coordination of work, arbitrary adjustment without a thorough understanding of the skills and propensities of the people involved can have detrimental effects on the company's long-term health.

Mr. Clawson is assistant professor of business administration at Whittier College in California.

RAISING SPIRITS WITHOUT RAISING SALARIES

. . . .

by Bruce Serlen

A mbitious *young middle* managers currently are facing a critical dilemma. Today there aren't enough promotions available from entry-level management jobs to meet the demand from qualified employees.

There wouldn't be enough higher-level management jobs

available in the best of times, as management hierarchies are structured like a pyramid (the higher you go, the fewer slots exist). But there certainly aren't enough available today—not with demands for leaner management ranks and increased productivity being heard far and wide.

Employees who don't like the way they're being treated are always free to leave the company. But these are often valuable employees. The company will hardly collapse if they go, but their particular department or division might certainly suffer from their absence.

Let's say one such disgruntled young middle manager reports to you. It's the day of his annual performance review. You know a promotion is the issue that is uppermost in his mind. How do you counsel him, trying, at the same time, to be hopeful and to avoid being patronizing?

Be honest. Young people know the company's policy on promotions as well as anyone, so there's no sense making it seem such a policy doesn't exist. If there's an actual freeze on promotions, say so.

Don't bother making promises about the future, if you're not sure the promotion freeze will be lifted. Promises about something happening "down the road a piece" or "when the economy turns around" may be well-meaning, but they're too vague and open-ended to make much difference.

Simple pats on the back won't help. We all like hearing we're "highly regarded," but such bouquets don't mean much when they're not backed up with a salary increase and a title change. In an odd way, such praise even makes the pill harder to swallow. If the middle manager *wasn't* doing such a fine job, he wouldn't feel justified in requesting the promotion in the first place.

There are a number of positive suggestions a supervisor can offer:

Assign new responsibilities to the employee to make the job more of a challenge. "What else can you do?" this reasoning goes. "You're already doing a, b, and c, now take a stab at x, y, z." Call on him to undertake a special project. Ask him to work up a strategic plan. Assign him to represent your department on a companywide fact-finding committee.

If you do add new responsibilities, be sure to relieve the employee of some of his other, more mundane duties at the same time. After all, what's meant as an incentive should hardly end up a punishment.

Why would the employee want additional work, if he's already feeling unappreciated? Because he wants the chance to broaden his area of expertise. He realizes he only has to gain professionally if he acquires new skills.

What's more, these particular projects are important. Not only are they timely and substantive, but they're likely to involve increased visibility for the employee and possibly even interaction with the company's senior officers. Middle managers are looking to make themselves as invaluable as possible—to the point where they become indispensable to the company. And this is one way to do it. What better way to take the future direction of your career into your own hands?

Other incentives you might be able to arrange? Attendance at a seminar, enrollment in a course or, better yet, a trip. Often, there'll be no money in a company's budget for salaries or promotions, but plenty for travel or education. These are concrete ways of showing your appreciation for an employee, shy of that actual title change.

One area of business life everyone is eager to learn about is the new technology—data processing, advanced communication systems, videoconferencing, etc. Any seminars or training programs you're able to offer the employee in these areas will be especially welcome.

One company went to great lengths to keep one of its stalled young managers happy. It "volunteered" him to a government committee in Washington as a public service. There, he spent a year on "special assignment" while remaining on the company payroll. When he returned to the company, the managerial bottleneck had opened up sufficiently and he was able to move up with a significant promotion.

A less drastic course is to try to get the employee a transfer to another department *within* the company, even though it will only be a lateral move. Again, he'll be broadening his experience. You'll regret losing him, but there's always the possibility he could transfer back at a later date—and at the higher level. You'll miss him in your area (you'll still be down one body), but at least he'll still call your company "home."

The important point to convey in all this is that you sincerely want to help. You appreciate the frustration the employee is feeling. Your experience coming up in the company was, no doubt, a lot different. So you can't know firsthand how difficult it must be trying to get ahead in today's economy. But you were and *are* ambitious enough to appreciate the frustrations of those caught in the current middle-manager crunch.

Mr. Serlen writes on management subjects from New York.

THE BEST CORPORATE CULTURE
IS A MELTING POT
. . . .

by Jack Falvey

Promoting from within has been a policy of misguided company loyalty that has damaged the foundations of organizations it seeks to build.

Because of promote-from-within policies, many companies are headed today by organization men of the 1940s. Many of these inmates-turned-wardens have never worked outside of the corporations they head. Is it any wonder they are having difficulty adjusting to a world marketplace? Take this example:

A major company introduced a new consumer product. The market for that product accelerated and soon a foreign competitor entered the arena. As the company's share began to erode, top management met to determine strategy. The competitor's clever advertising was to be countered with trade deals and deep price cuts. The decision was unanimous. Why? Because everyone in the meeting was with the company fifteen years before when a similar foreign product threatened another segment of the business. Everyone's experience was exactly the same. "We were successful before, so we will do the same thing again."

Unfortunately, the foreign challenge was slightly different this time and so were the results. There were layoffs, then several plant closings, and finally sale of the product, or what was left of it, to another company.

When I speak to management groups of established companies, the view from the podium is sometimes frightening. They look alike; they dress alike; unfortunately, they think alike. They are the products of a success profile. They are plain vanilla. But strength comes from diversity. When you face a problem, isn't it better to have five or six options rather than just one?

When, on the other hand, there is "cross-pollination," some wondrous things begin to happen: A consumer-goods president took over as chief executive officer of a computer company. He insisted that stock be available before a new product was launched, knowing that advertising backed by empty shelves was a waste. Consumer electronics companies usually had announced first, promoted and sold second, and delivered third. He reversed the order and filled the distribution pipeline first. He single-handedly caused a major shakeout of his competition by his product's success.

To compound the promote-from-within syndrome, companies have established traditional areas of the business from which all top managers will come. Organizations are headed by finance businessmen twenty years after they are no longer in the finance business. Engineers have headed computer companies that have consistently driven down prices and increased performance of their products with technical breakthroughs but that have failed to make the products usable in the marketplace. Family ownership imposes similar limitations when it gives each son a small division or sees to it that every cousin has an office somewhere.

Is it any wonder our industrial giants become targets of opportunity for anyone who chooses to pose a serious challenge to their products, services, or marketplace? (In some cases the challenge is directly to those companies' management teams in the form of takeover bids or green mail.)

One of the major moves in our business environment is the formation of ventures by talented, aggressive, well-trained managers who have left their companies. Most could not survive or contribute within an inbred organization. The proliferation of prospering companies that have been spun off should tell us something about the company men who were unable to make a success of those subsidiaries.

Between twenty percent and thirty percent of all openings should be filled from outside. The broader the mix the better. Every position should have outside talent included in the selection process. If inside people are not competitive, how can your organization be competitive in the marketplace?

Consultants who work across industry lines will confirm that the fundamentals in every industry are almost identical. There are no real barriers to mobility. Junior managers especially should be valued if they have three or four different work experiences, because they have found that managing their own careers produces far better returns than delegating that responsibility to a single organization.

The mobile manager of the 1960s, who did duty in six cities and then returned to the home office, should now be replaced by the mobile manager of the 1980s, who has worked across six different industries and deals comfortably in business on three different continents. The time of the generalist top manager is coming, and none too soon. Narrow specialists have always had difficulty with the big picture.

The rules of business have been shifting dramatically and rapidly for the past decade. Stable, secure management teams are remnants of the past. Dynamic, diverse management is needed for the present and the future. The rigid rules of organization construction must be broken.

The process of regenerating cannot be done overnight. Broaden your view and bring in more talent from nontraditional sources. Its addition will add new strength. It may already be long overdue.

Mr. Falvey, a writer, speaker, and consultant, lives in Londonderry, New Hampshire. His latest book is What's Next? Career Strategies After 35 *(Williamson 1987).*

MAKING SURE MINORITY RECRUITMENT
IS NOT JUST FOR SHOW
. . . .
by Thomas S. Murphy

Capital Cities—*like* most of the broadcast industry—was inexcusably late in coming to a full recognition of what is at stake for us, the issue of equal opportunity.

We had to be prodded into that recognition by others, and even today we are not beyond the need for an occasional sharp reminder. But there is a limit to what can be achieved by prodding. The barriers to equal opportunity did not grow up in a day or a year and do not crumble simply because a chief executive makes a speech, issues a memo, or otherwise cracks a whip. What we need above all is an understanding of what works and what doesn't.

It's easy to provide some examples of what doesn't work. It doesn't work to create jobs that perform no real function and give them fancy titles, so you can have a position into which you can place a minority person or a woman for statistical and bragging purposes. It doesn't work to promote a minority person or a woman into a job that he or she can't handle because of lack of experience and training or simply lack of capacity. And it doesn't work to sell a radio or television station to a minority-controlled enterprise that is undercapitalized, inexperienced, and programmed to fail in the business world.

It's much harder to suggest what does work—but I can offer some clues. Some years ago, Capital Cities made a special effort to locate and recruit, for the sales departments of our radio and television stations, members of minority groups who had had some experience in the sales end of nonbroadcast businesses. The premise of our effort was that sales had traditionally been one important route to broadcast management positions, that there were virtually no minority persons with experience in broadcast sales, and that people with some experience in nonbroadcast sales might (with a little help) be able to transfer that experience to broadcasting.

The people we hired were not trainees. We provided them with some orientation to the broadcasting business and gave them training on the job. While central management provided the impetus and the orientation sessions (as well as help in the recruitment process), the basic job was done by the senior management at each of our stations.

There is no way to keep an accurate score on such efforts, but we were pleased with the results. We had a number of success stories. Some have moved on to positions such as sales manager or general manager in our broadcast company or others, and one now runs his own station. Most important, however, once our station management learned how to deal with the issue, the process continued and broadened. Central management is no longer directly involved and the sources of recruitment vary. But nearly one out of six of our broadcast sales personnel is a member of a minority group.

Here's another idea that works. Starting in the late sixties, Capital Cities began to enter the field of print journalism, first with the trade papers produced by Fairchild Publications and then not only with other specialized publications but with daily and weekly newspapers of general circulation. We were becoming a large, diversified media company, in which no one knew what job opportunities were available on a companywide basis. At the same time, we were firmly committed—as we are today—to the principle that the managers of each enterprise we operate should be given the widest possible autonomy consistent with legal requirements and our overall goals. In that context, the notion of some centralized recruiting process designed to maximize the chances for minority recruitment made no sense.

Instead, we started a biweekly listing of every job opening in the company, which is posted at every employment unit and circulated to a wide range of minority organizations, to women's organizations, and to other potential sources of applicant referrals. To the best of our ability, we try to hold those openings long enough for some opportunity to get a response to those listings. We have not been inundated by frivolous applicants and have not stimulated (as some feared) a mass migration of talented younger people in our smaller operations to the larger ones. But we have found some very good applicants—both minority and nonminority—and we have given all our employees a healthy sense of working for a company in which there are lots of opportunities, even if the avenues for advancement at the particular place they work seem pretty well filled by long-term seniors ahead of them.

When we turned our attention to the question of minority ownership of broadcasting stations, we tried to apply some of the lessons we had learned in dealing with minority employment. We looked for sources of capital and business competence in minority-group members who had been successful in nonbroadcast fields, and we ultimately found a group of black doctors, dentists, lawyers, and business people who were willing to put up $1 million toward the acquisition of a VHF, network-affiliated television station. We offered advice and expertise from a variety of talented people in our organization, and the search for a station began. The road was long and bumpy, but Seaway Communications became the first black-owned company to be the licensee of a VHF, network-affiliated station (Channel 12, in Rhinelander, Wisconsin), and today Seaway owns another VHF station (in Bangor, Maine) as well.

There are several aspects to the Seaway story I would like to stress. There aren't a lot of black people living in or near Rhinelander, Wisconsin (or Bangor, Maine, for that matter). But while it's important for black people to be involved in station ownership in markets where black people live, it's also important for black owners to be involved in broadcasting as a national industry, to learn how to deal as business people with markets of all kinds. The second point is the importance of that million dollars that Seaway put in the bank before it started on its search for a station. No matter what anyone tells you, broadcast ownership is a risk proposition, and adequate equity financing is essential.

When we confronted the need to sell a large number of stations and cable television systems in connection with our merger with ABC, we tried to apply all of the lessons we had learned. We tried to make the process as open as possible, by searching out prospective minority buyers and letting them know at an early stage what was for sale, how we proposed to go about it, and the importance we placed on an adequate proportion of equity capital. Once again, the road was bumpy. There were some misunderstandings and some disappointments (many of them unavoidable), but we have been able to sell a television station in Buffalo, New York, to a company primarily owned by blacks, and an FM station in Detroit to a company owned by blacks and Hispanics, and a television station in New Haven, Connecticut, to a company owned by Alaskan natives.

I do not suggest for a minute that we have found all the answers. We have not yet found the right way to integrate minorities and women into the management of our radio and television news operations. But we do know that the solution has to be tailored to the special needs of individual operations and the special characteristics of the people who run them. For one thing we have learned from all our experience is that top management of a company can accomplish very little in equal opportunity or, as a matter of fact, in any other area until and unless it succeeds in enlisting the dedicated cooperation of the people who bear the day-to-day line responsibility for the company's operations.

Mr. Murphy is chairman and chief executive officer of Capital Cities Communications. These remarks are adapted from a speech he gave to the National Black Media Coalition.

EQUAL EMPLOYMENT RECORDS:
TO KNOW THEM IS TO LOVE THEM
. . . .
by William E. Blundell

Whisper *"Equal Employment* Opportunity" into the ear of American business and it can barely stifle a collective groan: All that record keeping, all that expense, all that bureaucratic horse manure, just to show that a company is not discriminating against minorities. However, a few wise managers and consultants may now be using EEO reports to their advantage. Some may even have found a pony in the manure pile.

Demographer and statistician Ross Stolzenberg, who recently became vice president of research of the Graduate Management Admission Council after a tour at Rand Corp., is convinced that lurking in the EEO files of corporations are data they could use to make far wiser decisions in managing employees. What type of person should be hired for a certain kind of job? Is a training program worth the time and effort put into it? What can be done to reduce turnover? Give the computer enough information, says Mr. Stolzenberg, ask it the right questions in the right way, and it can tell you.

But few employers bother to ask. "It's a pity," says the

bearded, thirty-eight-year-old researcher, "but there's little recognition that you can use computerized employee records for anything more than payroll and producing required reports." It would be easy, he says, to do much more at relatively little extra cost; large companies already have met most of the expense required by converting to computer records. And these records are filled with much essential data.

EEO reports are used to guard companies from charges of bias against members of groups protected by law—women, older workers, blacks, Hispanics, and others. Monitoring the shifting makeup of its work force, an employer can correct tendencies in hiring, dismissal, and promotion that could be seen as discriminatory. Computers make it relatively easy to produce external reports for watchdogs like the Equal Employment Opportunity Commission.

Smart companies collect much more employee data than the EEOC requires, and for good reason. If an employer has taken an action that might appear discriminatory—favoring whites for a certain job, for example—it will want to show that good performers in that job need to have advanced degrees, and that a far lower percentage of the available minority labor pool have the required schooling. So factors like education and a history of job performance are frequently added to required data on age, race, and sex.

Given histories of job performance and enough other data, Mr. Stolzenberg says, companies could tease out of their computers certain factors common in the backgrounds of highly productive workers and hire new people whose histories include these factors. They could reduce turnover by identifying overqualified applicant types who, when hired, do very well for a short period and then quit out of boredom or frustration. And, rules permitting, they could target poor performers who can be laid off in a business downturn instead of losing some of their best people.

Potential benefits run well beyond intelligent hiring and firing. A company could experiment with different deployments of workers, the researcher says, and adopt the one that works best. "Do you form an elite corps with your best workers," Mr. Stolzenberg asks, "or do you scatter them through the larger group as an inspiration to others? Is it better to have a quality control person within each production unit or should you separate that function?"

Comparative studies also could reveal whether employees receiving a certain incentive turn out enough extra work to justify the cost; which incentives work best; which benefits really do reduce turnover among specific classes of employees; whether a training program is paying off; and other matters now subject to seat-of-the-pants decisions based on sketchy or nonexistent data. Mr. Stolzenberg says, "We need to manage human capital with the same sophistication we use in managing physical capital."

Managers haven't been applying technical models to their personnel problems, he suggests, for reasons both practical and emotional. Many users, he says, may not realize the benefits of doing so because data analysts in the social sciences have done such a wretched job of marketing their ideas in practical forms. Others may be reluctant to pioneer; it is cheaper and easier to let front-runners make the initial costly mistakes and hire away their experts when the glitches have been eliminated. And there is the lingering taint of Big Brotherism, the feeling—unfounded, in Mr. Stolzenberg's view, but persistent nonetheless—that managing people with computers is somehow wrong, a manipulative tactic that is an affront to individualism.

A few users are pressing on, however. Mr. Stolzenberg knows of no company doing all of the things he believes possible, but he cites Texas Instruments (which he once served as a consultant) and Bechtel Corporation as two that have gone further than most. Neither concern will discuss its current uses of employee data. But the experience of Wayne Wright, former director of industrial relations at TI, suggests that managers in general would pounce on such an analytical tool if it were made available.

Mr. Wright helped set up an employee data base that included five-year employment histories and job performance ratings. It was intended solely for EEO work, but Mr. Wright quickly found himself besieged by TI managers who saw what it might do for them.

Some wanted to analyze the characteristics of successful production supervisors and use that profile in making such appointments, Others dug into turnover factors. Compensation specialists wanted to see if TI's merit-pay system really worked, or if it was being undercut by automatically rewarding seniority and "haloing" classes of employees—giving them more merit money as a group because they were somehow perceived as being more important than other groups.

Mr. Wright left TI in 1982 and doesn't know how all this research worked out, but he has come to believe in a detailed employee data base and creative use of it as a management tool. He hasn't been able to build such a base yet at his present job, vice president of human resources at Nissan's new U.S. operation in Tennessee. "We're just learning to walk here," he says. "We're real happy when we get all the names and addresses right."

Mr. Blundell is a national correspondent of The Wall Street Journal.

WILL EMPLOYEE STOCK OWNERSHIP PLANS PREVENT TAKEOVERS?
. . . .
by Frank Altmann

A*fter years of* vilification as an employer tax advantage—free-riding as an employee benefit—the employee stock ownership plan, or ESOP, has suddenly surfaced in a supposedly virtuous form—as a corporate defense against takeovers. The impetus is a recent Delaware Supreme Court decision in *Polaroid v. Shamrock Holdings Inc.*, which supported a trustee's voting of unallocated employee shares to thwart a hostile bid for the company's stock.

With this new use of the ESOP, management has found an ally in labor to support it in its battle against the "greedy" financiers. Has Main Street finally triumphed over Wall Street?

Assume for a moment that all the technical details—SEC and Labor Department requirements—line up favorably for the adoption of an ESOP. Are there any drawbacks—say, from the standpoint of corporate strategy—that militate against using the ESOP as a takeover defense?

If voting rights are unrestricted, it is presumed that worker-owned shares will be in safer hands, in the sense of being "on management's side." But to what extent will the workers identify with the firm on matters, say, of investment?

As an employee benefit, the ESOP is a profit-sharing or "defined contribution" plan. As such, company contributions of stock held in trust are construed as wages forgone. And the trustee has a commensurate fiduciary mandate to maximize the value of this stock, as deferred compensation. So what happens when a trustee is faced with voting unallocated shares in a munificent tender offer? It is the decision in *Polaroid*—letting the trustee off the "fiduciary hook"—that paves the way for an antitakeover use of the plan: The employees are *presumed* to be opposed to the buyer's offer, and the trustee votes their shares accordingly.

Enter the split personality of the worker/shareholder. As a shareholder, he puts his stock at the firm's disposal, relying on the board to make the decisions necessary to maximize its value. As a company worker in a takeover battle, however, he is presumed to reject the buyer's offer in favor of management. In *Polaroid*, the "worker" personality was predominant. The ESOP takeover defense represents an alliance between labor and management, with the shareholder in a supporting or implementing role.

How profitably can one expect the corporation to perform, given this reordering of priorities? Would labor increase its income at the expense of capital?

The mainspring of profitability is entrepreneurship, which involves balancing a prospective reward against the accompanying risk. The upshot of this risk-reward trade-off is, therefore, crucial in evaluating a coalition approach to profitability. Capital and labor view the matter from quite different perspectives. While the capitalist's risk extends into the indefinite future, the worker's is more immediate.

It is precisely the workers' risk-averse attitude that management counts on to thwart a takeover. The workers will be suspicious of a prospective owner's motive in wanting to acquire "their" company; their jobs and wages will be at stake. Suppose, for example, that a prospective owner plans to introduce revolutionary technology. The workers are not opposed to investment per se, but they will oppose decisions that shift investment in a direction unfavorable to their immediate interests.

Suppose the installation of an ESOP is successful in blocking a takeover. To the extent that labor's influence on the board inhibits innovation and long-run profitability, the return on capital will fall—also hurting the company's credit rating. Management will find itself caught between the need for, say, technological innovation and a desire for labor peace. In these circumstances, the "shared" requirements of productivity, employment, and wage and salary maintenance are likely to supersede the more "capitalistic" requirement of return on investment.

This brings us back to basics. It is necessary for corporations to balance incentives and controls with the factors of production to drive down the cost of goods and services. With regard to the supply of labor, this objective can be achieved only when hammered out through collective bargaining, leaving the shareholders in sole possession of excess gains. Any other arrangement will deprive the corporation of competitive access to funds.

The ESOP can be seen as a device for disseminating property rights among the workers, solely in the interest of equity. This objective might be considered an acceptable trade-off for some loss in efficiency, if it were feasible from the standpoint of governance. But who is going to be responsible for losses?

When outside investors are in sole possession of residual gains, they also suffer all the losses. In this case, it is not necessary to adjudicate disputes; the shareholders cannot sue themselves. On the other hand, dispersing property rights across an interest-group boundary creates a condition of potential conflict, inviting court action as a means of settlement. Given that recourse to the courts is both costly and time-consuming, it is apparent that considerations of equity and efficiency are difficult to separate.

While the ESOP has indeed found a place as a takeover defense, its significance is not to be found in a conflict between "Main Street and Wall Street." The conflict between labor and capital is actually much closer to home.

Mr. Altmann is head of a Kansas City, Missouri, consulting firm specializing in industrial organization.

NOTHING HURTS MORE THAN A BOGUS BONUS

by Sir Gordon White

As head of the U.S. branch of Hanson PLC, a transatlantic conglomerate with more than a hundred business units, one of my jobs is to help our divisional managers perform on their own, in keeping with our insistence on decentralization. Key to our success at doing this has been the way we have "incentivized" our managements—established a system of performance bonuses for our managers to maximize both profits and return on capital.

This incentive program is really rather simple, and is based on common sense. Still, I find that other companies routinely fail to use common sense when establishing bonus guidelines, and so I offer some pointers from our own experience.

- *Base yearly bonuses upon the performance of each individual business unit.* This is crucial. We do not expect our managers to be responsible for the profitability of the entire company, but for their particular profit centers. Today's environment increasingly recognizes that the value—and potential value—of a corporation may be seen by breaking it down into its individual assets. By fully appreciating the worth of each unit, and providing incentives based accordingly, we can most fully realize the potential of our entire company. Furthermore, this treats the individual manager more fairly, by neither penalizing nor rewarding him for the activities in areas outside his control.
- *Determine bonuses in a simple and straightforward manner.* Divisional managers should know exactly what to expect, as far as what they can earn in bonuses and how they can go about earning them.

For us, the first step in this process is the budget, produced by the management of the operating companies. That budget will indicate expected profit levels and the returns to be achieved on the capital employed. After review, the budget is agreed upon and each manager's potential bonus is based upon it. At Hanson, we set a great deal of store by our budgets; quite frankly, we consider them sacred. They are the foundation for all our operations. In the area of bonuses, strict adherence to agreed-upon budgets makes sure that everyone understands exactly what he is expected to work with and what the levels of profitability are expected to be.

By our demanding, through the budget, a specific return on capital employed, our managers find it to their advantage to secure a budget that is very realistic. If a budget is too optimistic, the divisional manager will suffer by not earning his expected return on capital. And if it is too easily achieved, he will not be able to maximize his reward from his potential productivity. Although we revise our budgets in the middle of every year to accommodate market conditions, our bonuses are based upon the budget set at the beginning of the year. This way, we make sure that our managers always maintain a very keen sense of what the actual state of their business is.

Our formulas for determining bonuses are also kept to a simple equation. To receive 100 percent of their potential bonuses—on top of their already competitive salaries—our managers must produce profits above a certain return on capital employed. At the start of the year, we set out very clearly for all our managers exactly what levels of profitability will result in 25 percent bonuses, in 50 percent bonuses, etc., all the way to 100 percent. This way there are no surprises at the end of the year.

In fact, as our monthly results come in, each divisional manager can ascertain exactly what his bonus would be at the end of the year, based upon results to date.

- *Allow no "discretionary" factors in the bonus equation.* In other words, bonuses are based strictly on bottom-line performance. This means that absolutely no one will receive a bonus that has not been earned according to our established formulas. Simply put, we look at bonuses as if they were dividends. If the additional money is there, we will gladly pay a proportion of it out. But if it isn't there, we will not.

As a result, there are no bonuses for being a nice chap. To the same extent, if a manager just happened to have a great year—if industry conditions turned out to be particularly favorable, due to old-fashioned dumb luck—so be it. That lucky manager will be rewarded for his luck.

Strict adherence to this policy has gone a long way toward improving the morale of our divisional managers. We have taken over a great many companies, and we always try to keep the divisional managers that we inherit. Time and again, we have found that these managers have consistently been short-changed on their bonuses while working for the previous parent company. Because of poor performance in other parts of the corporation, or due to discretionary factors (although divisional managers may have achieved their expected earnings levels), they rarely received full bonuses. This resulted in poor relations with corporate headquarters.

One manager we inherited stated that although he always achieved his full quota of earnings, he had never received a full bonus. When he came over to Hanson, he could not believe that he would receive his full bonus until he actually had it in his hand. You can imagine what the previous system did to his morale.

- *Don't allow bonuses to discourage a long-term relationship.* Certainly, when our managers achieve their full bonuses, they tend to be happy. But what about managers in those industries that just experienced lousy luck? For example, the U.S. shoe business today is extremely hard-hit by imports. Our Endicott Johnson subsidiary has been unable to achieve our expected levels of return on capital, and we cannot cast the blame on our own people. But until things do turn around, our managers will not receive any bonuses (unless they succeed in radically shrinking their capital employed, which may or may not be possible).

Yet we want our managers to stay with us, and not jump ship for more alluring packages that may be offered to them by other companies looking for top talent when times are hard. As a result, we also offer an options program for our managers. These options for corporate stock—which are not cash awards on a yearly basis—are not exercisable for at least three years. This encourages our managers to stay with us through thick and thin, so that they may reap rewards later on. It also helps them to make business decisions from the point of view of the shareholder.

As I stated earlier, our guidelines are really based on common sense. But they are fair and consistent, and help us realize the full potential of our individual assets.

Sir Gordon is chairman of Hanson PLC.

KEEPING FAVORITISM AND PREJUDICE
OUT OF EVALUATIONS

....

by Andrew S. Grove

O*ur society has* become what Peter Drucker calls a society of organizations. And our standard of living largely depends on how well these organizations perform. In my book *High Output Management,* I characterized performance reviews as the single most important form of task-relevant feedback with which we supervisors can provide our employees.

What I said has not been enthusiastically received in all quarters. A teacher friend of mine heatedly insisted that performance reviews—and compensation and promotional practices based on those reviews—would not elicit better work but only favoritism in her school system. Another objection was raised by a lawyer I know who haughtily announced that nobody, simply nobody, could judge the quality of his work. Comments of this type have reached me from other quarters as well.

In spite of the criticisms, I remain steadfast in my conviction that if we want performance in the workplace, somebody has to have the courage and confidence to determine whether we are getting it or not. We must also find ways to enhance what we are getting.

But let's examine these criticism carefully, taking the lawyer's position first. I am quite sure that in any sizable law firm, an experienced and senior partner can make a meaningful evaluation of my friend's work, no matter how arcane the work might seem. After all, professionals go through intensive series of evaluations during their education. And during their internship and subsequent professional practice, professionals acquire and share basic facts and values that provide a good basis for meaningful dialogue and mutual evaluation.

This is not to say that when professionals are faced with a complex problem, there is only one way to handle it. Assessing performance is not an *act* but a *process*; even if the opening barrage is off the mark, the resulting exchange is likely to tune and perfect the work performed. In fact, the more obscure and intangible the nature of the work in question, the more such an exchange is likely to contribute to its quality.

For example, some years ago when I was supervising a number of semiconductor engineers, one of them discovered a technique that turned out to be extremely useful in solving an important problem. This solution brought recognition, praise, and a lot of satisfaction to my subordinate.

However, as time went on, he fell into the pattern of attempting to solve all problems with the same technique, even though it had no relevance to them. This led to wasted effort and a lot of frustration. When I pointed out this pattern to my subordinate, he got defensive at first. He thought I was trying to minimize the importance of his earlier achievement. As we talked about my observation some more, I eventually succeeded in convincing him that his insistence on using the same technique over and over was counterproductive. Eventually, he managed to break his thinking pattern and address his new problems with a fresh approach each time, thus regaining his earlier effectiveness.

The very idea of nonreviewability of professional work means that only the most monstrous errors get evaluated—after the worst has been perpetrated, and then frequently during the course of malpractice litigation. I think we can reduce the waste and damage caused by this practice in our society by agreeing on a basic principle; namely that *all* work can and must be subjected to review by somebody.

As for the teacher's fear of favoritism, obviously power— and the right to evaluate *is* power—can corrupt. What we as managers have to do is build enough checks and balances into the system to minimize the influence of personal bias and distortion. At Intel, we use three safeguards.

Once an employee review is written up by a supervisor, the supervisor's boss oversees and approves the written evaluation. This manager is the second most qualified judge of the employee's performance—second, that is, to the employee's immediate supervisor. Being one level removed, he can put the employee's performance in broader perspective; he is in a position to compare it with the work of other people in a larger organization.

Our second check of the evaluation process stipulates that the personnel representative assigned to the employee's department approve the review. Although someone from personnel probably can't judge the quality of highly technical endeavors, he is likely to catch signs of favoritism and prejudice, and call it to the attention of the immediate supervisor's manager. For this to have real effect, we must endow the personnel department with enough status and clout to make its opinions and comments count.

The third check comes from setting up ranking sessions, where the supervisor meets with his peers and, together as a group, they compare and rank all of their subordinates. Of course, no one supervisor can assess the work of all subordinates of his peers. But collectively, enough will be known about each employee to provide additional—and frequently conflicting—points of view to the assessment process, resulting in a fair outcome for everybody.

Do such checks and balances weed out all bad evaluations? They do not. No system is foolproof, especially one that is necessarily laden with human judgment. Furthermore, such an evaluation process takes much more time and effort than simply listing a group of employees by date of hire and letting it go at that (the basis of a seniority approach to evaluating performance). At Intel, we estimate that a supervisor probably spends five to eight hours on each employee's review, about one quarter to one third of 1 percent of the supervisor's work year. If the effort expended contributes to an employee's performance even to a small extent over the course of a year, isn't that a highly worthwhile expenditure of a supervisor's time?

We're paid to manage our organizations. To manage means to elicit better performance from members of our organization. We managers need to stop rationalizing, and to stiffen our resolve and do what we are paid to do.

Mr. Grove is president of Intel Corporation in Santa Clara, California, and is the author of High Output Management *(Random House, 1983).*

A COMPLETELY NEW WAY
TO PURCHASE MEDICAL BENEFITS
. . . .
by Edward L. Hennessy, Jr.

A merica's *annual health* care bill climbed from $248 billion in 1980 to $540 billion in 1987—a 120 percent increase that far exceeded the rate of inflation. More than $100 billion of this outlay is shouldered by corporations that provide health insurance for employees. The huge, fast-growing expense is a heavy burden for companies, which are fighting to keep costs down to compete against highly productive foreign firms.

We hear talk about cost control from doctors and hospitals. But let's face it, we're not likely to get real help from that quarter. We've got to help ourselves. To escape the cost avalanche, a completely new approach to purchasing medical benefits must be taken, one aimed at increasing market pressure on the health care providers.

We at Allied-Signal Incorporated recently became one of the first to do this when we created a single, national health care plan. By arranging to make our U.S. employees customers for one insurer, Cigna Corporation, we've been able to negotiate more reasonable terms in the health care marketplace.

In areas of the country where there is a surplus of doctors and hospitals, it is possible to negotiate lower health care rates. But unfortunately most companies purchasing health care still aren't cost-conscious buyers—and those that are haven't yet taken steps to use their bargaining power effectively. As a result, many health care providers are not offering more favorable financial arrangements. And those who do usually compensate by increasing services and charges for other consumers. So the nation's health care bill keeps shooting up.

Consider the government's effort to cut hospital care costs. In 1983, Medicare initiated a fixed-fee program that has led to shorter hospital stays for its patients. But as a number of health care analysts have noted, hospitals have been making up for the revenue loss by raising charges to private patients. In addition, hospitals and doctors have been delivering a greater volume of higher-priced outpatient services, because these are less subject to Medicare cost controls.

Also, studies indicate that many unnecessary surgical procedures are being performed. Findings by the National Institutes of Health reveal that 60 percent to 80 percent of the 250,000 coronary bypass operations performed in the United States each year—at a cost of about $25,000 each—bring the patients no increase in life span beyond what could be gained through nonsurgical treatment. And recent studies suggest that more than half of the 120,000 pacemaker implants done annually at a cost of about $12,000 each are unnecessary or of debatable value. According to Dr. Sidney Wolfe of the Public Citizens Health Research Group, in 1987 as much as $180 billion was wasted on unnecessary surgery, hospitalizations, and other services.

Of course, there are many reasons why one physician differs from another over how to treat a particular case; questionable procedures are not necessarily motivated by economic self-interest. But without a doubt, "revenue-enhancing" moves have been a major factor responsible for the failure of government and private sector efforts to combat cost inflation.

Most company cost-containment programs have been futile because they've focused only on influencing consumers of health care. At Allied-Signal, for example, we have long offered incentives for employees to use cost-efficient material alternatives such as outpatient surgery for minor procedures, home health care, and direct contracts for prescription drugs. But we soon learned that the only way to achieve meaningful cost control was to give providers themselves a reason to work for this goal.

By offering volume business to Cigna, we've secured a three-year fixed rate of increase in costs for comprehensive medical and dental care for our U.S. employees. Cigna is able to share the risk with us because it in turn has contracted with a network of physicians, hospitals, and other health care providers to deliver services.

The new plan shields our company from dangerously ballooning costs for the three-year period. We're not looking for reductions in our health care bill, but we do expect to slow its growth enough to generate savings in the $200 million range over the next few years.

While the plan provides a complete package of high-quality health care services for employees, it does have one shortcoming. In some parts of the country, the providers our employees would prefer to use are part of the Cigna network. The only way to get more providers participating in cost-effective networks is for many more organizations to demand such arrangements.

Momentum is building in this direction. In Milwaukee, for

instance, Miller Brewing, Allis-Chalmers, and five other companies have joined forces with the municipal government to negotiate lower rates with a network of local hospitals and doctors. Southern New England Bell has created its own company network of providers for employees. And Southwestern Bell and May Department Stores are following Allied-Signal's course of purchasing an insurance carrier's provider network. In fact, this latter approach is currently being evaluated for possible adoption by at least fifteen more major companies.

Companies throughout industry need to start making better use of their bargaining power—to stop watering it down by dealing with many diverse insurers and HMOs. We need to make U.S. industry a customer that has to be reckoned with in the health care marketplace. If we're serious about this goal, it shouldn't take handstands to accomplish it. After all, collectively we pay the health care insurance bill for 69 percent of the population.

We must persuade the providers to take a seat beside us on the cost-containment bandwagon. Only then will we be able to bring health care cost inflation more in line with that for products and services in other sectors.

Mr. Hennessy is chairman and chief executive officer of Allied-Signal Incorporated.

HOW TO GET THE MOST
FROM AN HMO
. . . .
by Jacob Getson

A t *last the* health care field seems to be acting like a market. With hospital chains vying for patients and profits, it is vital that major employers now use their clout as consumers of health insurance plans to control the cost of care.

Chief among the new models emerging from this new competiveness are health maintenance organizations, which combine elements of health care services with insurance benefit programs. HMOs have been highly successful in reducing health care costs by stressing preventive care, avoiding inappropriate hospitalization, and eliminating unnecessary medical procedures. While some large companies question whether employee health benefit costs are really reduced by enrolling workers in HMOs, research data tend to support their cost-saving benefits.

Yet reservations and skepticism remain as many HMOs vie aggressively for a fast-growing segment of the marketplace. While the merits of the question of ultimate cost may be argued, it would be unfortunate to let the debate end on the basis of dollars alone.

Employers should make strategic choices in determining options for workers examining carefully the differing types of HMOs such as closed staff models—where doctors work on a salary basis—open independent and practice associations—where physicians work out of their own offices. Employers should draw comparisons with traditional health care programs. Not only do premiums vary from plan to plan, but so do the benefit structures, staffing patterns, accessibility of care. The business community must look beyond the glitter of high-gloss marketing campaigns and the temptation of simple short-term dollar savings in providing options for workers.

In examining the premium, or monthly charge per member, it is important to review and assess the rate histories for individual programs over an extended period, perhaps three to five years. Building a successful, cost-effective HMO can take that much time. This, and a careful examination of hospital utilization, will give corporate benefit managers a better idea of the ability of an individual health plan to control costs effectively. Strong and effective management controls that particularly influence the admissions to hospitals are needed to ensure that premium rates will remain within reasonable limits. These controls must also include a vigorous quality assurance and medical review—the ability to direct necessary clinical service to the most appropriate setting. Here again, simple analyses of immediate cost increase are shortsighted and will fail to reflect the impact of effective management controls over time.

In some instances employers may argue correctly that certain HMOs may end up costing them money by drawing the youngest, healthiest workers. On its face, this seems contradictory. However, when only the high-risk employees remain in the indemnity pool for the traditional fee-for-service insurance plans, the premiums based on the actual cost of providing medical services to that individual employee group would reflect an extraordinarily high rate of both utilization and cost of this unmanaged health care. This could offset the savings from an HMO program.

For that reason it is essential that prudent purchasers of HMOs be alert to the signs of "skimming" the most favorable health risks from the pool. These warning signs include mandating "health statements" prior to enrollment to screen out high-risk workers; the absence of key benefits, including prescription-drug coverage welcomed by older subscribers; geographic isolation of health centers; or poor access to clinical specialists. A single "community-rating" system for responsible HMOs to use in setting premiums for all members, without age-based or other forms of discrimination, is the best defense against such adverse selection and reduces the cost of care for everyone.

If studied and implemented effectively, offering benefit programs that include HMO options improves the quality of care for a business's employees and helps control benefit costs to employers. And because of the increased options for consumers, the health care field in general is stimulated to act more competitively, to maximize the efficiency of its own operations, to trim waste, and ultimately to reduce the cost of providing services.

Mr. Getson is senior vice president for U.S. Healthcare of Blue Bell, Pennsylvania.

THE HIDDEN COSTS OF
EARLY RETIREMENT OFFERS
. . . .

by Mortimer R. Feinberg and Bruce Serlen

A*s part of* corporate streamlining programs, many companies are extending early retirement packages to legions of senior managers. They see it as one relatively painless way to pare management ranks—certainly less painful than involuntary layoffs. No one, after all, faces the stigma that being let go after many years of service entails; for the employee, the "senior citizen" package is easier to explain to friends and family.

Then, too, the sweetened package that awaits those who elect to retire early—usually a combination of salary continuation and improved pension benefits—softens the financial impact of the decision. And these experienced employees—typically at least fifty years of age with twenty-five years or more of service—find themselves with a variety of options. They're often still young enough to start second careers, they can work part-time, or, if the financial package is generous enough, they can simply sit back and enjoy themselves.

But sometimes older managers' early retirement decisions aren't as voluntary as they might appear. The early retirement offer will be circulated first, with the specter of layoffs lurking in the background if the company doesn't meet its target numbers. Older managers are then put in a position of playing Russian roulette. If they pass on the offer and their names subsequently appear on the list of those designated to go, not only do they lose the financial incentives—they lose face as well.

The company is also taking a gamble since it may lose some managers it needs. According to law, when a company extends an early retirement offer, it must, for legal reasons, extend it to everyone who meets the established criteria. So, there's no picking and choosing whom management would like to see start marching.

Often, management will expect some of those eligible to take the bait, but much to the corporation's surprise—and chagrin— a much greater number will start emptying their desks. "Among these, no doubt, will be individuals whose talents and abilities the company honestly wants to retain, while others will be deadwood that management is happy to see head for the exit," notes Robert A. M. Coppenrath, president of the photo equipment company Agfa-Gevaert Incorporation.

It's entirely possible, therefore, that on the appointed day, companies find a mass exodus under way. And with the exodus can come an unhappy realization: A good part of the accumulated history of the organization has gone out the door as well. "Older employees in any company bring the past into the present," says John S. Chamberlin, president of Avon Products. "They are the carriers of the culture."

Companies, mindful of all the ambitious young managers eagerly awaiting more responsibility (and prestige), mistakenly believe these young people can effortlessly fill the shoes of those departing. To the contrary, companies cannot assume that the talent they are losing is redundant.

"Neither can they assume that young people are capable of breaking the code that is contained in the files," adds consultant Edward C. Schleh. By "the code," Mr. Schleh means the years of collected memos and reports that help to define and explain such things as marketing cycles, new-product studies, and research on competitors—all data that young successors are tempted to toss out in their efforts to "clean house" and "make a fresh start."

When it comes to anticipating who will go and who will stay, remember that statistical projections deal in overall numbers, not specific individuals. "Think the process through very carefully," advises William A. Schwartz, former president of Cox Enterprises. "If too many opt to go, the package was either too sweet or people were unhappier than the company realized."

Assume a worst-case scenario in which the new retirees include a number of critical decision makers. They decide that they're ready for a long-overdue career change and that the company's generous offer has helped them make up their minds to finally act. Their futures, they decide, really lie in establishing potentially lucrative consulting practices in which they can market their skills—the very skills the company says are expendable.

"Far preferable would be to pare employees with varying degrees of experience throughout the organization," says Malcolm L. Elvey, vice president and director of Hawley Group, a food service company. Entry level employees and those in the midrange of experience would then bear some of the brunt of the restructuring. While involuntary layoffs are certainly more traumatic for an organization in the short term, the company may well emerge on a sounder footing in the long run.

Organizations intent on offering an early retirement package also need to take these factors into account.

- *Counseling.* Give the seasoned managers ample opportunity to mull over the offer. Provide appropriate counselors—preferably from outside the organization—to review financial and psychological issues with each individual. One executive in such circumstances remarked, "I trained to be an Olympic swimmer and now I need time to adjust to the kiddie pool."
- *Succession planning.* As part of its contingency planning, a company needs to work out—almost with the precision of

a chess game—what reorganized departments would look like if a manager chose to go. Who is in line for succession? Is this person really qualified to take on the increased responsibility? Who will then replace this person further down the ladder?

- *Orderly transition.* Allow enough lead time between the day the managers announce their decision and their last day in the office. Have them conduct meetings with their appointed successors in this period to pass on "the tradition." Those departing will appreciate the respect the company is showing them. And in almost all cases, they'll be gracious and cooperative in return. Also, allow each person to determine how much of a celebration he may want with coworkers who are remaining. Acknowledge there may well be ambivalent feelings. Some may want a bash, others prefer a quiet folding of the tent.

- *Consulting options.* Companies are free to negotiate a consulting arrangement on a case-by-case basis with any manager who elects to leave. Be prepared, however, for this not to sit well with remaining employees who may view such arrangements as smacking of "special treatment."

Mr. Feinberg is chairman of BFS Psychological Associates in New York Mr. Serlen writes on management subjects from New York.

SYNERGY WITH THE ECONOMIC ENVIRONMENT

No *matter how* efficient your operations, you can't control the overall market. But that doesn't mean that you must be resigned to sit back and drift helplessly in the currents of market swings and economic change.

This chapter will show, as always by example, how successful entrepreneurs and managers read the market and act accordingly. These individuals reject the judgment that businesses are the product of their economic environment and thus can't fight history. Successful managers don't fight history; they make history by formulating inventive strategies to survive a down market and exploit an up market. They find a synergy with the market.

Recently there has been much discussion about whether our economy is entering a new historical phase in which a classic recessionary period can be avoided by a so-called "soft landing." That's a nice thought. But few managers can rely on rosy forecasts. They must have a game plan prepared for any eventuality. And unless business cycles have completely disappeared—a miracle that our good Lord is unlikely to grant—we must learn how to cope in the bad times.

This section first explores strategies taken to get through a pernicious market. Like laying in a good supply of firewood before a harsh winter, there are many precautionary steps that a manager can take if he senses rough times ahead.

But even when you're in the center of the economic doldrums, you needn't get stuck along with the rest of the crowd. In the early and middle 1970s, Donald Trump bet his savings on cheap real estate in a city which had, by most accounts, "dropped dead." He is now king of the hill in a city that became the center of the world in the 1980s. It is the myopia of the many in a depressed market that gives a comparative advantage to the few with vision.

The market of the 1980s was dominated by one element about which there is probably no greater contention among managers today: the mergers-and-acquisitions frenzy. At first this phenomenon was an interesting curiosity for managers, but not one which affected them in any direct sense. But by the end of the decade, as the corporate world became reshaped by the massive shifting of assets and control, few managers escaped without some brush with downsizing, new controlling interests, and hot shot investment bankers making more in one deal than most managers make in a year. It's tough to find anyone who's neutral about any of this.

The most radical views are expressed by the raiders themselves and those who have been displaced by raiders. The raider claims to represent the best interests of the shareholder by maximizing the share value. The displaced manager says the raider is only interested in short-term gain at the expense of the long-term interest of the company. Both views are explored to some extent in this section.

While few of us are active participants in the takeover game, we have learned the hard way that it's best not to be caught off guard by takeover attempts—even friendly ones. Such is the case with most market trends. We may not be directors of these dramas, but we are important actors in the production. As such, there are roles for managers to play, if only to be ready to guard their own futures. This chapter gives the reader the tools to be prepared.

MANAGERS—NOT POLITICIANS—
MAKE THE ECONOMY WORK
· ·

by Clark E. Chastain

Politicians are still arguing over who should take credit for propelling this nation into a period—if not an era—of strong growth with low inflation. However, business managers probably contributed more to promote today's strong economy than the Reagan Administration, Congress, or the Federal Reserve Board. Cost-saving programs implemented on an unprecedented scale were management's chief recovery strategy.

Lean inventory policies are paring variable costs. An outside consultant estimates that General Motors Corporation budgeted a slash in its total inventories to $1 billion from $3 billion. By Americanizing the Japanese practice of *Kanban*, or "just-in-time" inventory management, GM is greatly reducing material costs. The company has encouraged selected suppliers to locate nearby in Flint, Michigan ("Buick City") so that major parts and materials arrive at the assembly line just in time.

Further, GM has streamlined suppliers for all corporate units. High-quality suppliers are rewarded with exclusive and semiexclusive contracts over the five- to six-year product life cycle. In reducing the number of steel suppliers at some stamping plants to two mills from five, it has slashed its steel inventory to about two and a half days from twenty days. Another major improvement is computerization of inventory stock records, purchase orders, and matching of invoices and shipping documents.

Permanent reduction or containment of oversized labor costs has also helped strengthen the foundations of our economy. Many companies have successfully bargained for wage and fringe-benefit concessions, and negotiations for new pay increases have been more in line with productivity increases. Two-tiered wage contracts, vehemently opposed by unions, allow employers to pay newly hired employees less than current workers. Employers are also placing high priority on paring employee fringe benefits.

Computer networks, linked by robots and using computerized equipment, such as planned for General Electric's "factory of the future" at Lynn, Massachusetts, or GM's Steering Gear Factory at Saginaw, Michigan, assure significant cuts in labor costs. The automated factory of the future, promising immense labor savings, is the vanguard in paring fixed costs. Capital productivity will increase as much as 100 percent in computerized plants that operate continuously.

Computer automation is also the cornerstone in advancing productivity in the office. Daniel R. Coulson, Ford Motor Company accounting director, says Ford is continuing the trend toward overall corporate integration of computers. The automaker, says Mr. Coulson, is "developing a Corporate Financial Information Center that would make a centralized base of financial data available for analysis by various Ford locations."

Smaller concerns have less integration (or none) between accounting and operating computer systems than large companies do. Jeffrey S. Kellerman, controller of Goyette Mechanical Company, in Flint, comments that when Goyette computerized its estimating department, a mini-system compatible with its Burroughs B-90 was too expensive. So it bought an estimating program that ran on a microcomputer, as separate unit that was within Goyette's budget.

The controller of Industrial Techtonics, a precision ball bearing firm in the Midwest, found that integration of computerized accounting with computerization of purchasing, inventories, production scheduling, and sales freed employees for other tasks. Although the controller notes that no employee has ever been replaced by the computer in the ball bearing plant, he emphasizes that "utilization of computers has allowed us to grow in a controlled manner, whereas manual systems would have become ineffective or broken down given our rate of increase in business activity over the years."

John Smith, president of General Motors of Canada, was more specific in identifying cost savings. In the GM unit's Oshawa, Ontario, plant, the use of computers for trade payables and streamlining suppliers eliminated 75 percent of the invoices.

Robert L. Caruso, director of cash administration at Westinghouse Electric Corporation, reported in *Management Accounting*, April 1984, that through the use of electronic transfer payments, a growing process among corporations, the company could save up to $1.4 million annually in processing trade receivables, and the company saved an additional $880,000 a year for accounts payable.

The controller of a large multinational corporation headquartered in the Midwest said it uses the computer to translate foreign currency statements into U.S. dollars, reducing personnel from the twenty previously required at peak periods to six. The company also uses the computer to transfer detailed data from general ledgers of subunits worldwide to corporate headquarters. This saves approximately two thousand hours at the sub-unit level, and reduces staffing and overtime at the central office.

A new approach to cash management is the economic balance sheet developed by Harry B. Ernst, president of Compumetrics, Arlington, Massachusetts. Cash flow is monitored so a balance between growth and liquidity is maintained as an enterprise expands. To improve effectiveness in accounting for cash flow, some authorities also recommend that the funds statement be standardized with a cash orientation for both management and external reporting.

Fresh ideas to save costs, whether applied throughout an organization or within a single department, such as accounting, are being implemented to make businesses more competitive.

With such bold, progressive management tactics, it is little wonder that the economy has strengthened more rapidly than expected. Economists and analysts perhaps have not yet given managers proper credit.

Mr. Chastain is a professor of accounting in the school of management at the University of Michigan, Flint.

CORPORATE STRATEGIES FOR A SHRINKING MARKET

by B. Charles Ames

Regardless of upswings or downswings in the economy, there will always be certain businesses that have to restructure to reflect a shrinking demand in their particular markets. It is understandably difficult—and may be impossible—for managers to accept that their business has leveled out 30 percent to 40 percent below prior peaks, or that a big chunk of their market has been irretrievably lost to new competitors and/or technology. But betting on significant market growth while maintaining a cost structure for a larger volume of business than is realistically achievable is foolish.

In the case of my company, we first had to figure out how to earn a respectable profit on what is today only $150 million of annual volume in our traditional businesses, compared with about $400 million each in 1980 and 1981. Next, we had to figure out how to get a larger share of a smaller pie, or recover the capital employed and take our business into new markets with more attractive growth opportunities.

While the idea of restructuring is not difficult to understand, I have found it very difficult to carry out. There are several roadblocks I have witnessed that make it difficult to dismantle an infrastructure put in place to support a business environment that no longer exists:

Inadequate attention to the importance of being fully cost-competitive. We retained McKinsey and Company to conduct a study on "Manufacturing Competitiveness." The study showed that many manufacturers (ourselves included) have been operating at a 30 percent to 55 percent cost disadvantage to foreign competitors and are losing ground on productivity by a factor of two to one. Some of this disadvantage is obviously due to our hard currency and the stronger government support of some foreign competitors. But it should also be obvious that you cannot be cost-competitive with:

- Plant and equipment carried over from World War II.
- "All in" labor costs that are far out of line with competitors.
- A manufacturing process that chews up working capital beyond sensible guidelines (e.g., thirty-five cents of receivables and FIFO inventories per dollar of sales).
- Structured costs built up during the years when automatic price increases covered indiscriminate staff additions.

You can have the most innovative, brilliant, hard-working management team in the world and you can pursue the most ingenious sales and marketing strategies. But if you are saddled with these problems, you cannot be fully cost-competitive, which means you cannot be an effective competitor in a flat or declining market.

A bureaucratic approach to managing the business in a way that resists change and frustrates the entrepreneurial spirit. As I see it, this roadblock manifests itself in at least three ways:

First, there is the tendency of multidivision companies to build large corporate organizations that are bloated with redundant corporate, group, and middle management people doing many of the things responsible line managers are supposed to do. I am very suspicious of the real contributions made by any large corporate marketing, corporate public relations, corporate advertising, corporate manufacturing, corporate planning, or corporate development group. Of course, any company of size has to have some staff to fulfill its legal and financial requirements and to carry out special projects. But this can generally be done with a much smaller group than you find in most organizations. Certainly this was true in our company, where corporate staff was cut from well over a hundred to under forty.

A second manifestation of this problem is the excessive layering in many organizations that separates senior management from those on the line who are actually doing the work. As a general rule, I think that whenever you have more than five layers in an organization, there is probably something wrong. It doesn't take very long to find organizations with six, seven, or even eight layers between the top management and first-level line workers. In addition to being much too costly, I doubt any senior manager can really know what is going on when he is that far removed from the action.

The third manifestation of the bureaucratic roadblock is the reluctance of some companies to break down and manage their businesses around a number of discrete profit centers. My company has moved from five to twenty, which in my mind is still not enough.

Managing around a number of small discrete profit centers offers several distinct advantages: It streamlines the planning and decision-making process and avoids the middle-management "drag" that is inevitably found in big organizations; it provides a much better basis for planning and control, because someone with clear-cut responsibility is on top of everyday problems; and it helps to uncover more strategic options because more people are thinking strategically about what they can do to accelerate the profit growth in their particular business.

An overdependence on old products that don't offer anything new or don't begin to measure up to current competitive offerings. Many of these products contributed nicely when the demand curve was moving upward and capacity was strained, but now they are simply not competitive. I am not suggesting that all these products or businesses should be scrapped. There are obviously plenty of short-term opportunities to generate significant profits and cash by "milking the business." But you cannot build a business around these products.

A lack of drive, urgency, and competence in sales and marketing groups that have become conditioned to earning a living by simply taking orders. The high rate of inflation we saw in the late 1970s and early 1980s allowed too many sales and marketing personnel to look good in terms of increasing sales dollars. Actually it didn't take much skill or effort to ride the demand curve upward in that period, and a lot of dollar volume was generated through price increases rather than unit gains. A lot of our sales and marketing people grew too soft and complacent in this environment. Many others have fallen behind technologically as new products and technologies came into play.

Overcoming these roadblocks and gearing one's business for profit growth in the face of diminished or slower-growing markets and more intense competition will require many managers to think in a broader-gauged way and to be a lot more tough-minded than they have been in the past. However, I don't believe that it requires a whole new array of sophisticated techniques. Emphasis on management fundamentals, many of which have been forgotten or overlooked in recent years, should be enough to recapture the competitive edge.

Mr. Ames was chairman and chief executive officer of Acme-Cleveland Corporation when this article was written, and he is now CEO of Uniroyal Goodrich Tire Company.

WHAT IF WE'RE NOT IN FOR A SOFT LANDING?

. . . .

by A. Gary Shilling

With most economists forecasting a soft landing, is this a time when business managers can relax and enjoy robust sales and earnings? Not unless you feel comfortable forecasting with your head buried in the sand. If you believe, as I do, that the soft landing is more the product of hope than realistic forecasting, and that the economy may have just entered a recession of unknown depth, what can you as a business manager do to deal with it?

First, try to impress on your subordinates the similarities of current trends with past business cycles. I see many CEOs who are properly concerned, but their line managers have been lulled into complacency by better-than-expected sales and earnings. As usual, earlier tight credit has laid the way to a general business slowdown. In eerie similarity to past prerecession periods, the inflation-corrected money supply declined for most of 1988.

Other managers are getting sucked in by the rolling recession argument—the belief that just as agriculture, energy, and manufacturing suffered near-depressions earlier in the decade, financial services and other sectors will be squeezed now, but that no nationwide slump is likely. This argument reinforces the normal and all-too-seductive idea that everyone else's business but mine will decline. Unfortunately, the cautious attitudes spawned by the long and severe recessionary periods of the early 1980s have seriously eroded.

At the very least, business leaders should be prepared to show their subordinates how specific general economic trends can (and should) directly affect their planning.

The rise in interest rates since the 1987 crash has damped auto and other discretionary purchases while leading to a boom in individual savings. In the first quarter of 1988, individuals saved an eye-popping 54 percent of the rise in after-tax income from the fourth quarter, considerably more than the already large 34 percent average of the final quarter in the previous three business expansions.

With weakness in spending, inventories have been climbing in relation to sales, in normal prerecession fashion. True, inventories aren't yet thought to be out of hand, but they never are until the recession is under way and stocks in manufacturers' and retailers' hands soar as sales fall faster than production can be cut.

One of the key measures managers can take given these circumstances is to hold down inventories. Even if you miss a few sales as a result, slash production now or at least at the first sign that your inventory-sales ratios are rising. For reasons I can't understand, businessmen never seem to realize when inventory problems are arising until it's too late. Our clients always explain them away as the result of special sales promotions, transportation bottlenecks, temporary production glitches, style or model changes, etc. Currently, auto dealerships are blaming manufacturers and manufacturers are blaming dealers for a huge buildup of auto stocks.

Excessive inventories are an ongoing cyclical phenomenon, despite the vast improvement in control techniques. As a result, in the postwar era, 75 percent of the decline in economic activity in recessions has been due to inventory liquidation, and the next recession will probably be no exception.

Another indicator that has led some to expect a soft landing is that as in past cycles, capital spending and exports are still growing robustly. But these are lagging economic series that normally don't turn down until a recession is well under way. And as all major countries have been raising interest rates to fight overheating economies and inflation, the recession that may be starting in the United States probably will be global. Also, though protectionist pressures have been held at bay during the 1980s' worldwide expansion, the test of whether protectionism raises its ugly head will occur in the next recession, not during boom times.

Thus, while managers are encouraging capital outlays to get in on "expanding markets" in post-1992 Europe and Asia, managers must be extremely cautious with capital. Typically, high-capacity utilization at the end of expansion spurs capital spending zeal, regretted only in the sober days of excess capacity in the following recession. After the recessionary shakeout of the early 1980s, most U.S. manufacturers vowed to confine capital spending to cost reduction and productivity enhancement, and to never again get caught with huge capacity-expansion projects coming on stream only during the next recession. But prosperity has overwhelmed caution in industries such as paper and chemicals, which appear to have locked into the sad, old overexpansion cycle.

In addition to holding back on cost outlays, redouble your efforts to cut costs, especially overhead burden. True, cost cutting—especially in manufacturing—has done wonders to raise profit margins and lower break-even points in this expansion. But higher profit margins and lower break-even points do not necessarily mean reduced volatility of earnings in the face of recessionary declines in sales. Furthermore, the recession may be long and deep if financial problems—such as the S&L crisis, overleveraged U.S. corporations, overborrowed consumers, bankrupt Third World debtors, and vulnerable real estate investments—explore and seriously impair business and consumer confidence.

While cutting costs and inventory, managers should also clean up their balance sheets by reducing debt and increasing liquidity. Interest costs fall in the recession, but dollar for dollar this decline will be dwarfed in most businesses by the slide in revenues. In tough times, debt is a drag and cash is king.

If you must borrow, avoid long-term fixed-rate borrowing until much later. Long-term interest rates typically decline not only through the recession but into the early stages of the following recovery. Corporate treasurers, scared stiff by the prerecession rise in interest rates, have a knack for borrowing soon after rates start to fall but long before they reach their lows. The current stalling in the interest-rate decline may tempt many, but borrowing too soon could lock you into excessively high rates in a postrecession era of strong competition and low inflation, which will not allow those costs to be passed on through higher prices.

On balance, be extra cautious until the next recession comes and goes. The economy may be entering a soft, not a hard, landing. But running your business on that basis is betting against a lot of history. Even if the recession is a mild one, modest steps taken in preparation now could assure a soft landing for your company.

Mr. Shilling heads a New York-based economic consulting and portfolio management firm. His latest book is After the Crash: Recession or Depression *(Lakeview, 1988)*

CLOSING THE HOMETOWN PLANT MAY KEEP
YOUR COMPANY IN THE UNITED STATES

by Elizabeth Haas

T*his particular story* involves a company making industrial products, but it could have happened in Silicon Valley as easily as in America's industrial belt. The company's managers knew they needed to improve manufacturing and that the industry was way over capacity. Nevertheless, they were committed to keeping all current facilities operating, particularly the original plant in the town where most of them lived. The option of closing the plant seemed to be drastic, unnecessary, and harsh treatment of faithful employees.

The managers decided instead to renovate the plant. Key people were brought in, workers agreed to a wage cut, two layers of management were eliminated, product changes were made, and equipment upgraded. It was a remarkable effort, but volume kept dropping. Overhead was still too high because there were too many other plants, In 1985 the old original plant was finally shut down, and the company stopped making many of the products produced there. Ironically, in trying to save the plant, management lost the industrial-products business.

In contrast, in 1979 Goodyear closed its Akron plant, consolidated facilities, and saved its industrial-rubber business. It remains the leading supplier in an increasingly competitive market.

A sinister logic confronts our manufacturers. Forced to combat low-cost foreign producers, they automate, school themselves in Japanese manufacturing techniques, integrate their operations with the help of computers, and thereby increase the capacity of current facilities—frequently in an industry already burdened with idle plants. Carrying extra capacity is an expensive burden that few, if any, U.S. manufacturers can afford.

Top management usually knows this, but balks at taking action. Closing a plant ahead of time means upsetting something that is working—fixing it before it's broken. It may involve eliminating hundreds of jobs, overturning communities. The specter of firings, bad headlines, and loss of morale make putting off tough decisions more attractive.

Yet waiting until the closing becomes an absolute necessity means taking the only way out—buying parts from or building in countries with low labor costs. Market share is lost in the transition, publicity reflects poorly on the closing, and employees lose their sense of self-worth, not just their jobs.

These problems can be avoided if the decision to close is made before the situation becomes too critical. In 1986, Electrolux Corporation closed its largest facility, in Greenwich, Connecticut, not out of short-term necessity, but as part of its manufacturing strategy. Employees were given severance beyond what contracts required, retraining, and help finding jobs. Within six weeks of the closing, 70 percent of them were reemployed at salaries comparable to what they had been earning at Electrolux. In contrast, 60 percent of all workers involved in plant closings in the United States in the past five years have been reemployed, and only with a big cut in pay.

Electrolux worked with government agencies, an outplacement firm, other local companies, and community interest groups. The press reports on these programs were positive and reflected Electrolux's health—how volumes were at record levels, and how automation, just-in-time inventory practices, and the use of state-of-the-art material in the company's products had created excess capacity.

A large part of the success of this effort was due to good communications and attention to detail. For example, when it was time to announce the plant-closing decision, letters were hand carried to the governor's mansion and to his office to ensure that he was informed immediately. The governor was also told that Electrolux's chief executive was in his office and available to discuss the decision. An announcement to employees was followed by a press release, then a meeting with employees, and then a press conference.

This is not to imply that it was easy for Electrolux to close the Greenwich plant or that it was a matter of buying off a few older workers. Moving a major production activity, such as the making of a vacuum cleaner motor, requires considerable planning and risk taking. Contracts at some plants were renegotiated a year early and flexibility built into them. Adequate training and setup were factored in. Supplier relationships had to be reconsidered and transition inventory built. Electrolux made a twenty-five-year supply of parts for some old models and found homes for tools and dies with suppliers. Things build up in a plant over sixty years—it cost the company two hundred thousand dollars to dispose properly of waste that was potentially hazardous.

No matter how good the plans, something will go wrong. When machines from the Greenwich plant arrived in Virginia to be installed in the company's factory there, it was discovered that the ceilings were not high enough. Fortunately, production people had enough time to fix the problem—a pit was dug in the floor.

Because of this complexity and the possibility for mistakes, it's no wonder that the biggest obstacle to changing manufacturing strategy and configuration is the manufacturing people themselves, including the senior executive and the top plant people. Given the order to close a plant quickly, they will cut workers and reallocate production, but not change anything else because of the risks involved. Their efforts result in productivity gains and cost savings of 5 percent to 10 percent. But those actions that will result in 20 percent gains and savings, and increase quality and flexibility—often the actions needed to combat foreign manufacturers—won't be taken unless a company makes the decision to close early and uses a self-imposed deadline to reexamine its manufacturing approach.

Radical reconfiguration is not always the solution to a manufacturer's competitive difficulties. But it is an option that needs to be considered more often. The decision to close an old facility may in the end be the kindest and wisest action. If a company waits too long, it may not have the opportunity to act humanely and will not provide workers and communities the chance they deserve to find new jobs.

Update

Since the time I wrote this article, radical reconfiguration has become an increasingly important option to consider, and careful advance planning has continued to be key to successful plant closings. In fact, both my ongoing involvement in plant closings and early returns from the recently legislated Workers Adjustment and Retraining Notification Act (WARN) have underscored the value to both workers and companies of management's advance announcements, planning, careful execution, outplacement activities, and strong follow-up.

Initial WARN-related statistics indicate that:

1. Employees notified in advance have suffered substantially less severe consequences in terms of periods of unemployment, financial distress, and the need to relocate.
2. There has been no adverse effect on companies, and the most productive workers have not left early.
3. The labor market adjustments have been smoother.

Individual cases tell the same story—there are realistic options for management beyond either costing employees their livelihood or supporting a noncompetitive facility.

For example, Electrolux's plant in Brockville, Canada, had a flexible work force but constituted more capacity than Electrolux needed in this age of automation. When Electrolux closed the plant, it was sold to Almico, Incorporated. The sale was conditional on Almico signing a letter of intent to offer employment to the dispatched work force. Electrolux agreed to pay for the necessary employee training.

Even in more depressed areas like the industrial belt, the story is the same. When Allegheny International closed three of its plants in 1987, the outplacement programs it put in place led to over 70 percent of its workers being reemployed within thirty days of plant closing. When American Can closed its plant in a depressed area of Oregon and offered to transfer employees, a phenomenal 95 percent were reemployed, again within a thirty-day period.

In all of these cases, the financial costs to the companies of advance notice were lower than expected. Electrolux's program to retrain workers, which was more than 75 percent compensated for by support from the Canadian government, cost less than two hundred dollars per employee (a much smaller amount than paying severance) and prevented the early loss of any employee.

In the case of Allegheny International, the advance notice

bought the company time to reconfigure and upgrade its other facilities and resulted in an overall product cost reduction—much greater benefits than a straightforward, abrupt plant closure would have provided. And, American Can's transfer of workers resulted in a mix of skills in its Vancouver facility that has provided a new and unexpected flexibility in output.

These examples tell us time and time again that advanced planning truly facilitates plant closings for all parties involved.

Ms. Haas is a consultant with New York Consulting Partners.

IS THERE LIFE FOR CREDITORS
AFTER CHAPTER 11?

. . . .

by Richard Dafoe

C*hapter 11 of* the federal bankruptcy law has been a blessing for debtor companies. Since 1982, more than 126,000 businesses in the United States have filed Chapter 11, an increasingly popular management tool for companies needing protection from creditors long enough to reorganize and stay afloat. But for creditors, Chapter 11 is both a blessing and a curse.

A successful reorganization can provide creditors a greater return than they might have obtained from a liquidation, and it keeps their customer in business. But when creditors end up getting less than they would have had the company liquidated, then the only beneficiary is the debtor—and that happens all too often under the protection of the bankruptcy code.

Although it is increasingly important for creditors to know how to protect themselves in a Chapter 11, many do not know where to begin, or they overlook simple steps that are critical to their case. Creditors must make quick, informed decisions within days of a filing to have a chance at a reasonable return on their debt.

Preparing to make those decisions starts long before a Chapter 11 is filed. For example, consider all debtors potential risks, and monitor your accounts accordingly. If a debtor falls behind on payments, reassess the value of the collateral—not only its value to the debtor, but its market value to you. You may need additional collateral and, in a Chapter 11, you are in a significantly stronger position if your claims are secured.

Find out as soon as possible if a debtor intends to file for bankruptcy. Monitoring accounts closely will give you a clue, and there are always rumors about companies preparing to file. Check the rumors, Call the bankruptcy court or read the public records routinely to see if there has been a filing. Timing is critical; delays can ruin your chances of getting a return.

When a company does file, you might be tempted to say, "We've lost. Let's close this account." That might be appropriate if your claims are nominal, but take a hard look at your options before closing the books.

First, decide if your claim is worth fighting for. You might think so, until legal costs begin to mount. Don't throw good money after bad—what you receive from the debtor's estate may not be worth it in the long run. Make your decision based on what you know about the debtor's business and the business's ability to reorganize.

Participating in a bankruptcy case means choosing sides. Unsecured creditors often have no option but to align with the debtor and hope the company will reorganize with some payment plan. If you're secured, however, you do have an option. You might side with the debtor company in the hope it will successfully reorganize, or you may favor an immediate settlement through liquidation or return of your collateral.

Knowledge of the debtor's business helps you judge the chances of a successful reorganization. A debtor's plan may be to pay a percentage of earnings over the next two years. But if that doesn't work out, you could get only a fraction of what might have been secured two years earlier through liquidation.

You may be able to strike a deal. For example, you might agree to settle a debt for fifty cents on the dollar if you think you would get less under a reorganization. But such settlements may not be permanent. Provisions in the bankruptcy code allow the court to overturn such transactions if they occur within a specified time before the Chapter 11 filing. The assets or property in question would return to the estate for all creditors to share.

Here are some often overlooked points:

Filing a notice of appearance. Creditors must follow a case closely to learn if a debtor plans to liquidate certain assets. Filing can be as simple as writing to the bankruptcy clerk, the debtor, and other creditors requesting that you receive notice of all proceedings involving the case.

A notice of appearance is not always a guarantee you'll get advance word. In a case with a large number of creditors, the debtor might receive court permission to notify only the largest claimants. The aggressive creditor will go to the court regularly and read public records of the proceedings. A personal visit also helps to establish contact at the court, so you'll know whom to call if you need information.

Reviewing financial information. Throughout a Chapter 11 proceeding, the debtor is required to file various documents. A schedule of assets and liabilities, and a statement responding to questions about the debtor's financial affairs, must be sworn to and filed, typically fifteen days after the petition. Thereafter, monthly reports which contain operating information also must be filed. These filings can contain useful information for creditors.

Talking to other creditors. All creditors, regardless of their claims, should share information, assess the debtor's prospects, and determine strategy. The debtor's schedules—listing creditors and amounts owed—are available from the bankruptcy clerk.

Attending the first meeting of creditors. All creditors listed on the debtor's schedules receive notice of the first meeting of creditors. This is an informal, out-of-court meeting at which attending creditors can raise relevant questions with representatives of the debtor.

Filing a proof of claim. In many circumstances, if you don't file a proof of claim within the specified time, you lose. The filing is simple to do, yet companies have lost hundreds of thousands of dollars by neglecting it. The proof of claim ensures your chance at some recovery of debt once the company reorganizes or liquidates. You must immediately find out the bar date—the cutoff point after which no proofs of claim are accepted.

Seeking reclamation. The bankruptcy code allows creditors who supply goods, within ten days after the delivery of the goods, to reclaim them. Let's say you supply a company on a daily basis. If you learn of the filing and respond immediately, you might cut your losses. If you stand around for ten days, you lose your opportunity to reclaim products.

There's also the possibility a company will not finish a reorganization plan within the hundred and twenty days the law usually provides. If it does not, creditors may file a plan of their own. But those situations don't occur often, and it is up to you to protect your interests. In a bankruptcy case, no one is going to look out for you.

Mr. Dafoe is a partner with the Dallas law firm Vial, Hamilton, Koch and Knox.

HOW TO DRAW CAPITAL
IN A DECAPITALIZED MARKET
· ·

by Peter J. Sprague and Charles E. Harris

As the business community picks its way through the debris of the 1987 market crash, it is starting to reexamine the very raison d'être of Wall Street and, to the extent that the market has strayed from its purpose, to propose reforms.

One of the clear results of the crash is that capital is now at a premium. As a means of providing for those companies without huge reserves or assets, we suggest that small companies be allowed to raise capital from the stock market following the same procedures available to individuals under Rule 144 (which permits an insider to sell a minimum of 1 percent of a company's capitalization each quarter). While such expanded access would address a result of the crash, it would also help address one of its causes.

Wall Street, as opposed to Atlantic City, is supposed to perform two primary functions: facilitate the investment of savings, and raise capital for growing enterprises that create jobs and real wealth. The recent laissez-faire years have led to a distortion of these intentions. Like mutants created from a too-highly-charged radioactive environment, the distortions have (at least until the crash) been multiplying rapidly: insider trading battening on merger and acquisition activity; buyouts leveraged by junk bonds, transforming stable companies into debt-servicing financial fandangos spinning off divisions and employees; manic, computer-accelerated trading of derivative financial instruments; long-term investments in the actual shares of growing companies supplanted by commission-churning options and financial futures; the trading practice of betting on stock fluctuations without actually buying and selling the underlying shares (which is exactly what the "bucket shops" did at the turn of the century before they were outlawed, for the good reason that they siphoned capital away from legitimate investment activity).

In summary, the tail has been wagging the dog as financial maneuvering has often been taking precedence over genuine capital development.

There are two ways to deal with such a condition. One would be to load down a weakened market with yet more regulations and restrictions. Another method would be to allow a bit more freedom of movement for smaller companies—those without easy access to the exotic financial instruments used by the individual and corporate giants to raise capital. We recommend the latter course.

Specifically, if these smaller companies could enjoy the same access to the financial markets that their own insiders have under Rule 144, they could then have a meaningful—though limited—source of capital without the time and expense of preparing a registration statement and hiring an underwriter.

Rule 144 already has demonstrated itself as a workable mechanism for distributing limited amounts of stock in the marketplace. If individuals are permitted access to the marketplace in this manner, can it be less in the public interest to permit corporations to have the same access? A corporation and its officers and directors are responsible under the anti-fraud provisions of the securities acts for the accuracy of the corporation's filings. A passive investor selling unregistered shares under Rule 144 is not. The investing public's protections could not be weakened by this liberalization of Rule 144. Nor would it be difficult to implement for corporate officers, directors, and corporate counselors, who are typically quite familiar with exercising Rule 144.

If there would be little potential for harm in this liberalization, is there significant benefit to be realized? We believe so. Under current rules, only about fifteen hundred companies qualify for an S-3 shelf registration, which is rarely used for equity offerings, as it has been claimed that such offerings would depress the market by creating an overhang of shares. The more limited Rule 144 offerings have been shown not to overburden the market.

To illustrate the benefit of the extension of Rule 144, consider the benefit to a hypothetical corporation:

A corporation with $50 million in shareholders' equity selling at a market valuation of two times book value—or $100 million—and earning 15 percent on shareholders' equity—or

$7.5 million—would be able to sell a minimum of 1 percent of its capitalization each quarter, or some $4 million worth in a year. Assuming that the company is not paying a dividend, shareholders' equity would grow by $11.5 million instead of $7.5 million in the year, thus giving the company 7 percent more capital at the end of the year and permitting (all else being equal) 7 percent more growth in the following year.

While it is routine practice for Wall Street trading desks to call companies to see if they want to buy back blocks of their stock, the trading desks cannot buy stock directly from issuing companies. The ability of a company to sell a block at least equal to 1 percent of its existing equity capitalization in any quarter would make the commerce with trading desks a two-way street, making it easier for institutions to take positions in smaller companies without disturbing the market.

An additional benefit would be realized for the investing public through this liberalization. Corporate managers would have a continuous reason (other than fear of takeover) to be concerned about their financial public relations, instead of worrying about the stock price only once every few years when the company needs to do a financing or they themselves want to unload some stock. Thus, in post crash Wall Street, the interests of the investor and corporate manager would be brought more closely into alignment by allowing corporations to avail themselves of Rule 144.

Again, the idea is to address what we view as a fundamental problem in the market, something that may well have played a major role in the crash: Too much distance has been created between the producer and the marketplace. Takeovers and fear of takeovers, leading to fancy bond issues and other financial instruments, have begun to highlight, if not define, our stock market. After the smoke settles (and stock prices stabilize), the only people who really benefit from this activity are the folks in the middle of trades—the arbitragers, lawyers, traders, etc. Money that could have gone into real growth is lost in the black hole of "profit creation."

Small- to medium-size companies have been the engines of American industrial growth during the past decade. While the Fortune 500 have been reducing employment, companies with under five hundred employees created most of the new jobs in the 1980s. During the ten-month period before the 1987 crash, over $1.6 trillion of stock changed hands on the New York Stock Exchange. Public equity offerings during the same period raised only $22 billion on all exchanges. Companies need capital for growth, and the country will need their growth more than ever during the difficult years ahead.

Mr. Sprague is chairman of National Semiconductor and has been a director or officer of a wide range of companies. Mr. Harris is chairman, president, and chief executive officer of Harris and Harris Group.

HOW TO STAY ON THE RIGHT SIDE
IN MEGAMERGERS
. . . .
by Kenneth M. Davidson

N*o one can* know whether General Electric's $6 billion acquisition of RCA in 1986 will, in the long run, turn out to be a profitable strategy. We are told that General Electric understands the businesses of RCA, including NBC. Much is made of the fact that GE helped form RCA. But it should be noted that in 1979 GE sold most of its radio and television stations as part of a $5 billion divestiture effort to bring coherence to the company's businesses.

It is a truism that managers must understand the businesses they operate, but too often this truism is ignored. Many billion-dollar megadeals seem to reflect a failure of managerial wisdom. Rather than find or create new business opportunities that match their capacities, managers of very successful American corporations have simply spent their profits on a small number of breathtakingly large acquisitions. Takeovers on this uninspired basis have earned their unfortunate fates.

At the end of this decade of misconceived megadeals, some transactions have had brighter prospects than others. Three types of megamergers have the greatest potential to increase corporate profits: acquiring a target in a closely related business; acquiring a diversified firm to break it up; and acquiring a target to create a new industry.

The highest probability of a successful merger exists where a well-run company buys one of its direct competitors. Because the managers of the acquiring firm understand the business, they can make considered judgments about new products, research projects, and eliminating duplicate facilities.

For example, Shell Oil could reasonably pay billions more than the price at which its shares had traded to acquire Belridge Oil. Shell and the integrated oil firms against which it bid were developing new techniques to recover Belridge's reserves of very heavy crude oil and of light oil located at very great depths. Similarly, Chevron and Texaco could afford to pay large premiums in their 1984 $10 billion-plus acquisitions, in part because they could project savings that would result from closing down duplicate facilities. In contrast, acquisitions by the large oil companies in electric motors, department stores, and copper have failed primarily because of unforeseen problems in these unrelated industries.

Similar very large mergers with a potential for increasing profits or reducing costs have been undertaken in the transportation, communication, and steel industries. The airline mergers, like the oil transactions, have a potential to increase efficiency by combining business operations. Realizing that potential is not automatic, however, Pan Am did not benefit from acquiring National Airlines. The demise of low-overhead People Express may have been hastened by its takeover of more mainstream Frontier Airlines.

The prospects are brightest where a firm has a successful

formula that it is replicating in its acquisitions. Thus, Gannett and Newhouse have continued to add to their string of publications. G. Helleman Brewing has done well acquiring a succession of regional beer companies. And it looks as if Stroh Brewery will profit from its acquisition of Schlitz. But Philip Morris, despite its marketing success in introducing Miller Lite Beer, had had problems finding profits that match its market share. Again, it is difficult for an acquiring firm to create profits in industries with which it is unfamiliar.

Misunderstood businesses that are not realizing their full profit potential offer knowledgeable managers the opportunity of buying a poorly run division and running it properly or buying an overly diversified company and selling its components to competent managers. Victor Kiam, for example, turned around the declining sales and profits of Remington Shaver when he bought the company from the Sperry Corporation, as did the managers of American Safety Razor who bought their division from Philip Morris.

Indeed, corporate raiders have increasingly provoked overly diversified conglomerates to divest businesses they cannot manage. U.V. Industries escaped a takeover bid only because the value of its shares rose in response to an announcement that U.V. would sell off all of its businesses. Apparently its stockholders agreed that the U.V. properties would be more valuable if operated by other managers. Commenting on its agreement to be acquired by General Electric, RCA Chairman Thornton Bradshaw conceded that a higher total price could have been obtained for the company if he were willing to split divisions "up into little pieces and parcel them out to the highest bidder."

The profits from selling the "little pieces" of misguided megamergers can be enormous. John Kluge holds the record. After taking Metromedia private for $1.6 billion, he sold its television stations for $2 billion and its mobile phone and paging services for $1.6 billion. Other divestitures brought in another $1 billion.

Combining companies to create a new business is a partial exception to the requirement of industry expertise. The novelty of a new business necessarily limits the familiarity any manager could have with its operations and consequently increases the risks of the merged firm. These risks may be more than compensated for by the potential market for the new product or service.

For example, the national financial services companies being formed by Sears, Merrill Lynch, Citicorp, American Express, and others are undergoing a very difficult process trying to integrate banking, financing, investment, insurance, and real estate services. But if they succeed, it will be because these companies have recognized from the outset the need to accommodate skills and attitudes of very different kinds of financial professionals and to understand both the emerging technology and customer expectations that will define this industry.

There are limits to the time and talents of corporate executives. And the profits go to those managers who understand their limits.

Mr. Davidson, a lawyer who works for the Federal Trade Commission, is the author of Megamergers: Corporate America's Billion-Dollar Takeovers *(Ballinger Publishing Co., 1985). His views do not necessarily reflect those of the FTC.*

TAKING STOCK OF
YOUR COMPANY'S REAL WORTH
. . . .
by Alfred Rappaport

M*anagers looking for* some signal that their company is a takeover target should take note of a comment by Goodyear Tire and Rubber Chairman Robert E. Mercer after Sir James Goldsmith's bid: "I used to check the stock price maybe once a week, but I've started checking it every day, sometimes several times a day, after this Goldsmith thing got started."

A takeover threat manifests itself initially as an increase in the company's stock price, usually well in advance of a takeover announcement. But the challenge for a chief executive officer is to determine how much of the stock price increase may be evidence of a takeover threat. An increase may be due to any of three factors: more optimism about the company's future operating performance; a decline in interest rates; or the introduction of a restructuring premium—that is, a premium that anticipates major restructuring, either by incumbent management or by an acquirer.

An insightful interpretation of market signals emanating from a company's stock price provides management with an early-warning system for takeovers and a strategic opportunity to evaluate its own operational and financial-restructuring alternatives. Management thereby is able to look at what the stock price says about the market's expectations for a company's future performance. The question is no longer simply whether the shares are fairly valued. Management must first assess whether the company is being valued on a going-concern basis or on the basis of some anticipated breakup value or less comprehensive form of restructuring.

The market-signals approach can be illustrated by the example of a Fortune 500 company rumored to be a takeover target. The company's top executives were convinced the market was undervaluing the company's stock. In early 1986 the shares were trading at about fifty dollars each. Management found this price was justified by long-term projections for sales growth, margins, capital expenditures, and working capital investment that had just appeared in Value Line and other investment research sources. The company's own five-year planning projections were very close to Wall Street forecasts. Management thus concluded the company was fairly valued rather than undervalued.

By midyear, the per-share price had increased to about seventy-five dollars. It was clear that the substantially higher level of operating performance required to justify the new price would be beyond management's reach. Indeed, Value Line and other investment research services had not revised their operating expectations from beginning-of-the-year forecasts. Five dollars of the twenty-five-dollar-a-share increase was attributable to lower interest rates. Further analysis disclosed the first important signal to management: The remaining twenty dollars of the increase was attributable to the market's growing anticipation of a major restructuring program carried out by either current management or an acquirer.

There was another significant signal: While the stock was trading at about seventy-five dollars, individual investment analysts on Wall Street estimated the company's breakup value (that is, the sum of what the various businesses could be sold for) at eighty-five to a hundred dollars a share. The spread between the company's breakup value and its then current market value represented the potential profit to an acquirer and therefore signaled that there was a takeover risk.

To minimize the likelihood of a takeover, management naturally would like to see the stock price maintained at its current level, or increased; after all, there is no better means of avoiding a takeover than increasing the stock price. But this is likely to be accomplished only if management provides convincing evidence to the market that it will embark on substantial restructuring such as divestiture of under-performing businesses, spinoffs, and stock repurchases that are seen as creating value. Restructuring to create shareholder value is not a transitory fad; it will become a permanent part of management's strategic response to shifting economic forces such as deregulation, technology, and global competition.

Managements that resist value-creating change and signal an unrelenting desire to keep their companies independent by initiating antitakeover tactics such as poison pills and greenmail are likely to dissipate shareholder value. Gillette's blocking of Revlon's bid is an excellent example. The day Gillette announced its agreement to pay a premium for Revlon's 13.9 percent stake, Gillette's shares plunged almost 20 percent.

While many restructurings are motivated by a desire to foil a takeover bid, it is nonetheless essential to emphasize that increasing shareholder value has become the driving force for corporate restructuring. The first stage of the restructuring is largely based on one time transactions involving the buying and selling of businesses or changing the company's capital structure. In contrast, the next stage, creating shareholder value, is becoming the basis for managing the entire business.

A growing number of companies such as Kraft, Trinova, and Westinghouse are moving to the next stage by introducing the shareholder-value standard in planning and performance-monitoring of all business strategies on an ongoing basis. Top management and the directors thus will have more reliable answers to such basic questions as: Will the long-term corporate plan create value for shareholders, and how much? Which business units are creating value and which are not? How would alternative strategic plans affect shareholder value?

Successful execution of this second stage will accomplish two basic objectives. First, using the shareholder-value approach will ensure that management has met its fiduciary responsibility to evaluate corporate plans and performance on the same basis that investors use to value the company. Second, it will reduce the current concern that a takeover of an undermanaged company is imminent. Companies reluctant to enter the second stage of restructuring are likely to become the prime takeover candidates of the 1990s. And those that ignore the powerful market signals to management do so at their own peril.

Mr. Rappaport, Leonard Spacek professor at Northwestern University's J. L. Kellogg Graduate School of Management, is author of Creating Shareholder Value: The New Standard for Business Performance *(The Free Press, 1986).*

HOW TO AVOID CONFLICTS OF INTEREST
IN THE TAKEOVER GAME
....
by Ben W. Heineman

Directors *trying to* make astute buy-or-sell decisions during corporate takeover battles are often obstructed by strong conflicts of interest involving the management and professional advisers. The conflicts reflect two competing trends: the tendency in takeovers for directors to affirm the chief executive officer's policy decision rather than to initiate policy themselves, and the directors' recognition that the chief executive and his close management associates may have personal motives ranging from protecting their tenures to setting up "golden parachutes" in case they have to bail out.

Any meaningful takeover threat and its Byzantine consequences ultimately involve questions of value, and fairness to the stockholders. The key professionals are investment bankers and special takeover lawyers. Their interests and the goals of the officers who engage them may be closely allied and may conflict with the perceived interests of the directors and stockholders.

The investment banker's function is to give a reliable opinion on value and fairness. Nevertheless, the banker frequently has a conflict of interest that if faced by a director would prevent the director from participating in any way in the takeover decision and could compel his resignation. The conflict arises from the millions of dollars of fees contingent upon the completion of the transaction, and if the transaction succeeds, from the expressed or implied promise of major future transactions. One could reasonably believe that the potential benefits of the transaction to the investment banking firm might undermine the detachment and independence of its opinion. Fees in excess of $20 million are not unknown.

Not just years or decades but centuries of experience have taught us that those with a conflict of interest cannot effectively and fairly represent others. John Alden was not the proper representative for Miles Standish.

What to do?

Investment bankers should remember the history of contingent fees in acquisitions and divestitures. When ongoing relationships rather than individual transactions were the foundation of investment banking, modest contingent fees were designed for the protection of clients and to enhance the relationship between client and banker. The size of an individual transaction was small when compared with the value of the long-standing relationship. The transaction seldom involved the tenure and, hence, the personal self-interest of the chief executive. Today, transactions, and not relationships, are the foundation of investment banking; the value of most traditional corporate relationships pales in contrast to the benefits of a single transaction.

A recent *Wall Street Journal* story discussed the contingent or "performance" fee of millions of dollars charged by a leading takeover law firm in a major transaction. The fee would be paid only if the transaction took place. The chief executive of the acquiring company is quoted as saying that the lawyers "did contribute much" to the pursuit of the target, and that what they do "goes much beyond legal work."

Performance fees for corporate lawyers are too recent an innovation to know whether the concept will spread. I would hope that performance fees would die aborning so that directors could be assured of dispassionate and independent advice from their counsel.

Corporate boards should acknowledge the conflicts of interest of their professional advisers and take steps to reform these relationships. As a matter of internal control, these steps should include giving unmistakable policy guidance to the chief executive. The normal deference given by a board to a chief executive functioning in the usual course of business has no application to such extraordinary policy issues as the purchase of a major enterprise in an unfriendly takeover or the sale of the entire business.

When faced with such situations—with the powerful, and perhaps overriding, conflicts of interest of the lawyers, investment bankers, and even management—the directors' alternatives are difficult but clear: The directors may oppose the transaction as a matter of principle on the ground that the board's professional advisers are as disqualified from participation as the directors themselves would be; they may vote for the transaction with the nagging fear that the professionals' opinions have been unduly influenced by the huge contingent fees and other perquisites; or they may seek to retain yet more investment bankers and lawyers to review—exclusively on behalf of the board—the professional opinions that the corporation already has obtained.

In one widely noted case, "outside" directors at Owens-Illinois chose the latter route, retaining additional investment bankers and lawyers unrelated to the company or its management. The bankers chosen by the directors reached different conclusions from those of the bankers selected by management. Each set agreed with the objectives of its patrons, although each was representing not its patrons but the corporation and its stockholders.

I would urge all those concerned in a takeover to reexamine their corporate relationships with utmost care. It is only a matter of time before a dramatic economic downturn, or some other drastic event, will bring a sea change in current mores. This will call into question many of the transactions that will have taken place, including many that will have seemed secure. The result could easily be external intervention, investigation, and regulation, accompanied at the very least by extreme embarrassment to many prominent but shortsighted people.

Whatever their reasons, in initially opposing management

and its professionals and following their own independent views, the outside directors of Owens-Illinois have increased the value of the company for the shareholders by at least $180 million.

Mr. Heineman was founder, chairman, and CEO of Northwest Industries, a Fortune 500 company, until 1985.

TAKEOVER WARS IN THE BOARDROOM
....

by Thomas J. Neff

"My *first time* through a takeover, I was personally very apprehensive," says one veteran outside director who so far has experienced five buyouts of companies on whose boards he was serving. "I was deeply concerned about my personal liability in case of stockholder lawsuits. I was concerned about the time it might take from my job [CEO of a Fortune 200 company]. I was nervous about the politics of the thing—my relationship to the inside directors, some of whom I was close to and who I knew were dead set against any takeover. About the last thing I thought about was the takeover bid itself, the issues it presented, and how they could best be resolved."

Once a takeover bid has been received, outside directors quickly displace inside directors and senior managers as the company's supreme authority. However, often they are quite unprepared for their new responsibilities and apprehensive about taking them on. Just as outside directors tend to echo one another when discussing their first takeovers, they tend to agree on how takeover and leveraged buyout bids should be dealt with, including the do's and don'ts most likely to contribute to a responsible conclusion. Board members and other executives of companies that have yet to go through the ordeal of a takeover may find a few of these views of practical use at some point down the road.

• *Where will I find the time?* Responding to a takeover or leveraged buyout bid is both time-consuming and nerve-racking. The crisis may take months to resolve or—as with the Irving Trust-Bank of New York marathon—more than a year. Board meetings may occur two or even three times a week, often at short notice. For tactical reasons or out of necessity they may be convened at unusual times (the Macmillan board, on which I served, met for nine hours on Memorial Day).

Between meetings there are memorandums from lawyers and investment bankers to be read; telephone briefings as the situation changes; private discussions with other directors to hash things over, and lengthy depositions to be given as the inevitable lawsuits are filed. Meanwhile, the company's stock is trading at unprecedented prices, and reporters and investors are clamoring for news. And there is always a chance that the bidder may withdraw or new bidders may appear and step up the pace even more.

Outside directors who hold full-time jobs can't possibly be full participants in such hyperactivity. As a result, leadership quickly passes to the ones who have retired from business and are accountable to no one but themselves. From this it follows that a company board should include among its outside directors a cadre of three or four able elder-statesman types whose time is their own.

• *What is my legal liability?* In 1985, in response to a minority shareholders' suit, the Delaware Supreme Court found the outside directors of Transunion personally liable for $23.5 million—the difference between what the shareholders received from Transunion's takeover by the Pritzker family of Chicago and what the court determined the holders might have received if the directors had properly represented their interests. (Liability insurance covered

$10 million and the Pritzkers contributed $10 million, leaving the balance for the directors to pay on their own.)

The message of the Transunion decision is that shareholders are entitled to a thoughtful and rigorous probing of any takeover or LBO bid and also of any alternatives that might produce a superior value. The court's emphasis was not on the final result but on the process leading up to it—for which it held the outside directors strictly accountable.

- *Ordering golden parachutes.* Within limits, it hardly seems unreasonable that CEOs and other senior officers should be compensated for losing their jobs as the result of a successful takeover attempt. Federal law itself presumes golden parachutes lessen the self-concern top executives otherwise might feel. But in many cases the golden parachutes are ordered so late that they get mixed up with the takeover itself, generating extra complications for the board and often bad publicity as well.

A better method is to arrange for the necessary protection on a contingency basis, before any sign of a takeover bid. That way, it can be treated as a perk within the context of the company's overall compensation package and the practices of the company's industry. Managers' anxieties about the personal consequences of being taken over will be minimized and, should a takeover in fact occur, the cost to the shareholders probably will be less than protection negotiated while the company and its board are under duress.

- *Outside directors versus management.* After an initial period of distress and anger, the CEO and other senior managers of a company targeted for takeover usually respond to the threat in one of three ways:

  (1) They may resign themselves to the company being sold and cooperate with the outside directors in maximizing shareholder value; (2) they may investigate every conceivable method of restructuring the company in hope of blocking a takeover up to and including asset sales, stock buybacks, the paying of a massive onetime dividend,

and leveraging the company to the hilt; (3) they may become a competing bidder by obtaining loan commitments from banks in order to make a leveraged buyout of the shareholders' equity interest and take the company private.

A management that concludes that resisting a takeover would be futile presents no problems to the company's outside directors. But should it become clear that the CEO and other inside directors have their own agenda, they no longer can be treated as allies and colleagues by the rest of the board. Members of the management group may see themselves as potential saviors of the company, but the outside directors are obliged to judge their restructuring or LBO proposals purely in terms of shareholder value.

When a chasm of this kind opens between two sets of individuals accustomed to working together and often personally friendly, it is hard on both. Misunderstandings are frequent. Disagreements often turn bitter. For outside directors, the best policy is usually to distance themselves from management as much as possible—including socially—until the episode has come to an end.

Among other things, this means the outside directors will review management's proposals without management being present and won't reveal to management in detail the proposals of other bidders. It also means if management formulates its proposals based on the advice of the company's legal counsel and outside law firm and the financial projections of its investment bankers, the outside directors will retain their own separate legal counsel and investment bankers to help them examine and appraise the management offer.

- *Are takeovers good or bad for business?* As everyone knows, there are plenty of heavyweight economic, political, and philosophical arguments—and arguers—on both sides. Some maintain that today's apostles of "corporate restructuring" are the true builders, like the Morgans and Rockefellers, while others view corporate raiders as simply manipulators of assets.

While plenty of outside directors can be found in each camp, on one point they agree: Since most takeover attempts are successful, the stress felt by management at the outset tends to become more acute and spread further through the organization as the noose tightens, with progressively ill effects on company operations. "It's not a pretty sight" is the comment of more than one outside director.

On the other hand, as any student of economic history knows, waste and disorder are just as characteristic of capitalism as creation and organization are. The lifeblood of our economic system—the unique characteristic that makes it so much more productive than any other system—is its ability, even its propensity, to keep changing and strike out in new directions. This extraordinary nervous energy leads to achievement and error alike, and both appear to be necessary for capitalism to grow and progress.

Mr. Neff is president of SpencerStuart Executive Search Consultants and was retained to find a new CEO for RJR Nabisco.

MORE POWER TO THE STOCKHOLDERS

. . . .

by Mark S. Nadel

To *which group* does Time Incorporated's board of directors owe its first allegiance: shareholders or management?

Since Time's board is elected by its shareholders it would certainly seem accountable to them, particularly since directors have a legal duty to represent the interests of their shareholders. Directors are reminded of that duty by a 1985 Delaware Supreme Court decision, which held ten directors of Trans Union Corporation personally liable for $23 million lost due to their negligence. Yet directors of large public corporations often feel their loyalty is to management.

This is because of the way directors are selected. Although shareholders elect the board, the proxy solicitation process provides shareholders with little more choice than voters in the Soviet Union. A single slate of nominees is presented for their approval and they rarely are informed of the candidates' views on corporate policies. Often the shareholders blindly ratify candidates selected by management and the incumbent board—or throw their proxy ballots in the trash.

Corporate laws vest the board of directors with the power (1) to determine the content of the proxy statement; (2) to nominate the candidates of their choice; and (3) to use corporate funds to promote their positions. Not surprisingly, all this means they are able to nominate loyal directors. Shareholders who oppose management nominees are at such a disadvantage that the "Wall Street rule" recommends they simply sell their stock.

Directors chosen under the current system resemble a corporate cabinet or club rather than a body of shareholder representatives. Most directors are inclined to feel accountable to those responsible for their nominations. Of course, very often shareholder interests coincide with those of the management-appointed directors—when, for example, the stock price is raised (through buybacks or some other method) to fend off a raider.

Pressure Has Helped

Historically, attempts to eliminate director bias have not been very successful. The pressure placed on corporations by shareholder movements to recruit more independent "outside" directors has helped. But as long as management retains a strong voice—if not veto power—in their selection, directors are still likely to feel more accountable to management.

Various regulations have been placed on the conduct of

directors. States typically prohibit them from authorizing fundamental corporate changes, such as mergers and liquidations, without a shareholder vote. A bill introduced in the House in 1987 would have required direct shareholder approval of specific takeover defenses as well. Both the House bill and a related Senate bill would have required such approval before greenmail payments could be made. Neither bill made it to a floor vote.

The Securities and Exchange Commission's 1988 "one share/ one vote" decision—prohibiting publicly traded corporations from issuing shares carrying multiple votes—prevents directors from attempting to increase the voting strength of parties supporting management.

Rather than focusing on additional legal checks, efforts should be made to address the cause of such director bias: lack of director accountability to shareholders. Adolf A. Berle and Gardiner C. Means in their classic 1932 study of the corporation, *The Modern Corporation and Private Property*, felt that shareholders' powerlessness is a necessary result of the diffusion of ownership. But that diffusion might be overcome by reforming the process for selecting directors to encourage them to favor shareholder interests over management. The major stumbling block to more open shareholder elections is the need to insure that board candidates are qualified to provide the sage advice upon which management traditionally depends.

The key to producing directors who represent the interests of shareholders without denying management access to a cabinet of experienced advisers is to recognize that the roles of loyal cabinet advisers and public shareholder representatives are separate, distinct, and often conflicting. American corporate laws should follow the European model by recognizing this distinction and dividing corporate responsibilities so that management can select *advisers* of its choice while shareholders can choose *supervisory directors* to represent them. The advisers appointed by management would act more in the capacity of peer counsellors, while the shareholder-elected directors would intervene more as judges, dispensing edicts without passion.

To elect this more independent variety of director, proxy statements must be made more open and informative to shareholders. Insiders should still be permitted to offer nominees, but corporate ballots should also be open to all individuals able to secure some minimum level of support (3 percent or five hundred thousand dollars of a corporation's stock were the levels offered in the House bill mentioned above). Moreover, nominees should be permitted to submit brief statements of their positions on specific relevant corporate policies—such as the level of dividends or corporate debt, or whether the firm should seek to acquire other firms or to be acquired by them.

Such a system is practical. Some universities use similar systems for selecting their boards of trustees, and these work quite well. Alumni nominating committees recommend candidates, but the ballots—circulated at university expense—also include the names and short statements of any other candidates able to secure some specified number of alumni signatures.

All this need not add great additional expense or confusion to the proxy process. Nor should it diminish the quality of the directors willing to participate. Adding names and statements to proxy materials would add no more than a few extra pages to proxy booklets. Nominations could be made only by those who represent—either individually or collectively—substantial stock holdings. And such owners would be unlikely to nominate candidates apt to waste corporate funds self-servingly.

Limits on the number of candidates who could be included on the ballot would be unnecessary. Shareholder proposals can now be made by anyone owning a thousand dollars in stock, and it has not proven impractical to include all such proposals in proxy statements. Only when an important issue is to be decided would the cost be high, but probably not much higher than the cost of the proxy fights that arise under the present rules. And while ballots and proxy statements could get confusing in such instances, shareholders would always have the easy option of supporting the slate of nominees supported by management or someone else they trusted.

As for the effect of contested elections on the quality of candidates, it should first be noted that the proposed reform would, if anything, make it easier for management to select the advisory cabinet members of its choice. This is because such advisers would no longer be forced to assume direct fiduciary responsibility to shareholders.

Furthermore, since management could rely on its informal cabinet for the traditional advisory functions of a board (e.g. whether and how to spin off a subsidiary, etc.), shareholder-elected directors would no longer need to be called upon as frequently as they are now. Nor would a director's expertise need to exceed that of, say, a retired business executive or college business professor. The advisory cabinet would assist management on the really tricky questions.

Directors could always intercede in decisions made by management and their advisory cabinet if they believed shareholder rights were at risk. If the directors were occasionally faced with a decision they did not feel qualified to make, they could commission outside consultants to act as advocates for the position opposed by management and then listen to and question both sides—like an appellate court—before reaching a decision. If the elected directors devolved into a group of interfering busybodies who questioned every little management decision and actually began to drag down the company, they could always be replaced by the shareholders.

Not Deterred by Fear

Under this proposal shareholders would be able to select from among candidates who articulated different views about how to supervise management; the directors chosen would be advocates for shareholder interests. Management, meanwhile, would be able to recruit an advisory cabinet of its choice and those solicited would not be deterred by the fear of shareholder lawsuits. Finally, when management disagreed with policies favored by shareholders, management, not shareholders, would be expected to move on.

Mr. Nadel is a lawyer who works as a policy analyst at Congress's Office of Technology Assessment.

A PRIVATE CONCERN
STILL NEEDS A PUBLIC PROFILE
. . . .
by Henry O. Timnick

Huge, *billion-dollar* leveraged buyouts (LBOs) were a major feature on the financial landscape of the 1980s. Names like Viacom International and Owens-Illinois continue to steal headlines as tax reform and takeover fears fuel LBO announcements and speculations.

Yet behind the headlines is the fact that well over two hundred of the approximately three hundred and fifteen LBOs announced in 1986 were divestiture LBOs, in which over-grown conglomerates sold parts of their empires to division managers.

Where managers are resourceful and energetic, and believe in their capabilities as directors and owners—rather than as employees—LBOs have worked well. After the glow of pride fades from lining up the numbers and putting the deals together, what can corporate managers expect to find as the new owners of their former company stores?

One serious threat to success is the inability of some managers to make the transition from company men to entre-preneurs. Others become so absorbed with cost cutting and debt reduction that they forget to reinvest in the underlying business. Many managers also miss the abundant opportunities for reducing operating costs in areas where they have no technical competence, such as pensions, medical programs, and insurance. Substantial savings can be realized in each of these areas without reducing benefits or coverage.

But the biggest danger in going private lies in management becoming close-mouthed. Many buyout groups react to freedom from quarterly earnings statements and shareholders by constructing moats around their companies. Building real value, whether a firm is public or private, means not only communicating company strategy to employees but talking with outsiders as well.

In 1979, I was a group president of Mead Corporation, in charge of Virginia-based Stanley Furniture Company. Stanley was healthy but had not achieved its full potential as part of a big paper company. When I studied the situation I quickly realized that Mead would be better off without the $120 million contributed by furniture and fabric sales, and that Stanley would be better off without Mead's corporate structure. Stanley no longer fit Mead's strategy. It was also clear to me that furniture divisions of large corporate entities usually did not perform well. Therefore, Stanley's managers opted for a leveraged buyout.

The risks our buyout group faced then were enormous—personally and professionally. None of us was wealthy. We all had to take out second mortgages to help finance our investments in Stanley. Interest rates had surged beyond 20 percent and business was in its worst slump since World War II. Gone were the security, perks, and resources of the parent company. If the venture failed, the two thousand jobs that supported the economy of Stanleytown, Virginia, would disappear along with our investment. But I was confident that a revitalized Stanley, even as a highly leveraged enterprise, could prosper.

As an owner I learned that we needed to do more than agree on management objectives—we had to communicate our resolve to everyone working at Stanley. This came to a head during an early planning session when a production manager asked what company policy was on a particular matter. "I don't know," I said. "It's our company now; we have to create the policy." From that point on we set in motion an open-door communications program to get both our managers and employees thinking like spirited owners. This type of aggressive dialogue wasn't necessary under corporate rules where everyone knew his place, but it was an essential ingredient in our new company.

I made a special effort to keep our banks informed of our progress, much the way the chief executive officer of a public company gives updates to securities analysts. We discussed the results of marketing plans and new products with the banks and improved their feelings of confidence toward us at critical stages of our development. Similarly, we kept the press, customers, and local officials informed of company developments.

When I had been a division president I rarely had time to spend with retailers, but as a manager-owner it was important for me to keep customers informed of our long-range plans. We also didn't forget Stanleytown. Civic programs, such as scholarships and recreational facilities, were maintained and, in many cases, enhanced. In essence, Stanley was a private company with a public profile.

Our dialogue with employees extended to company finances as well. We opened the books to all managers and they in turn began to appreciate what cash flow was all about. Soon, they were no longer talking about what they had to have, but about what they no longer needed. We also set up performance incentives that reached well down the chain of command—incentives based on long-term profitability, not just revenue growth.

Companies that undergo leveraged buyouts must learn quickly to cope with their problems in order to maximize cash flow and pay off debts without compromising growth. Many of the executives in these newly created private companies will protest that they don't have the time or resources to waste on communicating their goals. But it is the obligation of management groups to talk candidly to employees and the outside world, especially during the early stages following a buyout. That's when the greatest opportunity exists to shape an LBO company into an entrepreneurial enterprise.

Mr. Timnick, former chairman and CEO of Stanley Interiors Corporation, is a principal of the New York-based private investment firm Clayton and Dubilier.

TAKING THE RISK OUT
OF LEVERAGED BUYOUTS
....
by B. Charles Ames

L*everaged buyouts are* routinely criticized for being the product of financial engineers with sharp pencils but little appreciation for running and improving enterprises. There's little doubt that a number of transactions have been completed at exceptionally high purchase prices by investor groups just hoping to divest divisions at even higher prices. Worse still, some LBOs are so highly leveraged that investment funds for crucially important product, market, and manufacturing improvements are simply unavailable; the burden of debt service takes priority.

But not all LBOs fall into these categories, and it is unfair to tar them all with the same brush. I am a partner in an LBO firm that invests only in friendly, management-involved situations and prefers businesses where we can see significant opportunities to improve performance and enhance value over the long haul.

How have we done this? By making sure that we have the right blend of operating and financial skills deeply involved in all phases of our LBO activities. Our financially oriented partners take the lead in structuring, negotiating, and financing the deal. But once the LBO is an entity, our focus shifts and our operating partners move into the lead position.

Emphasizing operating insights in building new ownership ventures can take much of the risk out of leverage. That was certainly the case with Uniroyal Goodrich Tire Company, an LBO we sponsored that would have seemed discouragingly risky to most financial buyers.

The tire industry is known as a dog-eat-dog business. Moreover, profits were declining at the time we invested in this company. Despite the bleak picture, two of our operating partners became convinced that performance could be improved dramatically if management were freed from a fifty-fifty partnership structure that led to endless arguments and inaction. In late 1987, our firm began arranging the details for an LBO, and I was asked to take over as the CEO.

I had three initial objectives: (1) to be sure we had the right team in place, and that it was functioning as a team; (2) to make sure we had the right marketing strategy; and (3) to develop a production strategy that supported the marketing strategy.

Since Uniroyal and Goodrich had competing products, some said they could never be sold by the same company. But I was convinced we could support two brands if we clearly delineated their market positions and developed marketing programs to support their specific needs. Profit performance turned up the first quarter after the LBO was formed and has continued upward. More important, a market-driven business strategy has been developed that will ensure continued improvement over the long term.

The Oklahoma Division of Safeway Stores, now Homeland Stores, also improved through a management-led change in ownership structure. The company operates a hundred and six supermarkets in Oklahoma, the Panhandle region of Texas, and southern Kansas. About two years ago, we acquired Homeland, along with its managers from Safeway. We also gave our hourly employees an equity interest so they would be a part of ownership.

Pride of partial ownership among labor and management was a crucial factor in the complete transformation of the Homeland culture. One measure is the pilferage rate, which can be a big cost for grocery chain operators. Since the buyout, pilferage has dropped to about half the industry average. At the same time, Homeland's earnings before interest and tax have more than doubled. The company has added twelve hundred employees, and by 1990 invested $50 million in new stores, remodelings, and other capital projects.

Certainly the sense of proprietorship that management buyouts foster is a powerful motivation for successful restructuring. Call it self-interest, or American ambition, or magic: The fact is that managers who become owners are often capable of prodigious performances. And the further down the corporate ladder equity is pushed, the better. We make sure that the managers buy equity in the company the same way we investors do. What's important is for all managers to have a personal stake in the company's future.

The biggest risk is that the buyout sponsor snuffs out this spirit of proprietorship by unwittingly getting in the way of managers. Operating people usually have little patience for investment bankers, particularly young ones with beepers on their belts and lap-top computers in their briefcases. The six- to twelve-month transition period is most successful when the investment firm that organized the buyout provides an entrepreneurial environment for the management team.

Without the total respect of the new owner-managers, the sponsor will have little success penetrating the information fortress to get accurate profit-and-loss forecasts, identify problems early, or persuade the managers to institute changes when they are necessary. As a former CEO and operational man, I was asked by management at Uniroyal Goodrich to take over as CEO to set the new structure in motion. But I am stepping into the background now as operating management takes on a momentum of its own.

What is the role of the buyout sponsor beyond knowledge-able counselor? First, to nurture a strong profit consciousness. In some respects this is the easiest part of our job. In a tightly financed management buyout, managers quickly focus on cash coming in and out of the box.

To overcome some of the restrictive thinking of the past, we encourage managers to think differently about their businesses. Take the example of the manager who buys an industrial tool business that as a division of a larger company historically sold a wide range of commodity-type drills. After the buyout, should he shift into special-purpose drills for difficult applications or new materials? Or should he decide to help customers make holes in the most efficient way possible and consequently move into laser or fluid drilling systems? While he eventually may decide to choose neither option, the point is that they won't even be seen if the manager can't get beyond yesterday's strategy.

The ultimate challenge of the operationally astute LBO sponsor is to help the new owner-managers recognize that there are no benefits in defending past attitudes, habits, and practices. I can't speak for all LBO sponsors, but we encourage the managers of the businesses in which we invest to turn their visions of the company upside down and to trust their intuition. As a matter of history, style, and practice, nothing could be further from the values of most large public corporations today.

Mr. Ames, CEO of Uniroyal Goodrich Tire, is a partner of a private investment firm specializing in management buyouts. He is coauthor of Market Driven Management *(Dow Jones/Irwin, 1989).*

OWNERSHIP ISN'T ALWAYS THE BEST STRATEGY
· ·

by Peter Bisson

There were many dramas in the contest for RJR Nabisco, but the bitterest battle was over executive ownership. A group of top RJR executives were rebuffed in their efforts to buy the company they served. While clearly a special case, the RJR buyout highlights an assumption that deserves scrutiny: Most managers assume that the best way to control a key asset is to own it. Not necessarily.

In some cases, companies can control assets perfectly well without owning them—and without making the commitments of capital and management that ownership entails. The result: leaner companies with better business strategies.

Marriott Corporation is a prime example. Beginning in the early 1980s, Marriott took advantage of a strong real estate market to bolster the performance of its hotel business. Hotel companies traditionally had owned both the land their hotels were constructed on and the buildings themselves. But Marriott came to recognize that while it added value as a developer and operator of hotels, it was not an optimal hotel *owner.* As a public corporation, it could not benefit from the tax advantages available to private owners. It had to maintain a more conservative capital structure than did private real estate concerns. And most stockholders were not especially eager to speculate on the possible appreciation of real estate.

Marriott acted swiftly. In just a few years, it sold most of its hotels, but retained long-term contracts for their management. This initiative, involving a variety of transactions tailored to the interest and tax situations of particular investors, helped to boost the price of Marriott's stock. What is more, it reduced the firm's capital investment by several billion dollars, enabling it to focus more intently on its true value-adding skills—in site selection, design, construction, and management. Today nearly 85 percent of Marriott-operated hotel rooms are owned by others. And by deciding to own less, Marriott was able to grow more and faster than it could have otherwise.

There's a term for what Marriott has done—decapitalization, which can be defined as reduction in the capital of a business unit relative to the unit's capacity to generate value. And it's working.

Another company where things go better with decapitalization is Coca-Cola Incorporated. The firm wanted to optimize its control over its bottling system and at the same time minimize its commitment of capital to that end. The solution? Coke created Coca-Cola Enterprises, which now has majority ownership of Coke's bottling facilities. The original firm—Coca Cola Incorporated—retains partial ownership; its control over the bottling assets is assured by a carefully crafted franchise agreement with CCE.

The benefits of this arrangement are manifold. Coke avoids dilution of its high returns and, with the removal of interest expenses and goodwill deductions, enjoys an improved book performance. More substantively, it has spun off a separate company that because it is concerned with bottling only is better able to stress the skills that activity requires. Moreover, the new company can use a more aggressive capital structure than Coca-Cola Incorporated and can function as an equity vehicle for future purchases. Coke now has more control than ever over pricing, promotion, and marketing, and can look forward to a less fractious relationship with CCE than it had with some of its independent franchises. In sum, Coke has been able to enhance its strategic flexibility while minimizing its investment requirements.

Marriott and Coke are not isolated examples of successful decapitalizations: Other firms in other industries—restaurant companies, utilities, oil, and gas businesses—have taken similar initiatives and met with similar success. As the market continues to develop more sophisticated ways to separate ownership and control, managers will have more opportunities to retain the latter without the former. But in order to take advantage of such opportunities, managers must first find them. That means doing several things:

First, a manager needs to dissect the business system of his or her company in order to determine where—at what stages and in what activities—the firm adds the most value. Independent operations that specialize in only one aspect of the company's business can serve as useful points of comparison. And this analysis should not be confined only to those aspects that the company is now in; it should encompass what the firm's suppliers and distributors are doing as well. Are there elements of their businesses that, if controlled, could greatly enhance the manager's strategic degrees of freedom?

Next, the manager should determine whether the assets used in current or prospective operations have to be fully owned in order to be controlled adequately. Subsumed in that formulation are two questions about each category of asset: How much control is necessary or desirable? And how much ownership is essential to attain or retain that much control? It may be useful in this phase of the analysis to consult with financial advisers and to look carefully at what other firms are doing to decapitalize.

Third, the manager has to ascertain whether there are alternative owners of an asset to whom the asset might be worth more. This could be a matter of another company having a tax position that it can exploit, a greater debt capacity, a different risk profile, or a greater ability to manage risks because of a naturally hedged position or special skill. Or it could be a matter of something as simple, and as easy to spot, as this: a private company's ability, because it doesn't have to report regularly to Wall Street, to take on an asset expected to generate poor earnings in its early years.

Finally, the manager has to address the question of means: How—through what transaction form or instrument—can the manager's company meet its own needs for continued control over the use of an asset while satisfying the special requirements of a potential investor? This is where the going gets tough.

As the contours of a potential deal are considered, what may have seemed a somewhat abstract exercise ("That Jones sure comes up with some interesting ideas") becomes starkly real ("You mean Jones actually wants to do this thing?") The manager can expect colleagues to develop cold feet (relinquishing ownership of an asset is not part of the culture at most companies) and financial advisers to raise all sorts of complicating considerations. The manager has to be persistent—and focus on why the decapitalization makes strategic sense, if the right mechanism can be fashioned. This last point is crucial. The standard against which decapitalization needs to be measured, from start to finish, is whether and how it will enhance the strategy of the company

Mr. Bisson is an associate in the New York office of McKinsey and Company.

SURVEYING THE EXECUTIVE RECRUITMENT JUNGLE
....

by Gerard Stoddard

I*n 1986, like* the other half million or so Fortune 500 corporate staffers suddenly looking for a job thanks to a takeover, restructuring, or whatever, I found myself talking to a lot of headhunters. In my somewhat confused state, executive search people seemed possessed of mystical skills, somewhere between those of Santa Claus and the guy who does your triple bypass. After all, they had the power, I thought, to reattach my corporate life-support system.

For those who will follow me into that jungle where headhunters hold sway, here are some pointers, and a description of some of its denizens. The first thing you are going to have to understand is that executive search is a business set up to serve employers, not would-be employees. The recruiter's problem is to satisfy his client: the company with the opening. If you can help with that, you are very important to him. If you can't help, don't expect to be treated like someone who can.

Second, it is one of life's ironies that good things happen most to those least in need of them. As the Texas philosopher put it, "Them as has, gits." In the employment jungle, this translates into the cruel axiom that people who are unemployed are infinitely harder to place than those already happily at work elsewhere. One recruiter describes his client's ideal candidate this way: "He has to be dragged kicking and screaming from his present job so that his sneakers leave skid marks." People who point out that the practice also creates another vacancy for the headhunter to fill risk being considered rude.

In a few months of interviews, I came to know enough different types of search people to start placing them in categories. Here are some of those you're likely to encounter:

• *The Brother-in-Law:* This is the headhunter who isn't really needed on an assignment because the hiring executive knows several well-qualified candidates personally. But, because management has a policy and lives by it, or because it's the professional thing to do (and, besides, you get the feeling the headhunter is the brother-in-law of somebody important), he gets the assignment anyway.

Let's say the hiring executive follows the most logical way of filling a vacancy: He decides on what he wants and asks senior people in similar firms, consultants, and suppliers if they know anyone who qualifies. You emerge as a candidate and are interviewed at the highest level, perhaps even by the president or chairman. Things seem to be going along smoothly. Then you're suddenly told you have to be interviewed by the headhunter, too.

Not daunted, you visit the headhunter, who blandly explains that the company wants to have you "packaged"—i.e., presented in the same way as others he has uncovered. Now, if a headhunter has his own candidates and is asked to evaluate you—who came in on someone else's recommendation—you're dead in the water. Brother-in-law or no, he has to prove himself worth his fee. Otherwise someone in the company asks, "What are we paying this guy for if we found the best applicant ourselves?" To avoid that embarrassing possibility, the headhunter has no choice but to find just enough negative about you to "save the client from a big mistake."

- *The Expert:* Watching a former corporate personnel type pretend to be well versed in a specialty you've spent twenty years learning about would be mildly amusing if you could get over the fact that he stands between you and a chance to meet the client. He manages to imply he could handle your job as well as his own if only he had an additional fifteen minutes a day. What bothers you is that he believes in his expertise but will never have it tested. When you spot this type, button your lips. Challenging a know-it-all who knows nothing is a self-defeating exercise.

- *The Philosopher:* The really successful headhunters take pride in looking beyond a candidate's mere technical qualifications. How the candidate reacts when his hostess deliberately overfills his demitasse, for example, is thought to reveal how he will react to stress on the job. It is entirely coincidental that such scrutinies require the headhunter to host many tax-deductible entertaining events at home, on ski weekends, and during sailing parties.

- *The Turf Guardian:* Woe betide the job seeker whose résumé finds its way to the employer, but not through the headhunter. Most job hunters spread their paper around in the hope that a friend or business acquaintance will pass it along to someone they know is looking to fill a job. But if a headhunter has been retained the employer is likely to refer the résumé to him. And if the headhunter thinks you are trying to go around him to negotiate directly with the potential employer, he is likely to take a dim view of you and your quest. "You must remember," one recruiter told me following such a misunderstanding, "there are substantial fees involved in transactions like these."

Of course, if executive recruiters delivered as little value as all this suggests, their business wouldn't be booming as it is. There are recruiters who really get to understand not only the nature of the job that's open but the real needs of the organization doing the hiring.

Because hiring people can be as stressful and difficult as firing them, corporate executives tend to leave as much of it as possible to specialists. However, executives make a mistake if they avoid seeing the three or four candidates recommended by trusted colleagues just because they bypass the headhunters' list. By getting more directly involved, executives would at the very least gain a better feel for the requirements and the possibilities of the job. And they might even end up saving the company a "substantial fee."

Mr. Stoddard, formerly vice president for corporate communications at SCM Corporation, is a communications consultant for law firms.

SYNERGY
IN THE
WORLD MARKET

T*he bad news* is that there have never been more competitors for your service or product in the history of mankind. The good news is that there have never been more customers for your service or product in the history of mankind. Depending on your point of reference, the world market is either a curse or a blessing.

But even the worst news is not so bad. As Professor Michael Porter of the Harvard Business School has already told us in the section on marketplaces, a good competitor is not always a dead competitor. This applies just as readily to foreign competitors as it does to the homegrown variety. Mr. Porter reminds us that managers at Caterpillar have an easier time keeping employees on their toes with Komatsu breathing down their necks.

Nevertheless, for some reason, we have a tendency to accept behavior from our domestic competitors that we find unacceptable coming from foreign competitors. When pricing our product, we may undercut a local competitor at a loss to gain market share. That's called smart business sense. But when a foreign competitor does the same thing, cries of "Dumping!" are shouted from the lobbyists that businesses send to Washington to protect their interests.

Money spent on lobbyists and lawyers would be far better spent investing in synergistic fits with foreign competitors who are becoming part of your market. Not only can protectionist fervor end up doing a lot of harm to the economy as a whole, but managers lose valuable opportunities for expansion. This chapter includes articles which explore the many opportunities that now exist for expansion and integration within the global market.

One of the reasons so many of us are afraid of foreign competition is because we know so little about how business is done outside the United States. Naturally we fear the unknown. Especially, when myths portray the unknown as an invincible creature of some kind. Such is the characterization of Japan, Inc.

While the Japanese culture is, in some ways, profoundly different from our own—their emphasis on the group, for example—when it comes to basic business strategy, some things never change. This chapter seeks to demythologize Japanese managers by showing their weaknesses as well as their similarities to managers elsewhere. The more we get to know the Japanese, the better equipped we will be to work with them and, if need be, outmanage them.

Welcome to the World Market.

BRAVING THE NEW WORLD

. . . .

by Robert B. Horton

From *currency fluctuations* to trade statistics to stock crashes, the late 1980s provided many object lessons about the interconnections among the triad powers. And in all three of the world's economic powerhouses—America, Europe, and Japan—every traditional businessman is mumbling to himself that the world has gone crazy.

The traditional American businessman was primarily a producer, a product innovator. He was an optimist. Leadership in his company consisted of creating a management able to cope with competitors who all played by the same rules. U.S. laws and regulations governed the game. Moreover, it was an American game. The competition was fierce, but knowable. If you played your cards right, you could win a hand.

The European always knew the deck was full of jokers. He knew he could trust no one—not his government, and certainly not his local competitors. He did not subscribe to the idea that a rising tide lifts all boats. Too often, he saw an ebb tide.

Cartels were a beloved European business strategy. (The fact that they inevitably fell apart through cheating wasn't important; to a European, everything always falls apart.) The European businessman was less focused on customers—less market-oriented—than the traditional American. He hoped to manage the market, not serve it. Cooperation, not competition, was his goal. And the European was quite willing to make government a partner in his plans, rather than merely a policeman. Unaccustomed to a level playing field, the European worked to tilt it his way.

Japan's viewpoint was a picture of crystalline simplicity. The Japanese saw their strength as a vast capacity for slogging hard work. They conscientiously set out upon the classic course of every developing economy, mercantilism: Close your own borders while exporting to the rest of the world. The Japanese businessman knew that he could figure out how to make other people's products cheaper than other people could. And he knew that through hard work, he could learn how to satisfy customers better than anybody else.

Today, to the American, foreigners are breaking American rules right and left. And the traditional Japanese businessman feels betrayed by the Europeans and Americans, who no longer play by the rules he learned to exploit.

Into this miasma strides the new breed of nontraditional businessman: the global manager.

As an Englishman, I must say I suspect that most of these new global businessmen are Europeans. This is simply because a good manager is one who both innovates and recalls past mistakes. And Europeans have made more mistakes than most. They have learned, through hard experience, what not to do.

Some of the European businessman's experience will have given him expertise in particular aspects of business based in one country or place. And some of his experience will be in the overall operation of his kind of business, an aspect that ranges across the globe. The concepts are not national boundaries, but rather identifiable advantages and disadvantages.

While the new internationalist may not be a font of knowledge himself, he learns very quickly. He may not know the average Frenchman's favorite dish, but he knows if any Frenchman, Englishman, American, Japanese, or Korean is making his product, or a substitute. He may not know the words to "The Star-Spangled Banner," but he knows that the world's cheapest TV-set production plant is in Indiana. And he knows that probably the world's most cost-effective auto plant is in Marysville, Ohio, and makes Hondas.

He knows, too, that the Japanese are moving their plants into nations in which they hope to continue marketing. That the British are leading in investing in America. That the Germans are not far behind, concentrating on high-tech machinery and chemicals. And he knows why.

The new international manager also knows his own operation. He learns by hands-on experience how to make the product, where the raw materials come from, the parts, how they get there, the alternatives and choices, where the funds come from, and what their changing relative value does to his bottom line.

In making decisions for the global company he searches his armory of plants in various nations for the most cost-effective mix of supplies, components, transport, and funds. And the constant awareness is that the choices change and have to be made again and again.

This problem of constant change disturbs some managers. It always has. But today's global manager has to anticipate it, understand it, deal with it, and turn it to his company's advantage.

The international manager must be comfortable with a high degree of uncertainty, particularly about economic variables. He must make decisions with maybe only 70 percent of the facts. And he must be flexible, because mistakes will have to be corrected on the run.

So where are our global managers coming from? How do you bring on younger people to make them better than you were, quicker in their careers?

I suggest that corporations put their young aspirants on a track so fact they need skates to keep up. Let them go through five to ten years of broadening and deepening, with postings to various operational jobs and an introduction to finance and strategic planning. Send them to various parts of the world as well. Let the best of these graduate into another corporate education, supervised by a committee of the most senior executives.

They should be taught knowledge, and grace. They will need both to succeed in our shifting but glorious new world. They must be comfortable with a host of nonquantifiable talents as well as fundamental skills. They should be shown an array of examples, piled with opinions and case studies. Their education should afford them as much breadth as possible. I believe a real business leader must love science, history, and biography as well as finance and strategy. An awareness of literature and the arts makes better business people.

After the global traumas and explosions of the 1980s, we know better than ever that no nation or business is an island. And in this new world grown close, better businesspeople make for better business.

Mr. Horton is deputy chairman of British Petroleum.

COMBAT PROTECTIONISM WITH GLOBAL ALLIANCES

· ·

by Daniel A. Sharp

A *new pattern* of corporate alliances is emerging around the world, creating unprecedented challenges and opportunities for U.S. companies and U.S. government policy. To be competitive, U.S. corporations must join "networks of international coalitions" and learn how to manage them. Otherwise, erosion of our markets—both international and domestic—could further threaten our world influence and standard of living.

While corporate alliances are not new, their pattern has changed significantly in the past few years. The number of corporate marriages is accelerating, with close to two thousand such arrangements springing up between U.S. and European firms alone in the last half of the 1980s. They are found especially in high-technology and information-technology industries, such as office equipment, electronics, automobiles, and banking. Previously, industry leaders such as IBM, General Motors, Europe's N.V. Philips, and Japan's Nippon Telegraph and Telephone marched to the macho "go it alone" tune. But there is no company now large enough to be truly competitive globally on its own, so the giants are joining forces with many other companies, often including major competitors, in various niches of their product lines.

Why is this happening? Dramatic changes in the external business environment have accelerated the need for global strategic alliances. The world has gone beyond interdependence to an international market in many sectors operating within one global financial system. Yet the protectionist and nationalistic policies of many governments threaten the global market. In response, corporations are using alliances to help head off or jump over protectionist barriers (e.g., the many new Japanese investments in the United States).

Converging technologies require companies to integrate a full line of products, rather than, as in the past, selling one stand-alone machine. The Xerox copier, for example, is now part of an integrated office information system that processes documents from creation to transmission, including storage and retrieval as well as reproduction. No company can cover the complete line competitively without help from other companies.

The increased power of these new alliances is putting even greater pressure on corporations to join, since a company outside the network is barred from selling into it. To become truly competitive, U.S. corporations have two urgent new requirements. First, they must quickly join the right team—or network of alliances. It is no longer enough to pick the right partner. Now companies must assess the networks of each prospective partner for their competitiveness. Second, companies must develop sufficient numbers of seniors managers who combine a knowledge of their own companies with the ability to work with foreign partners who have different goals, values, customs, and languages.

Whether the trend toward alliances helps or hurts U.S. competitiveness is a controversial issue. Robert Reich of Harvard argues that we are giving away our technology, particularly to the Japanese, who will use it to dominate us in industries in which we were once the leaders, such as aeronautics, just as they have done in microcircuits, Mr. Reich and others argue that the United States must maintain its strength in such industries not only for reasons of national security, but also for the economic health of the industries themselves, which depend on domestic U.S. markets for a major part of their revenue.

Mr. Reich's critics counter that by being more competitive globally through strategic alliances, U.S.-based companies are actually preserving jobs in the United States and contributing to increased competitiveness at home. One recent study appears to show that U.S. corporations, measured globally rather than just in terms of local U.S. production, are competitive. In any event, without such alliances the international strength of many U.S. companies might rapidly decline.

And there are broader possible advantages to transnational corporate links:

- Countries can be brought closer together by combining business and financial institutions. This can help build confidence to overcome our trade fights with Japan and Europe and lay a much-needed foundation for the new U.S. role in shared management of the world economy.
- Corporations can help preserve an open trading system by jointly lobbying their multiple host governments against protectionism.
- Corporate alliances often facilitate finding components at lower cost, in Asia and Latin America for example, U.S. companies can thus become more efficient in the short term and can invest more to improve competitiveness of other aspects of their business.
- By joining with foreign companies, U.S. firms can acquire global marketing and extra technological expertise.

If U.S. companies are to be able to participate fully in the new game, some U.S. Government impediments to such cooperation may have to be removed. Antitrust laws are already being interpreted more gently. However, new industrial associations are under development in the United States that will test that antitrust flexibility as they move into coproduction and other forms of cooperation. New laws permitting such actions may be necessary. And tax laws may have to be revised to facilitate U.S. personnel working overseas in their new partnerships, and, of course, in terms of how to tax these transnational entities.

National security issues also arise. The U.S. Government does not want to support foreign companies or become dependent upon them for its defense technology. The Defense Department already views this as an issue (e.g., the rejection of Fujitsu's offer to buy Fairchild Semiconductor—although this may have been veiled protectionism inspired more by the Commerce Department than Defense). Yet Defense is farming out strategic defense initiative contracts to our allies, including Japan.

Inevitably, national governments, beholden to their domestic electorates, will continue to think along the vertical dimension of the nation-state when making decisions about taxation, antitrust, industrial, economic, and other policies to protect the national interest. However, new economic realities force corporations increasingly to think and act along horizontal, global dimensions. Narrow-minded nationalist loyalties may be eroded as both shareholding and corporate alliances become increasingly global.

Mr. Sharp is director of international relations for a major, multinational corporation.

RETHINKING GLOBAL CORPORATE STRATEGY
. . . .
by Kenichi Ohmae

Cheap labor, *abundant* natural resources, expanding domestic markets, and hospitable governments have made developing regions attractive to multinational corporations. Increasingly, however, they are retreating from these areas. Many Japanese companies, for example, are pulling out of countries in Southeast Asia that offer low-cost labor and investing in automated production plants back home or in the United States and Europe, right in the middle of the big markets. Should their U.S. and European counterparts do the same?

Cheap labor has proved to be a mirage. In the early 1970s, Singapore was widely believed to be the ideal location for ship-building and assembling consumer electronics. But then everyone moved in, tightening the labor supply and driving wages up. The migration of the U.S. textile industry from New England to Appalachia, Japan, Korea, Taiwan and on into Indonesia, the Philippines, India, and Sri Lanka shows the futility of chasing cheap labor. In one country after another, labor costs rose, forcing the industry elsewhere about every five years. Perhaps capitalistic China will be the last hope for those companies seeking only low-cost wages.

Labor costs in developing nations now come up to as much as one third of those in developed nations. The advantage of this narrowing differential has been reduced by the decline in the labor content of traditional assembly operations. In many industries it has dropped to less than 10 percent of total manufacturing costs and no longer offsets the cost of transporting key components and products to and from low-wage countries. Even in the traditional labor-intensive footwear and plywood industries, the labor content of manufacturing costs has become less than 25 percent.

At the same time, local governments have grown increasingly inhospitable by imposing tariffs, local content laws, and ownership requirements on foreign companies. Mexico requires its foreign car manufacturers to use locally produced parts and materials equal to 50 percent of each vehicle's value. Indonesia requires any exporter selling more than $750,000 of goods to the state sector to buy an equal value of local goods. Saudi Arabia is now insisting on local partners and is seeking local manufacture of oil-field service products such as rock bits, valves, and tools. Similar requirements are being pushed by Brazil, India, and Nigeria.

These barriers are often coupled with political instability and overnight policy changes. The policymakers in many developing countries have no business experience and tend to have difficulty understanding the realities of today's fiercely competitive and yet cooperative international marketplace.

More and more the question is whether it is worth overcoming these barriers. Even though the population growth of developing regions has been substantial, their share of the free world's gross national product had not grown at all. Europe, Japan, and the United States represented 75 percent of the free world's GNP in 1960. Today, thirty years later, it is 72 percent. The small slippage is almost entirely attributable to economic problems in Europe, particularly in Britain in the 1970s and in France in the 1980s.

More important is what has been happening outside the developing regions. The "triad" of Japan, Europe, and the United States represents not only the major and fastest-growing market for most products, but also an increasingly homogeneous one. Gucci bags, Sony Walkmans and McDonald's hamburgers are seen on the streets of Tokyo, Paris, and New York. Machine tools and silicon chips have fewer country-specific variations.

Skyrocketing costs of development and large-scale production in many industries make it essential that companies crack all the major markets. To do that they must become insiders in each region, either directly or through partners, to tune into consumer and technological developments. They can't afford to waste resources in developing regions. Some companies have learned this the hard way. While taking advantage of low-cost labor and materials, and capturing large shares of small markets, they (particularly the European multinationals) lost touch with their competitors and customers in the major markets. A good example is Adidas Shoe Company, which enjoys a high market share in Brazil. But it came at a big price if it slowed Adidas's response to the trend toward fashion in sports equipment, which showed up first in the United States.

Some corporations lost sight of the importance of the triad markets. They were misled by macroeconomic data that showed the growth of developed nations slowing considerably. Most realized that the United States' growth was slowing, but few understood that this was a net result of the declining Midwest and East and the rapidly growing West and Sun Belt. Opportunities are great in some booming states such as

California, which is bigger than Brazil, and Texas, whose gross state product is bigger than the combined GNP of the Association of Southeast Asian Nations.

Not many countries belong to the ten-thousand-dollar-club of nations whose per capita GNP exceeds this level. Even the champion of the newly industrialized countries, Korea, has only a two-thousand-dollars-per-capita GNP and does not have the luxury of discretionary income that forms the basis for high-tech equipment markets, as well as for high-value durables and perishables.

What role then do developing regions play in the future of multinationals? If corporations already have a strong position in a developing region, they should keep it but should not expect these subsidiaries to enhance a global competitiveness.

Unless they do something like Matsushita Corporation has done. It built an advanced world-class compressor plant in Singapore comparable with its Japanese facility. With a capacity of 3 million units, it is aimed at not only the ASEAN, but also the Middle East, Europe, and the United States. Since it has the advantage of low labor costs in addition to economies of scale in a state-of-the-art production facility, it was possible for Matsushita to use this plant to penetrate a very difficult U.S. market. Today, Matsushita sells more than 30 percent of the low-end compressors used in the United States for refrigerators. Shin-Etsu Chemical Company in silicon wafers and Toshiba Corporation in discrete and hybrid integrated circuits have also used this golden combination of a state-of-the-art production facility and relatively stable, low-cost labor to produce globally competitive products in Malaysia.

The new global enterprise will be more deeply and strategically involved in fewer countries, choosing a few and getting to know their institutions and leaders well. It will distinguish its global-scale operations in these locations from opportunistic, small-scale plants that companies used to build to enter restricted markets. It will be as prepared to contribute to the host nation's goals as to its own home country. Over time, it will build relationships with neighboring countries for raw materials and supplies of low-cost components, as well as marketing and distribution.

This kind of serious and rational commitment to a few developing nations gives them some hope and could reverse the widening disparity in income between northern and southern countries.

Mr. Ohmae is the managing director of McKinsey and Company's Tokyo office.

PROFIT NOW FROM EUROPE'S 1992 OPENING
. . . .

by Michael Bartholomew

E*urope is finally* coming together—much faster than expected—to form one marketplace of 320 million consumers. If companies from countries outside the European Community are to take advantage of the emerging opportunities, they must act before the Single Market's deadline, 1992.

The goal for 1992 is a uniform economic space across the twelve European Community countries where people, goods, and services can circulate unhampered by national frontiers. The potential benefits for member states are enormous. The Common Market estimates its overall gross national product could rise as much as 7 percent, or $285 billion, while creating 5 million jobs and vast U.S.-style economies of scale.

For non-EC members as well, these changes merit attention. Of the 279 barrier-bashing legislative proposals designed to establish the Single Market, more than half have already been passed. But many of the most far-reaching and controversial directives—ranging from international bidding for public contracts to harmonized duties and excise taxes—have yet to be adopted. Since the EC turns to its business community for input on all 1992 draft directives, those non-Common Market companies already in Europe are well positioned to influence the making of these important policies. Those not already established here must make strategic decisions now if they want to compete in Europe later.

What should American compaines do to prepare for a new Europe?

- *Get into the European marketplace now,* especially while the dollar is low and American prices competitive. Current trading terms are favorable and the European economy is growing at a steady rate of 3.7 percent. Experience gained now will prove valuable as 1992 approaches.

- *Try to establish a solid foothold within the Community as soon as possible—before European protectionist measures crystallize.* For the large American multinational, a European presence might mean branch offices, subsidiaries, or even direct acquisitions. For smaller companies, opportunities are also there. Use one European country as a distribution base to penetrate all the EC markets. Many European countries do just that in the United States. Another way to reinforce the competitive edge of small American companies in the Single Market is to combine with similar-sized EC companies, many of which welcome U.S. know-how and financial muscle.

Joint ventures should boom after the twelve Common Market nations adopt plans making it easier and cheaper to legally set up a Pan-European company. As things stand now, only the largest corporations can afford to do this.

American companies that team up with European partners could qualify for seed money under the Community's multibillion-dollar high-tech research and development programs. Many companies overlook the numerous grants, loans, and EC tenders generated by Brussels.

- *Many American companies established in Europe are likely to be treated as domestic companies under the Single Market program.* This is one of the main reasons why AT&T, with a keen eye on 1992, decided in 1986 to jump into Europe by expanding its Brussels headquarters more than 60 staffers.

- *Think in terms of Continental strategies.* Veteran American companies such as IBM and Ford have always treated Europe as a single market. First-timers should do the same. American Express, for example, is launching a Pan-European advertising campaign for its credit card and financial services. Other American companies are reviewing their production and distribution networks. Boston-based Gillette has recently switched from country-based subsidiaries to a system organized along product lines.
- *Understand and be sensitive to regional differences in Europe.* Borders may disappear, but national identities will remain. Although English is the lingua franca, American managers with language skills can open more doors.
- *Stay informed about Europe's market landscape.* There are dramatic shifts on the horizon, with wide-ranging implications for business. For American exporters, bureaucratic costs and delays should plunge with the advent of the Single Administrative Document, which replaces seventy separate customs forms across the Community. For financial services, the Common Market has decided to remove all capital and exchange controls and throw open large chunks of its banking, securities, and insurance industries to cross-border competition. Manufacturers will benefit enormously once transportation is deregulated and value-added taxes are harmonized.
- *Monitor events to protect your interests.* To take advantage of market opportunities in this rapidly changing environment, American companies must closely follow developments as they unfold within EC institutions and—when necessary—make their views known.

Firms armed with such reliable information will be ahead of the game and ready to compete.

Mr. Bartholomew was assisted in the preparation of this article by fellow journalist Brooks Tigner. Both men monitor the Common Market from their base in Brussels.

LOBBYING BRUSSELS IN ANTICIPATION OF 1992

· ·

by Michael Bartholomew

The *European Community's* 1992 program for a border-less single market has spawned a lot more than new legislation. It has also strengthened Brussels's fastest-expanding industry: lobbying.

Lobbying is nothing new in Brussels, but its size and energy have changed dramatically. In 1988, EC lobbying and consulting services generated about $250 million in revenues, up nearly 100 percent from 1987. While there are nearly twenty-five hundred trade, industry, and nonprofit organizations in the Belgian capital, there are only a handful of professional lobbyists. Their numbers, however, are rising as consulting companies, law firms, and independents flood the city.

Prices for lobbying services—still cheap by American standards—run anywhere from five hundred to sixteen hundred dollars a day. How long these rates will hold depends in part on the eventual success of the twelve countries' Single Market program. The need is growing for more sophisticated "ears and eyes" in Brussels. That's because laws are moving at a faster clip through the community's legislative machinery, following changes in 1987 to the EC's constitution.

Here are some "do's" and "don'ts" of lobbying the Common Market, culled from specialists in the field:

- *Don't export Washington-style lobbying.* That muscular approach usually involves unabashed enthusiasm and financial largesse. Low-key is the name of the game in Brussels. Europeans are more reticent. Officials see things in European shades of gray, not American black and white. That's not to say Eurocrats are less open to traditional methods of persuasion than their Washington counterparts. They love champagne and caviar as much as anyone else. But don't dump it over their heads. And if you are not sure where and how to entertain Brussels official-dom, one long-time lobbyist offers this advice: "When in doubt, don't spend the money."

- *Know whom to lobby and at what level.* Many Common Market officials are approachable, particularly those at the lower level who are drafting legislation. Do not try to contact an EC commissioner directly unless there is an exceptionally important problem. In any case, it is best to brief a commissioner's chief assistant beforehand, prefer-ably in written form.

The EC is in fact actively seeking views from industry for its directives of eliminating trade barriers. The EC Commission is open to lobbying because it wants advice from and a rapport with people who are earning money. Some of the most imagi-native and successful EC research and development programs, such as ESPRIT, RACE, and BRITE, were promoted by industry.

Given the Common Market's expanding power, it's worth noting that key officials must make decisions in areas where the community is sailing into uncharted waters. A carefully planned information and lobbying campaign aimed at key people can be most effective. But make sure you are talking to the right officials.

- *Act quickly to influence decision making.* All European Community laws used to require unanimous agreement among the twelve member states. Today, though, those laws dealing with the Single Market now pass by qualified majority. This has speeded up the process.

The European Parliament has also received new powers. Lobbyists used to bypass Parliament with last-minute inter-ventions at the final decision-making level, the Council of Ministers. Now Parliament can amend all 1992 proposals through two mandatory readings before sending them to the council. The challenge comes because 1992 laws cannot be significantly amended after the first reading. Therefore a lobbyist must make his case early on. The second reading is often perfunctory.

Therefore it is more important than before to monitor—and intervene soon after a proposal is submitted to Parliament. Lobbying can yield results both in Strasbourg, where Parliament holds its plenary sessions, and in Brussels, where it holds its committee meetings. Parliamentarians are generally open to such approaches.

Input at the ministerial level must be provided at national capitals. Unlike the United States or Britain, where power is centered only in Washington and London, the EC has many centers of power scattered across its twelve member states.

- *Pick your representative carefully.* The ambassadorial approach often doesn't work well, for EC officials can resent official delegations. Don't automatically rely on high-powered consulting agencies. Contact by the individual or organization directly concerned is often more effective.

Don't, however, engage in overkill. For example, one major U.S. trade association flew a dozen tough-talking lawyers and executives from Los Angeles to Brussels to make their case before lower-level officials. All those represented got for their pains were some large bills—and little sympathy or understanding from the EC. This approach is already beginning to change. American companies are starting to use European associates to make their case, as well as U.S. citizens practiced in European ways.

Trade federations are powerful channels, but they have the concerns of many to represent. Remember that they often take time to act.

- *Establish a presence in Brussels.* It is impossible to stay on top of developments without daily monitoring. Unlike in Washington, getting information from the authorities in Brussels is a complicated affair. You can't just demand a complete file from a directorate, something you often can do in the United States under the Freedom of Information Act. Getting key documents and other information means a lot of running around. Use or create experienced Brussels hands to do this, and don't rely only on companies offering slickly packaged, and recycled, information.

The main message: The advent of 1992 means you cannot get enough information about the EC from your own government or trade association.

Mr. Bartholomew and his journalistic partner Brooks Tigner monitor the Common Market from Brussels.

EUROPE 1992: A CONTRARY VIEW
. . . .
by Victor K. Kiam

In the year leading up to the opening of the London Stock Exchange, economists and financial reporters worldwide were bursting with stories about "The Big Bang." It was hyped to the heavens.

In anticipation of the onslaught that would deliver fresh business and new clients, many American financial institutions opened up new offices or expanded existing operations in Britain. But the avalanche never got rolling; within a year, most businesses found themselves cutting back. The Big Bang had delivered a few tremors, but none were potent enough to register on the fiscal Richter scale.

Now, it seems we are being asked to hold our breath in anticipation of another momentous happening. By the end of 1992 we are slated to witness the birth of "Fortress Europe"— a Europe made rapturous with the miracle of economic unity.

Just think of it: Project 1992 will deliver a commonwealth of nations without economic borders. In this single-market Utopia of 335 million consumers, people, capital, goods, and services will move as freely as they do within the United States. Companies will be able to compete in a free, open, and equitable market; passports will be passé. American companies are already being warned to solidify their European presence now or miss out on the greatest thing since sliced bread.

Well, pardon me, folks, but I don't buy the whole loaf.

Yes, there is going to be a more-closely-knit European Community featuring fewer barriers on all aspects of living. But this is neither surprising nor new. The evolution toward this semiunification has been going on for the past forty years. There are, however, some walls that loom as obdurate as Stonehenge. Consider the many differing rules by which Europe's players are governed.

In Britain, my company—Remington—has seven accounts that make up 85 percent of our business. In Italy, however, no organization can own more than six retail stores, which means we have to deal with a plethora of mom-and-pop shops. This means our distribution network there is completely different from the one we use in Britain.

In Britain, sales representatives can be terminated with ninety days' notice. In Italy, the law doesn't let us dispose of reps so easily. They, in effect, own their territory. To fire a rep requires paying a penalty based on the rep's anticipated earnings over a long period of time. In France, anyone who gets fired must receive severance pay, an amount borne solely by the company. In Britain, when a worker is made "redundant" the government picks up part of the check.

Retirement and benefit programs also differ from country to country. Will these suddenly change in 1992? Hardly. There probably will be a long period of adjustment.

As Fortress Europe is being assembled, Spain and Portugal are joining the Common Market. These countries have a lower standard of living than do their new economic allies. How will their suddenly accessible low-cost labor pool affect the unemployment rate across Europe?

All European Community members have some form of taxation on goods and services, called value-added taxes, or "VATs." These vary from country to country. For instance, Spain's VAT is about 12 percent, while Ireland's is twenty-five percent. The European Commission, the group in charge of planning the 1992 extravaganza, is trying to harmonize these figures. Some countries would be forced to raise their rates and others to lower theirs. This suggestion is causing quite a brouhaha. British Prime Minister Margaret Thatcher is on record as being opposed to such mandatory changes; she is not about to give up her government's power of taxation.

Mrs. Thatcher is also determined to retain some border controls. She feels they are necessary to stop illegal immigration, the inflow of drugs, and the easy transit of terrorists. And she is voicing the concern of many European leaders on these delicate subjects.

The value of the various European currencies is another problem yet to be solved. Several members of the European Commission are pushing for a unified monetary system and a European central bank. Few European leaders are dancing in the streets over this suggestion. Mrs. Thatcher is diametrically opposed to any such changes.

And then there are product approval controls and stringency standards, which vary widely from country to country—not to mention the approval procedures for pharmaceuticals, which also differ widely.

In America, managers are now hearing how "you must be placed in Europe RIGHT NOW!" What's the hurry? Fortress Europe should help facilitate the exchange of goods among its member nations, not make it tougher. Remington, like most U.S. companies, shouldn't have to open up a factory across the Atlantic in order to take advantage of this. Like most American companies, Remington can benefit by shipping to one European location, from which we will then distribute our products to other countries.

Some observers warn that a united Europe could slap heavy duties on goods coming in from outside its realm. I don't see this happening. If it did, I'm sure the United States would respond in kind. And since the United States is Fortress Europe's largest potential customer, a European-initiated duty war would be suicidal.

If there is a major, immediate impact, it will come in the number of mergers across national borders. We are already seeing signs of this: French companies acquiring British companies, British businesses acquiring German enterprises. With the lifting of various restrictions, these transactions are becoming more common; wider access certainly will be possible.

In today's global economy any American company that wants to be a player must have a finger in international marketplaces. But you don't have to catch the next Concord to remain competitive.

Remington isn't doing anything differently to prepare for 1992. We have a base in Britain and do some assembling there. If we were to lose a duty war, we might have to see about establishing a manufacturing plant there as well. It would probably take only about six months to accomplish this. We'd have plenty of time, as would the rest of corporate America. Europe 1992 may serve very well as a symbol and an ideal: it remains to be seen how it will function in reality.

Mr. Kiam is CEO of Remington Products.

THE CHALLENGE OF MANAGING FOREIGN NATIONALS

. . . .

by John Lenkey III

The *challenge of* managing foreign nationals can present itself in three ways: when a U.S. company sets up business abroad; when it hires foreigners in the United States, and when it is acquired by foreign owners. Of concern to U.S. managers is whether they will be accepted and respected as competent managers either overseas or by foreigners working in the states.

To begin, let's examine how U.S. managers handle subordinates overseas. To understand these subordinates one must look at their motives in working for a nonlocal company. Play to your employee's interests (trips abroad, for example, can fulfill a desire to travel). But beware the native who badmouths his homeland. He may be ready to emigrate. Your unit needs a native manager if it's to be properly integrated into the marketplace. Find a stable manager who will stay put.

Next, there is the nationalism phenomenon. When you place an Englishman in a French operation, or a Swiss in a Korean one, a strange thing can happen: Nonnationals abroad tend to become even more nationalistic than they were at home; your Swedish employee in Belgium may act more "Swedish" than if he were at home in Stockholm. A smart manager will take this into account and use it to his advantage: He will reinforce individual national traits when giving praise.

One must avoid strict stereotyping, but certain national characteristics have been noted more than once and may suggest ways of accommodation. For example, for many Brazilians, direct orders are a slap in the face, to which they respond with the threat of leaving work and "going to the beach." Thus, never order a Brazilian to do something, suggest instead. Japanese generally respond to short-term assignments better than distant goals. Thus, be specific—if you think you have loaded in a week of work, separate it into five daily tasks. Koreans, I've found, can be commanded as if they were Americans. Concerning Israelis, former premier Yitzhak Shamir advised me in 1985: "If you have seven Israelis in a meeting, you will have twelve opinions." Thus, don't ever use a committee for decisions in Israel.

One must always avoid using one's own criteria for success when promoting foreigners. My own blunder occurred in Belgium. I decided to promote Omer, a product engineer who had developed a good flair for customer contact and sales. Applying U.S. procedures, I promoted him to marketing manager. You wouldn't believe the howling reaction! Apparently, Belgians feel engineering has more status than marketing. We found a new title. Kenneth J. Matejka, a behavioral psychologist at the University of Richmond, has a suggestion: "Make sure your reward is not punishment, and vice versa, before applying it, especially cross-culturally."

Pass this along to an American manager going overseas. The manager—and his spouse—will have to learn not to consider "wrong" what is merely different. They must listen, and think a lot before acting. At the same time, they must pledge not to "go native." I have met American presidents of Japanese subsidiaries who embarrassed both sides by trying to become more Japanese than the Japanese.

When transferring an American overseas, I suggest a contract stipulating a three-year minimum stay to overcome the roller coaster of euphoria on arrival, depression after four months, then stabilization, with rising performance by the end of the first year. Five years should be the maximum, or the transfer becomes permanent. As part of the contract the U.S. company is generally wise to guarantee return to the home office upon completion of the assignment. Unless the manager is promised a job in the United States at a level he probably would have earned if he had stayed home, it will be difficult to recruit a good candidate for the job abroad.

Finally, don't pay your U.S. manager via your foreign subsidiary. Local managers, generally paid on a lower level, will get wind of your American manager's salary and want more for themselves. Pay your employee through a U.S. bank, so he can convert only the cash he needs.

When it comes to managing non-Americans in the United States, the key is maintaining proper respect for your employee's culture. A Chesterfield County, Virginia, joint venture that makes electrical products provides a good example. Swiss and Germans are the owners, but the employees are almost entirely (legal) Vietnamese. Because management reinforces their nationality and helps them become Americans—including use of subsidized education—their productivity is exceptional.

If your U.S. firm is acquired by a foreign company, the international-operations department loses its authority, and research and development may be axed in favor of the new master's priorities. If you survive the almost-inevitable downsizing, it would pay off for you to bone up immediately on the national preferences of the acquiring company and learn all about the work ethics. In the case of a Japanese buyout, all you have to do is work ten hours each day, eat lunch quickly, and come in on Saturdays to do follow-up. Don't take sick leave or vacation days, do not complain—and never have an extramarital affair. Come to think of it, had you worked that hard for your U.S. boss, your company probably would not have been sold.

Mr. Lenkey, a Richmond, Virginia-based business consultant, is an adjunct professor at the University of Virginia's McIntire School of Commerce.

TOO FEW U.S. MANAGERS PRACTICE ABROAD
. . . .

by Stephen J. Kobrin

T*wenty years ago,* a visitor to an overseas subsidiary of an American firm was likely to find Americans in most significant managerial positions. A return to the same subsidiary today would find the situation radically changed. The visitor often has to look hard to find an American—and those who do pop up are often on short-term assignment.

There has been a dramatic replacement of Americans abroad by local or third-country nationals. There are many positive reasons for this shift, but one important reason is less appealing: American corporate experience with overseas assignments has been disastrous.

On the whole, replacement of expatriates with locals has been seen as positive—lowering costs, increasing managerial effectiveness, minimizing conflict with both employees and the local community, and contributing to managerial and technical development in the host country. It is viewed as a reflection of the maturation of American multinational corporations. The number of "non-American" employees is often taken as a measure of internationalization.

But much of the change is due to the fact that many Americans have not been able to handle working and living in other cultures. A high failure rate has meant enormous expenses in terms of direct costs, management time, and, most important, human misery. In the end, U.S. multinationals have found it easier to replace Americans with locals than to make an effort to solve the underlying problem.

In an initial 1984 study of a hundred and twenty-six large, U.S.-based international industrial companies and banks, I found that half had reduced their number of expatriate employees in the preceding ten years. About 26 percent reported no change and 23 percent an increase. When asked about expected trends from 1984 to 1994, 41 percent projected a continued reduction, 40 percent no change, and 18 percent an increase. Later studies have confirmed this trend and suggest that American firms have gone much further in reducing the number of expatriate employees than have their European or Japanese competitors.

As managerial and technical competence in many countries has increased, proficient managers have become more available. All things being equal, a local person who speaks the language, understands the culture and the political system, and is often a member of the local elite should be more effective than an alien.

The sharp reduction in expatriate assignments, however, has important implications for the global strategic management and competitiveness of U.S. multinational corporations.

First, a surfeit of local managers can make it difficult for corporations to meet their longer-term, worldwide objectives. Few locally hired mangers in U.S. multinationals identify with the global organization. To a local in a subsidiary, the corporation as a whole is an abstraction; it is local performance that matters. At the top, mangers in turn find it difficult to form and implement a global strategy. Having locals in charge increases the difficulties multinationals face in creating informal organizational links across subsidiaries. Although any diversified corporation serving a large geographic area faces challenges of this sort, the multinationals' problems are exacerbated by greater distances, time changes that make communication by telephone more difficult, and, especially, cultural and linguistic differences.

Take the example of Europe's plan to complete an internal market by 1992. A Belgian manager of a U.S. firm in Brussels may have a better understanding of the 1992 opening than he does of the products his company sells outside of Belgium.

Without a clear understanding of the latter, he may be ill-equipped to take full advantage of the former.

Another problem has arisen with a proliferation of local managers: Corporate control of local subsidiaries has become more difficult. Strategic control in a multinational often depends on control over personnel. But geographical and cultural differences, along with political and legal jurisdictions, may limit subsidiary responsiveness. Locals may feel caught between conflicting corporate and local interests; they may find themselves allied with local policy makers against corporate headquarters.

Nevertheless, this is not a problem without solutions. Working with local managers on their career planning, development, and assignments can help put them more in tune with their company's international environment.

Another solution is the creation of a core of international employees that includes "third country" nationals. This simplifies problems of strategic control through personnel and facilitates the socialization needed to build a common organizational structure worldwide. Expatriates will not (and should not) automatically identify with their home country over their host country; rather, at their best, they should be able to assess local interests in the context of global strategy and identify with the worldwide organization. Occasional assignments at headquarters would help international staffers assimilate corporate culture and objectives.

In practice, it is doubtful whether American multinationals and the U.S. economy would be willing to tolerate the logical results of this internationalist strategy. To the extent that international expertise is a prerequisite for top managerial jobs, this policy would favor non-Americans. In reality, however, U.S. companies show a strong bias toward Americans. But since fewer Americans are doing stints overseas, American executives may simply be less qualified in the future.

This is not to recommend that the old model of a quasi-permanent core of long-term U.S. expatriates be resurrected.

But it must be recognized that the core of expatriates served important functions and their departure leaves a vacuum that must be filled.

Mr. Kobrin is professor of management at the University of Pennsylvania's Wharton School. This article appeared in longer form in Human Resource Management.

WHEN THE BOSS IS A STRANGER
IN A FAMILIAR LAND
. . . .

by Robert Shuter

D*irect foreign investment* in American companies has soared from $90 billion in 1980 to $304 billion in 1988. As a result, American managers increasingly are finding themselves employed by British, Japanese, Dutch, German, and other foreign companies operating in the United States. Many of these managers are not prepared for the experience and suffer corporate culture shock, particularly if they have never before worked for a foreign employer. Most quickly learn that foreign companies frequently operate much differently than U.S. corporations do.

Take promotion, for example. "Moving up" is an inalienable managerial right, or so U.S. managers think. Traditionally, U.S. companies have accommodated managers by providing an array of titles and positions and a deep chain of command. Not so in many foreign companies.

Swedish corporations, with more than five hundred subsidiaries in the United States, usually have much fewer managerial positions and a leaner chain of command than do U.S. companies. This is to ensure efficient, speedy operations at a lower price tag. However, American managers usually do not see it this way. They feel the prospects for promotion are dim because there are fewer managerial positions to jockey for.

To complicate matters, many foreign corporations often fill key managerial positions with Europeans, Japanese, or other non-Americans. Not surprisingly, American managers see top foreign executives as obstacles to their own promotion, and they do not like the situation one bit. In one Japanese company, the American managers were up in arms because key management positions were always filled by transferred Japanese. To calm the troops, the Japanese created job titles that had little authority—like assistants to the vice president—and promoted American managers to these positions. It did not work. The troops did not fall for the false titles and remained disgruntled.

While U.S. managers are title-conscious, they usually see through the title game played by some foreign firms and aren't satisfied until they get the "perks" of the position: more money and power.

One of the most difficult aspects of an American manager's job is supervising non-American employees transferred to the United States for three to five years. The manager often assumes that language is the biggest problem and is relieved when a foreign employee speaks adequate English. While language is immensely important, American managers and foreign personnel are at odds over more subtle cultural differences in corporate protocol.

Consider the Norwegian or Swedish employee who "end runs" his American manager whenever he needs information. Imagine how surprised the manager is to learn that the sacred American corporate commandment—thou shalt not go over thy manager's head—doesn't exist in Scandinavian companies. On the contrary, Norwegians, Swedes, and other Scandinavian employees are encouraged to solve problems, not ingratiate themselves with managers, and are free to consult with almost anyone in the corporate hierarchy without first clearing it with their manager—a team coordinator, not a boss.

American managers also are used to "making" decisions; in

many Japanese and European companies, decisions are "taken," not made. In these companies, managers are expected to sound out employees before a decision is "taken"—a bottom-up approach. For U.S. managers, this means more meetings with employees and a change in psychology and style.

American managers also learn that the management techniques they acquired in business school may not work well with foreign employees. Visualize an American manager who does all the "right things"—holding regular meetings with personnel and staying on top of employee projects—and then finds out that the Swedes and Norwegians think he or she oversupervises and is too controlling. When this happens, and it does, the American manager sometimes learns that Swedes and Norwegians are used to working independently on projects far more than Americans are, and have few formal meetings with managers before a project is completed.

Also in jeopardy is the American manager who sandwiches employee criticism between two slices of praise, especially during performance reviews. For German employees, who are usually direct and to the point even with criticism, this approach is considered unnecessary and time-wasting: "Get to the point," they urge their American managers.

On the other hand, American managers in Japanese companies are viewed as being too direct and harsh, particularly when disciplining a worker. Japanese believe employees must learn to be self-critical, and that gentle managers, who do not embarrass employees with direct criticism, can help workers achieve this.

American managers must also cope with American personnel who regularly complain about the "foreigners" in their midst and wish they would disappear. For example, managers regularly deal with American personnel who are angry and jealous about the relocation benefits foreign employees receive when they transfer to the United States. Generally, these employees hear about a relocation package through the grapevine, and the benefits are magnified each time the story is told.

Even skillful managers have difficulty convincing their employees that such relocation benefits as purchasing an employee's major appliances or giving him vacation subsidies are reasonable incentives to motivate foreign personnel—or Americans for that matter—to leave family, friends, and country for several years.

And when a foreign language is spoken in the workplace, watch out: American employees generally hit the ceiling. They complain about being locked out of the conversation and imagine that the "foreigners" are discussing something they do not want the Americans to understand.

Managing in a foreign company is frequently like working overseas without leaving home. To be successful, it takes sensitivity, flexibility, and a healthy dose of cultural awareness.

Mr. Shuter is director of the Center for Intercultural Communication at Marquette University and business consultant for American, European, and Asian firms.

IMMIGRATION LAW MAY ALIENATE
YOUR FOREIGN PROFESSIONAL STAFF
. . . .
by Lawrence P. Lataif

A*n international oil-tanker* company in the United States recently needed a director of maintenance for its worldwide fleet, someone who specialized in Japanese shipyard engineering and architecture, and it needed him immediately. Delay was stranding the entire fleet.

Several years ago, many companies would have hired a foreigner with the requisite skills, put him to work, and then applied for a visa. However, just before the dawn of the new age in immigration law, the company in question endured the downtime, not daring to proceed without careful prior compliance with the tough new Immigration Reform and Control Act of 1986.

The act, which took effect June 1, 1989, rewrites almost a century of American immigration law. It transforms the business of hiring foreign executives and professionals from a matter of routine personnel processing to a vexing, often urgent issue requiring the involvement of top management. Successful corporate compliance with the new act and its regulations will demand a high level of coordination among top management, personnel managers, and legal counsel. Most corporations are neither prepared for nor, in many cases, even aware of the need for this level of involvement.

The act, in general, has the following provisions:

- Every employer, under threat of perjury, must verify in writing that all employees—U.S. citizens as well as aliens—are eligible to work and that the required documentation has been examined.
- Every company must develop an extensive "Employment Verification System" and keep records of work authorization.
- Failure to comply can, in the extreme, land corporate senior managers in prison.

One significant reason why increased coordination and centralization are called for arises from the fact that the act generally holds parent corporations responsible for the violations of any of its subsidiaries or divisions.

The Employment Verification System affects recruiting, promotions, transfers, and terminations of every foreign employee except those who have permanent-residence visas. Currently, violations of the verification system can trigger sanctions ranging from fines for paperwork violations to criminal misdemeanor and felony prison terms for senior managers of companies repeatedly violating the law. Top executives, therefore, need to monitor and set policy for employment verification and business-visa processing for foreign employees.

While the old immigration law theoretically required visas before hiring, employers could hire first and apply for visas second with no threat of sanctions against them. Consequently, many if not most foreign executives were routinely offered employment before consideration was given in the appropriate business visas.

As with the oil-tanker company, critical initiatives may be stymied or delayed pending application for, and issuance of, the visa. One major European electronics company saw its carefully planned multimillion-dollar research and marketing program for a new computer product jeopardized because fifteen key executives and professionals with specialized knowledge had not yet obtained work visas.

In another case, the buyer of a major U.S. company refused to sign the contract to purchase until it received assurances that two key foreign executives would have indefinite work authorization to manage the company after acquisition.

Promotion and transfer decisions affecting foreign workers who want to move to the United States or are already in the United States no longer can be made without advance planning, with the paperwork delegated after the fact to the personnel department. This is true because many categories of nonimmigrant visas are limited to the specific job for which the person initially was granted work permission. Giving the foreign employee a promotion or a transfer to a different job could invalidate the work visa.

Along with the new law are regulations that have received little publicity but that also will require a high degree of involvement by senior management. Under these regulations, any immigration filing (for example, a company's application for a visa) becomes a permanent part of the company's immigration compliance profile. The Immigration and Naturalization Service's evaluation of the company's current and future applications will take into account prior filings—whether they were made before or after the act became effective. Senior management, therefore, will have to live with the representations made in all filings.

In this strict new world of American business-visa law, exaggerated boilerplate claims such as "He's critical to the operation of our division" will not stand up to INS review, especially if after two months the employee is gone and the division continues to function smoothly. Given the potential for a company to be tainted by past filings, it is now advisable, if not necessary, to conduct an internal audit of prior immigration filings in order to calculate potential exposure.

In short, business-visa and compliance procedures will become a constant corporate concern. The steady stream of expected litigation and regulation changes will require permanent channels of coordination and centralization among top management, legal counsel, and personnel departments.

In the same way that discrimination, tax, securities, and other areas of government regulation have become routine responsibilities of corporate management, so, too, have immigration and business-visa matters.

Mr. Lataif is the partner in charge of immigration law in the Washington, D.C., office of an international law firm.

PROTECTING A FOREIGN BOSS
FROM THE INS
. . . .

by *Lawrence P. Lataif*

In the summer of 1988, a major U.S.-based hotel chain found itself in need of a controller following the unexpected resignation of the incumbent. No U.S.-based replacement was available, so the foreign conglomerate that had recently acquired the hotel chain decided to send a senior finance executive from London to supervise the accounting function temporarily. The chain's vice president for human resources had to deliver the news that it would take one to three months to get a work visa. Headquarters did not take the news well.

By contrast, in January 1989, a large California-based consumer electronics firm developed an unexpected vacancy when a senior vice president in the United States suddenly became incapacitated. An executive from the firm's overseas parent was able to fly to California within two days to take charge of the division. When the foreign company had bought the California firm, it had anticipated just this kind of problem and put in place an "E visa program" for top executives, along with a "Blanket L program" for other executive and managerial transferees. When a European was tapped to fill the position at the California company for the next several years, he was sent to the United States under an L-1 visa obtained in *one day* under the Blanket L program.

While this alphabet soup of visas may seem like a mix that most managers would rather avoid, immigration issues of the type mentioned above are very relevant to every U.S. business that is foreign-owned or that may become foreign-owned, as well as to domestic companies with substantial international operations.

While it would be helpful to know the exact number of U.S. companies owned by foreigners and their total number of employees, no such figures exist because there are no federal reporting requirements. However, an article by Victor J. Riley, Jr., in the November-December 1989 issue of *Chief Executive Magazine* states that purchases of U.S. firms by foreign companies in 1987 totaled $42 billion. In 1988, the British alone spent more than $32 billion to acquire four hundred U.S. companies. Foreigners accounted for about 20 percent of all takeovers in the United States in 1989. In Cleveland alone there are a hundred and forty-one foreign-owned firms. Approximately four hundred foreign banks are operating in the United States today.

These foreign owners are discovering the importance of

being able to move trusted senior people into the United States quickly to respond to unexpected developments. Ironically, foreign companies that espouse autonomous and independent functioning of their U.S. subsidiaries are most vulnerable, for it is these companies that are least prepared for unexpected high-level vacancies.

U.S. managers often cope with the shock of foreign acquisition by embracing the offer of autonomous operation whole-heartedly. The foreign owners and executives are under-standably reluctant to be offering autonomy on the one hand and appearing to be preparing to sent replacements with the other. Little attention is therefore paid to visa issues by either side at the time of acquisition.

But when an unprepared foreign parent decides it does need to send an executive over, there is likely to be shock and disbelief when it learns that work visas did not become available on demand when the U.S. company was acquired. Acquisition documents running hundreds of pages typically make no mention of visa issues for the acquiring owners or executives. When the inconvenience of this omission sinks in, U.S. management is likely to be held accountable.

What's a manager to do when faced with the prospect of foreign ownership? The following practical suggestions should help.

- *Raise the issue of immigration with foreign executives and management—and do so at the earliest opportunity.* When posed in terms of "How can we maintain the maximum flexibility to deal with unforeseen situations?" the foreign owners will be very appreciative. They realize much better than Americans the importance of arcane U.S. visa requirements, and the manager who raises this issue is likely to be perceived as savvy by the new foreign owners.
- *Suggest putting in place special corporate programs to facilitate the temporary transfer of foreign managers and executives.* The most useful of these are a Blanket L-1 program for intracompany transfers, an E-1/E-2 program

for treaty traders and treaty investors, and an H-3 training program. In conjunction with the array of individual visa petitions available, these programs will speed up dramatically the transfer of key personnel.

* *Centralize control of your company's current business-visa cases.* For a company that's not foreign-owned, a routine immigration mishap may be only a minor annoyance. However, for foreign owners these mishaps can cause serious delays if the Immigration and Naturalization Service scrutinizes the company's every visa application. By taking control of immigration filings, U.S. managers will be perceived as helpful and understanding. This is particularly important given the often-perceived cultural gap between U.S. managers and new foreign owners.

* *Make certain you are complying with the Immigration Reform and Control Act of 1986.* The act requires that every U.S. employer comply with certain recordkeeping requirements for every employee, whether alien or citizen. While the act's audits and enforcements have not been massive, they can be very troublesome to foreign owners if they result in immigration officials concluding that the company is playing fast and loose with the immigration laws.

These suggestions can't guarantee a harmonious relationship between U.S. managers and foreign owners, but they can go a long way toward achieving the shared goal of harmonious relations.

Mr. Lataif is the partner in charge of immigration law in the Washington, D.C., office of an international law firm.

HOW TO DEAL WITH THE SOVIETS

. . . .

by John Goodchild

T he *1989 joint* venture agreement between the Soviet Union and a consortium of U.S. businesses—Chevron Corporation, Eastman Kodak Company, Johnson and Johnson, RJR Nabisco, Archer-Daniels-Midland Company, and Mercator Corporation (which is also the consortium's merchant banker)—is expected to lead to U.S. investment of between $5 billion and $10 billion over the next fifteen years. The question is no longer whether businesses in the non-Communist world will be dealing with the Soviet Union: They are. And investments in the Soviet Union will be growing. The only question remaining is, what should the ground rules be for trade?

In my position as an advisor to a number of prominent CEOs—some of whom are contemplating Soviet ventures—I find myself fluctuating between two points of view: My capitalistic instincts say go, but my experience warns me to be cautious.

Because of these mixed feelings—shared by many of my colleagues—I've come to see the wisdom of adopting a set of rules to guide us in dealing with the Soviets. What I have in mind are the Slepak principles—seven rules of conduct to help American businesses do it right. Named after Vladimir Slepak, a founding member of the original Helsinki monitoring group in Moscow, the Slepak principles assert that if we're going to the Soviet Union to make a profit, we ought to lay the groundwork for something enduring. In business parlance, developing a solid market share should be a bigger concern than immediate profit.

It's important to remember that the old-line Soviet leader-

The Slepak Principles

American companies engaged in commerce with the Soviet Union:

1. Will not produce goods or provide services that replenish the Soviet military.

2. Will not use goods or products manufactured by forced labor in the Soviet Union.

3. Will safeguard Soviet employees prone to hiring or dismissal based upon politics, religion, or ethnic background.

4. Will decline to participate in a commercial transaction if the place of work is a Soviet-confiscated religious edifice.

5. Will ensure that methods of production do not pose an irresponsible physical danger to Soviet workers, neighboring populations, or property.

6. Will refrain from making untied loans to the Soviet government—loans which may be used to subsidize Soviet non-peaceful activities.

7. Will attempt to engage in joint ventures with private cooperatives rather than institutions connected directly to the Soviet state.

---

ship does not have the support of the people, as demonstrated by the humiliation of so many Communist Party pros in the recent elections. We don't want to be seen associating with the most conservative Soviet officials, who are being shunned by their own people. We also don't want to be seen collaborating with a system that sometimes jacks up the price of American imports tenfold, making ourselves the targets of consumer indignation.

Circumventing that system is a big job, however, because the old-timers still run most of the show. It's important to recall that American businessmen generally do not deal with Soviet businessmen, but with agents of the Soviet government. That's why rule number seven of the Slepak principles, for example, suggests that American businesses "will attempt to engage in joint ventures with private cooperatives rather than institutions connected directly to the Soviet state."

Established in May 1988 as part of Mikhail Gorbachev's *perestroika*, the new cooperatives are self-governing businesses allowed to keep their own profits. They are the closest thing to private enterprise in the Soviet state. According to Soviet economists, the private co-ops now represent 1 percent of the Soviet GNP, but are expected to represent 10 percent to 15 percent of GNP in ten years. The problem is that when they begin to compete too successfully with state-run enterprises, they are either closed down by the authorities or taxed to death. Supporting the co-ops would mix ethics with good business.

In fact, with human rights and corporate responsibility so keen a topic these days, the remaining six rules of the Slepak principles alert American businessmen to the wisdom of combining American business acumen with American values. American businessmen must win the support of the Soviet consumer by eschewing joint ventures with Soviet agencies that employ slave labor, that hire or fire on the basis of bigotry, and that use confiscated churches and synagogues as places of business.

If we're after an enduring business relationship with the Soviet Union, our best bet is to place ourselves on the side of the people. Read "people" as in "consumers."

Mr. Goodchild is president and chief operating officer of the Philadelphia-based communications company, the Weightman Group.

WILL BUSINESS EVER GET BACK
TO USUAL IN CHINA?
. . . .
by A. J. Robinson

I*n June of* 1980, I spent six months traveling around China researching and writing case studies for China's first business school in Dalian. I have vivid impressions of a country which was thirsting for knowledge and trying so hard to catch up.

Since then, I have participated in the creation of Shanghai Center—a $200-million multiuse project in the middle of China's largest city, featuring a hotel, apartments, an exhibition hall, and retail and office space. It has not been easy: Almost five years of off-again, on-again negotiations followed by three years of construction.

While engaged in this project, I have witnessed the transformation of a nation—from a colorless, ambivalent people to a well-informed, ambitious society eager to catch up with the rest of the world. I have also witnessed the start-up of our own venture, the transfer of over forty expatriates and their families to Chinese soil. When complete, the project will employ over sixty expatriates and fifteen hundred local Chinese. Our group became part of China's most cosmopolitan urban environment. We even put a banner on top of our building welcoming Gorbachev to Shanghai!

We all watched in amazement student protests in 1986 and 1987. With the rest of the world, we were moved by the dramatic, nonviolent demonstrations in Tianamen Square. Could this really be China? Free speech? Free assembly?

I left Shanghai on the morning of the Beijing massacre. What went on the rest of that week will be debated for years. Was China really close to revolution? Civil war? Will we ever know? Had our hopes for China been wrecked? Or had we all just been terribly naive, witnessing for the first time on our television screens a scenario of government brutality and its subsequent cover-up that has been committed on a grander scale many times before?

It's pretty obvious that the Chinese leadership has risked its image with the world, its growing ties with the United States, and its relationship with its own people in order to consolidate its control over the society. How long that control will last and in what form is anybody's guess at this point. Chinese government officials, as a rule, do not respond to ultimatums, but we must make our disappointment and concern known to our Chinese friends in a frank and candid manner. If we don't, we will seem to be condoning the actions of the government. One thing is certain: We are not going to change the current climate by sitting on the sidelines, merely bemoaning recent events.

Our company had four criteria that had to be met before we returned to China. I suspect that other companies had similar conditions.

1. We did not return until we were persuaded that the safety of our expatriate workers could be guaranteed.
2. We had to be assured that China offered us a stable and productive environment for our work.
3. Our Chinese partner had to advise us to come back.
4. Finally, we received an official statement from the local municipality stating that the city was safe and open to foreign interests.

But Chinese leaders are clearly anxious to draw business back to the country and may be willing to concede a few points in order to do so. Before returning, or for those contemplating or negotiating new deals, consider the following:
- *Expand the terms of your venture.* All China ventures—be they cooperative or joint ventures—have a limited term, some as short as five years. The Chinese govern-

ment overnight could ease current investors' concern worldwide if it unilaterally doubled the term of every foreign venture in the country.

- *Negotiate a reduction in your venture's taxes.* Many provinces and cities have the ability to waive certain administrative taxes. What better time to ask? Again, the government could unilaterally reduce taxes in the joint venture and cooperative venture laws by as much as 20 percent across the board in an effort to appease investors. In addition, what better way to attract foreign workers back to China than to reduce by 50 percent the amount of personal income tax they pay in the PRC?
- *Ask for more control in the management of your venture.* Many Sino-foreign joint ventures are hampered by bureaucratic decision-making processes which tie the foreign manager's hands in many routine matters. Now may be the time to push for better control.
- *Ask your partner, and foreign trade officials, for help in solving the foreign exchange conversion problems that almost every venture faces.* That is, extract some guarantees and assurances in your contracts so that earned local currency can be reasonably converted and remitted efficiently.
- *Encourage officials to undertake a "Promote China" campaign aimed at tour operators, businessmen, and tourists alike.* Consider travel incentives, government advertising, and other promotional methods in selling a safe, stable image of the country.
- *Urge officials to make special appeals to overseas Chinese (particularly in Hong Kong, Taiwan, Singapore, and the United States) not to give up on the homeland.* China desperately needs the emotional support, capital, ingenuity, and good favor of these communities outside of China. Their confidence must be restored quickly and dramatically with concrete programs so as to reduce the disappointment, frustration, and anger that most are feeling.

Specific programs, not just rhetoric, should be implemented.

All of the above advice may fall on deaf ears of the present government, but it's worth a try.

We are all worried about China. But so many times I have heard colleagues, both in and out of the government, tell me that never again will they suffer what they collectively went through during the Cultural Revolution. The next generation in China deserves a better chance than the last. We in the West should not turn our backs on this country. Those of us who think we know China should hang on. We may yet be proved right.

Mr. Robinson is executive vice president of Portman Overseas, an international real estate firm in Atlanta.

A DAMN YANKEE
CAN MAKE IT ANYWHERE
. . . .
by Jay R. Tunney

On a hot, humid Saturday not long ago, about three hundred well-wishers gathered at the main outlet of my Hobson's ice cream franchise in Seoul to celebrate one year of its being alive. Some people had told me it never would open. Others said it wouldn't last six months. I often wondered myself.

When the regional tax office came with ten men and ripped down my thousand-dollar banner, claiming it was illegal, and when the Korean bureaucracy turned down the tenth appeal to import Hobson's flavorings needed to manufacture the premium ice cream, I was angry. Another time, a second-echelon bureaucrat almost forced me out of business before I even opened. But when the same government authorities extended my deadline to take on a Korean equity partner, I was relieved.

These mixed feelings of frustration with and gratitude toward the authorities are part of the everyday life of a foreigner doing business in Korea. In fact, such contradictions are what seem to make the Korean world go round. A Western businessman needs to be ready for them. Here are a few hard-learned facts of Korean business life:

- *Don't expect instant success. Gear your thinking to the long term.* My first objective was to understand what motivates Koreans to buy Western-style consumer products. What I discovered was a tradition-bound suspicion of foreigners, especially foreigners who peddle foreign products. Success, I learned, has to be a grinding-it-out process of years, not weeks, with the hope that the quality of the product will win out.

This disinclination toward foreigners will change as more Koreans travel abroad to see and touch the world, and as more foreigners are seen dwelling easily in their midst. Koreans interact more easily with Westerners than do other Asians, possibly because Koreans and Westerners tend to share such personality traits as spontaneity and a lively sense of humor and fun.

- *Tread the political waters carefully.* Influential Koreans and expatriates deny the significance of anti-Americanism because responsible people in Korea feel pro-American. But anti-Americanism is significant. I see it daily in the Korean customers who pointedly interrogate our counter help, questioning why and how an American should be allowed to make money off hard-working Koreans.

Another example is when I put my children behind the counter, thinking it would add a certain American flair. But I noticed many Korean customers were unnerved to see them there, as though it were not a foreigner's place.

Members of the younger generation don't remember the anguish of the Korean War, nor do they sympathize with the gratitude their elders bestow on Americans for helping save them from Communism. They want their own identities in a new Korea. They do not want foreigners setting the pace.

- *Keep an open door and an open ear to labor.* The visible, often violent labor battles plaguing Korea contradict the tradition of a work force motivated by gratitude to a benevolent, paternalistic employer. That old Confucian ideal has given way to new democratic ideas of organized labor rights. That does not mean, however, that labor strife is inevitable.

In my still-growing fast-food operation of twenty employees, labor disputes don't exist. I am a working and participating boss who personally tends to the employees' private needs and problems. The atmosphere is kept informal; there are no closed doors, no secrets.

On a much larger scale, such a paternalistic structure still can be followed in Korea. The clearest example is Samsung Group, the largest company in Korea, where there have been no labor problems, because of the company's sensitivity and attention of maintaining harmony and a high level of motivation among company personnel. Properly motivated, the Korean labor force is one of the most productive in the world, and the expatriate executive should not lose sight of this despite the current labor problems.

- *Handcuff your lawyer and follow the spirit, not the letter, of the contract.* Foreign businesses find it most difficult to adjust to the interplay between written contracts and personal relationships. Because personal relationships, not legal contracts, guide their behavior in society, Koreans prefer to develop closeness with foreigners before dealing with them. I spent sixty hours over three and a half months negotiating a partnership with a large Korean food-processing company. The first third of the time was spent getting to know one another, going out to lunch, dinner, etc., to see if we could live together from a "personal" standpoint. Koreans want to be friends so that if conditions or circumstances should change the original premise of the agreement, they can improvise.

- *Consumerism in the land of thrift is new and sometimes threatens old ways*. For the first time in Korea's recent history, domestic consumption had exceeded export consumption, 48.7 percent to 48 percent. With export growth slowing and consumption at home exploding, foreign businesses should keep in mind that local demand is increasingly the engine of Korea's continuing rapid development. (Korea is Asia's second-largest domestic market after Japan.) This turnabout has been propelled by an average urban household income of twelve thousand dollars a year (compared with only sixteen hundred dollars in 1975) and a strengthened won, making Korean exports more expensive and imports cheaper.

The inherent contradiction of all this, however, must be considered. The new consumerism puts pressure on Koreans to behave contrary to all they've been taught and trained to think over centuries: the Confucian values of moderation and thrift. Suddenly there is a new generation that enjoys shopping and instant gratification. There even is modest wealth among the working classes because of recent hefty wage settlements. There is more leisure time: Workweeks have been reduced to forty-four hours from fifty-five. For foreigners, tapping into this expanding market can mean opportunity, but beware of the pendulum swinging back.

- *If you don't have any teeth, use your gums*. The government's liberalizing policy toward imports beckons foreign merchants of consumer goods. These new businesses provide jobs for Koreans and provide a certain joy to people's lives while raising their standards of living. Koreans are beginning to believe that they don't lose by importing. They gain by learning foreign technology, designs, and know-how, which they can absorb into their can-do culture. It's the same culture that provided the spectacular 1988 Olympics, the same one that proclaims "do it even if it is impossible," and "if you don't have any teeth, use your gums." One can think of no better formula for success than such an attitude . . . even for a foreigner.

Mr. Tunney has spent most of the past twenty years in Korea, Hong Kong, Burma, and Japan.

JAPANESE STRATEGY WAS
MADE IN THE UNITED STATES
. . . .

by Sam Kusumoto

A*merican managers continue* to flock to Tokyo and Osaka, searching for the business secrets that many believe have given Japan a competitive edge over American products. All this activity puzzles knowledgeable Japanese who realize that the secrets of Japan's economic success originated right here in the United States.

W. Edwards Deming is an American not nearly as well known in this country as he is in Japan. In fact, since 1950, Japan's most prestigious industrial award has borne Mr. Deming's name. Mr. Dening is known in Japan not only for the impact his quality control principles have had on raising the standards of Japanese industrial products, but also for his role in furthering close economic ties and improved understanding between the two countries.

Qualifying for the Deming Prize means measuring up to the tough standards Mr. Deming set for "total quality control"—an ironclad commitment to quality by top management along with an effective network of quality control circles and an employee suggestion system. The pervasive use of statistical methods, employee and subcontractor education geared to improved performance and product, and a strong customer orientation are also required. Companies typically invest three to five years in upgrading operations just to be deemed worthy of applying for the Deming Prize.

In the postwar era, Japan had a reputation for exporting cheap, shoddy goods. In part because of adherence to Mr. Deming's principles, the high standards of Japanese products have since won a dominant role in many international markets. Toyota's pursuit of quality has helped it in seizing nearly 50 percent of Japan's domestic auto market and in pursuing 10 percent of the world market.

The management principles that Mr. Deming has preached and Toyota Motor has practiced so successfully in Japan are just beginning to catch on in America. Officials at Ford Motor Company, for example, have applied such Deming principles as statistical quality control, long-term operating budgets, and close relations with suppliers to the development of "Team Taurus." The resulting award-winning car sparked a turnaround that has made Ford the most profitable of the major American auto companies.

Donald E. Petersen, Ford chairman, describes himself as a Deming disciple. He told Mary Walton, author of *The Deming Management Method* (Dodd, Mead, 1986): "We at Ford are committed to his principles, particularly to the ethic of continuous improvement and the involvement of all employees."

The "team concept" has also caught on at General Motors Corporation, under the name "simultaneous engineering," and at Chrysler Corporation, where it's known as "process-driven design." At GM, where Mr. Deming has worked with both the Fiero and Cadillac divisions, his principles have been incorporated into a training film entitled *Road Map to Change*.

The concept involves getting representatives from every area of the company—design, engineering, manufacturing, marketing, finance, and even suppliers—working together simultaneously rather than sequentially in developing a new product.

Mr. Deming is scornful of efforts to blame labor for shoddy

goods or to achieve quality control through end-of-the-line factory inspection. He insists that quality control must be applied at every step of the process from design to delivery.

He is critical of American management's absorption in hostile takeovers, short-term profits, annual performance appraisals, and management by objectives. He decries entrusting to freshly minted MBAs managerial roles that cry out for seasoned engineers. And he calls American management "retroactive," citing its dependence on reports and the avoidance of responsibility and leadership. He even warns against the adoption of quality control circles "detached from management's responsibility."

The latest trade figures from Tokyo indicate that American products still have a hard time competing with Japanese imports. The sharp rise in the value of the yen, which has forced up the cost of imports for Japan, has been a factor in the decline of Japan's overall trade surplus. But Japan's trade surplus with the United States remains high, primarily because Americans continue to pay what are now premium prices for Japanese imports considered superior in quality to domestic products.

We can't hide from the problem of America's growing trade deficit with Japan. It must be remedied. But protectionist legislation, for which there is growing support, won't improve the competitiveness of American products in the global market.

Some American observers of the success of Japanese manufacturers take a pessimistic view. They say the techniques that work in Japan would never work in the United States. They contend that the cultural differences between the countries are too great, Japanese workers are more dedicated, loyalty to the company and the work ethic are far stronger, and so on.

But the fact is that the real secrets behind Japan's competitive edge originated right here. And, as Ford and other

Deming clients have proved, the ideas that originated in America can work in America.

Mr. Kusumoto is president of Minolta Corporation, the U.S. subsidiary of Minolta Camera Company, Osaka.

COMPETING WITH THE JAPANESE
ON THEIR OWN TURF
· · · · · · · · · · · · · · · · · ·

by Julian Gresser and Andrew Osterman

H*aving your own* Japan operations is less expensive than you might think and more important than you might realize. Japan presents both a threat and an opportunity for small American high-technology companies. The threat is in the increasing Japanese competition in semiconductors, office automation, telecommunications, biotechnology, pharmaceuticals, and aircraft. The opportunity is equally apparent, although unfortunately few American high-tech companies have understood how to convert their most aggressive competitors into technological partners, manufacturing subcontractors, or captive customers.

There are several reasons for seriously considering starting operations in Japan:

Controlling the transfer of your technology. Most small American high-tech companies blithely file patents in Japan in the mistaken belief that such actions will protect rights to their technology. Such actions, in fact, create a dangerous exposure. The average patent in Japan takes about seven years to issue; in the interim, a small foreign company's technology is seriously at risk due to the weak legal protection of trade secrets and know-how, the requirement of early patent disclosure, and the uncertainties in translation and poor communication between Japanese and foreign patent lawyers. Small American companies must establish an active presence in Japan simply to police the transfer of their technology.

Reaping the benefits of Japanese manufacturing. Small U.S. companies increasingly can take advantage of rapid advances in factory automation and flexible manufacturing systems in Japan. By leveraging its Japanese manufacturing base, a U.S. high-tech company can gain the benefits of lower cost, higher quality, and faster throughput with virtually no capital assets at risk.

Developing the Japanese market. The principal deficiency of most U.S. high-technology companies' business plans is their failure to address the Japanese market. Few American companies today recognize the danger of permitting powerful competitors to strengthen their businesses in a captive home market. A presence in the Japanese market must be developed early before standards, distribution channels, and manufacturing commitments are made.

Most American executives write off Japan, citing lack of information and expertise about the country. Accurate information about the Japanese market, however, is readily available and inexpensive. Many American high-technology companies have some contacts in Japan, such as customers, distributors, licensees, and so forth. These are fertile sources of information. Moreover, any Japanese bank, securities house, or trading company with a U.S. operation also can provide inexpensive market research and other information.

Selecting a suitable partner before your exposure in Japan is vital. Most able, smaller American high-tech companies have supplier or sales relationships with large U.S. or Japanese companies that have already established a strong position in the Japanese market. These relationships should be carefully cultivated with an eye to launching Japan operations. Although most American companies focus narrowly on a joint venture when planning their operations in Japan, today there may be better structural solutions.

One solution would be for a small U.S. company to first

establish a 100-percent-owned subsidiary. Its primary initial contributions to the unit would be licensing of key patents, trademarks, know-how, and associated rights in the Japanese market.

Next, the U.S. company sells 10 percent to 20 percent of the stock of the subsidiary to the larger American or Japanese company with which it has discussed its intended Japan operations. The investing company receives for its investment a window on the parent company's basic technology, the expectation of shared profits, and the long-term prospect of capital gains, should the stock of the subsidiary itself be publicly traded at a later time. In consideration, the investing company also will contribute its customer lists and distribution network, and make office space available.

The next most important step is to find an experienced manager with the initiative to develop the business. He will have to understand the Japanese market, to be familiar with the parent's business and style, and preferably have a technical background. Ideally, he will later bring in a team of experienced middle managers.

All major companies in Japan rely extensively on subcontracting, and they themselves are subcontractors.

Production and process technology and manufacturing capacity are regularly brokered and bartered, not only within Japan but also offshore.

Creative subcontracting brings a number of benefits. First, it minimizes loss of control of the applications of an American company's fundamental technology and allows a Japan subsidiary to maintain its customers, market, capacity, cost structure, and distribution channels. Second, subcontracting allows a small American company to capture the benefits of Japanese manufacturing capacity without the substantial incremental investment of capital and human resources. The minimum investment to produce the first silicon wafer from a new state-of-the-art plant is $150 million and requires eighteen months and two hundred people. By subcontracting, the same wafer can be purchased at its competitive market price. Third, subcontracting permits the Japan subsidiary to avail itself of the highest skills for any task.

If it is well conceived and structured, there will be excellent chances for the subsidiary to sell another 20 percent to 30 percent of its stock to a leading Japanese venture capital company. Working capital is critical to foster growth in Japan, because most Japanese companies are heavily leveraged and cash-poor. Japanese venture capital companies today are stepping all over themselves for opportunities to invest in creative new enterprises. By associating itself with a well-known and well-established Japanese or American company, the Japan subsidiary will gain credibility, which is especially critical for success in Japan. Involving a Japanese venture capital company also permits the subsidiary to capitalize on this company's banking and other connections.

Most U.S. operations fail in Japan because senior management in the United States does not understand the requirements of the Japanese market and is unwilling to commit sufficient resources to support a Japanese operation. Any American company wishing to succeed in Japan must therefore appoint the brightest senior manager available and give this individual sufficient resources to support the effort. This person would need to visit Japan frequently to develop his understanding of the market, meet key customers, facilitate communication with the parent company, render support to management, and explore the ways in which the new Japan manufacturing base can reinforce the parent company's global operations.

By leveraging its assets creatively, a small American company can capture the benefits of Japan operations at an investment that is modest by any standard.

Mr. Gresser is a lawyer with offices in San Francisco and Tokyo. Mr. Osterman set up subcontract production for Intel Corporation.

GOING PUBLIC, JAPANESE-STYLE

· ·

by James E. Schrager and Julian Gresser

G*oing public on* the Japanese over-the-counter market (OTC) is among the most effective ways of raising large sums of money today. Avon's December 1987 public offering netted the company more than $200 million, and Shaklee Japan, Baskin-Robbins, and Nippon Avionics (a joint venture of NEC and the Hughes Aircraft division of GM/Hughes Electronics) have all raised in excess of $80 million each. Moreover, such offerings can boost the parent companies' stock prices on U.S. exchanges.

Given the relatively lax regulatory requirements for listing on Japan's OTC, and the prospect of enormous capital gains, many non-Japanese companies are hurrying to take advantage of that country's liberalized financial environment. Such haste, however, can spell trouble.

Although these offerings earned substantial capital gains for the parent companies, many are viewed in Japan with embarrassment, indicative, the Japanese say, of Americans' penchant for the easy fix. In one case, a parent company's need for funds to retire debt in the United States led to an offering in Japan that was ill-timed and consisted of far too many shares.

Our experience with presenting American offerings on the Japanese OTC has taught us that the issuer must focus its attention foremost on how its public listing will support its overall Japanese business. Capital gains will follow.

If properly implemented, public listing in Japan will reinforce important alliances with key financial institutions; expand an issuer's customer base; build the confidence of employees, officers, and directors, and help recruiting. The strengthened ties with Japanese financial institutions will greatly help the non-Japanese issuer raise low-cost debt in the face of a weakening dollar. Finally, promoting the issue properly can place the listing company and its products in the very best light before a broad spectrum of Japanese investors.

Investment bankers in the United States generally feel that the best time to make an offering is "as soon as the market is ready." The usual test of market readiness is when the total proceeds projected are about equal to the amount the company requires. But the Japanese underwriter's concept is different. The business objective of the issuer is matched by the Japanese government's concern for protecting the investor. The underwriter's principal concern is to answer all questions about the new offering raised by financial and industrial institutions, the Japan Securities Dealers Association, and the Ministry of Finance. An issuer's uncomplaining patience is assumed.

The major flaw of American offerings, say Japanese critics, is that they fail to build a proper foundation of *antei kabunushi*, "stable shareholders." Stable shareholders are those who will keep the stock of an issuing company for a long period, usually ten years or more. Such shareholders traditionally receive a 30 percent discount from the public offering price.

By holding stock, or making it available to an issuer on demand, stable shareholders help to buffer and support the market, particularly during periods of rapid economic change. In exchange for being secure shareholders, the banks and insurance companies stand to increase the volume of their transactions with the issuer as its business expands. Stock ownership associations for employees strengthen worker morale, and for some workers the prospect of capital gains upon retirement improves productivity.

Involving customers as stable shareholders can also be a useful means of consolidating key relationships. Some venture capital companies have begun to offer their expertise in financial analysis and business introductions, along with a promise not to sell their stock for several years, in exchange for an opportunity to buy at the secure-shareholder price.

In Japan, because the market is more consistent than in the United States, underwriters are able to be rather firm about price at a very early stage of the offering. In fact, price quotes from a prospective underwriter at the first meeting can be viewed as binding. In the United States, the market changes so fast that few long-term value questions can be calculated so precisely in advance. A careful approach to value considerations can make the difference between an ordinary and a spectacular price-earnings ratio under the official price formula set by the Japan Securities Dealers Association.

In the U.S., the doctrine of full disclosure, upheld by the courts and backed by the Securities and Exchange Commission, checks the misconduct of underwriters and issuers. In Japan, securities litigation is rare, and the protection of investors is largely the responsibility of the Ministry of Finance. In the case of the OTC, however, there has been a clear delegation to the Japan Securities Dealers Association—which, in turn, can delegate its power to the four major securities houses: Nomura, Daiwa, Nikko, and Yamaichi.

As a result, Japan's major securities companies have the unusual role of judging the suitability—in the public's interest—of the very underwritings for which they are responsible. This delegation of authority, combined with the Japanese practice of administrative guidance (a customary "paralegal" form of official governance), can create an atmosphere of great risk and uncertainty, particularly for the foreign issuer.

A confounding factor is that the "rules of the game" in Japan are rapidly changing. Indeed, the written rules are the ones that are subject to change, while the unwritten rules appear to be more inflexibly construed.

Despite the difficulties, the timing could not be better for a successful American company to consider public listing in Japan. The Japanese economy is booming, along with the Japanese stock markets (not nearly as decapitalized as the U.S. exchanges after the crash of 1987). Beginning in April 1988, for the first time in sixty-seven years, Japanese savers are being taxed on the hundreds of billions of yen they have salted away in bank accounts; this will free up much capital for the equity markets. Strong government-sponsored import policies will open new opportunities for foreigners and boost the prices of foreign issues, particularly of joint ventures. And new financial transactions can be crafted today in ways that would have been impossible a few years ago.

Going public may be the high road of access to Japanese industrial and consumer markets that twenty years of U.S. governmental wrangles with Japan have yet to open.

Mr. Schrager is vice president and chief financial officer of a trading firm in San Francisco. Mr. Gresser is a lawyer with offices in San Francisco and Tokyo.

JAPANESE EXECS:
FINANCIAL WIZARDS, THEY'RE NOT
· ·

by Scott Powell

Many American managers assume that the success of Japanese firms must be related to superior financial management and sophisticated approaches to capital budgeting. Part of the reason for this is the growing awareness of the degree to which many Japanese companies use financial leverage to raise capital.

While the proliferation of LBOs and junk bond financing has heightened concern about corporate American's overreliance on debt, the Japanese are comfortable with far more leverage than are Americans. Many of the successful Japanese multinationals carried debt levels in their early years that would be considered reckless by U.S. standards.

This tradition continues. The fast-growing Daiei and Seiyu Japanese mass-merchandise chain stores have debt-equity ratios three or more times those of Wal-Mart and K mart. And while corporate debt has been generally reduced in Japan as a result of the explosion of equity offerings in the booming Tokyo stock market, the largest and most successful trading companies carry huge amounts of debt. For instance, Mitsubishi and C. Itoh have debt-equity ratios of 324 percent and 479 percent, respectively.

One reason the Japanese seem better able to work at long-range goals than Americans may be that debt and bond holders tend to be more patient than stockholders. In contrast to American managers, whose feet are kept to the fire of quarterly profits demanded by Wall Street, Japanese managers have more latitude to pursue long-term growth strategies. This has allowed Japanese corporations to operate on lower margins and enabled them to take market share away from American corporations.

Japanese firms also are now spending increasing amounts on research and development—a key factor in securing and maintaining a competitive advantage over the long run. Today, the Japanese spend 20 percent of their gross national product on private research and development, compared with the 1.6 percent of GNP spent by Americans. The reverse was true just fifteen years ago.

But all this should not lead to the conclusion that financial management is the key to success in Japan. In fact, there are relatively few business schools in Japan, and Japanese corporate heads are less concerned with quantitative modeling and the intricacies of financial management than are Americans. Ironically, this may be one of the hidden strengths of Japanese business, according to Wharton professors Toshiaki Taga and N. Bulent Gultekin, who presented their research findings at the 1989 annual meeting of the Association of Japanese Business Studies in San Francisco.

While a visiting researcher at the Japanese Ministry of Finance, Mr. Taga prepared and sent out a questionnaire to a sample of two hundred publicly owned nonfinancial corporations listed on the Tokyo Stock Exchange and included in the Nikkei average. The survey specifically sought to query Japanese managers on how they estimated the cost of funds and how they made decisions on capital projects. In principle, capital budgeting is fairly straightforward: Corporations seek to invest in projects that will break even in a reasonable period of time and generate a positive cash flow, taking into account adjustments for risk and the time value of money. However, because there is no one right way to assess risk and determine the outcomes of future cash flows, managers rely on different techniques for capital budgeting.

The four most commonly used techniques are payback period, return on investment, internal rate of return, and discounted cash flow analysis. Capital budgeting techniques in U.S. corporations have become increasingly sophisticated, shifting emphasis from calculating payback period and return on investment to more elaborate models of calculating the internal rate of return and the discounted cash flow.

The survey results that trickled in puzzled Mr. Taga. He attributed the vagueness of answers concerning questions on financial management to traditional Japanese evasiveness regarding proprietary information. So Mr. Taga followed up his survey research with interviews. To his surprise, he found that Japanese managers were confused about many basic concepts concerning financial management.

For instance, most thought the weighted cost of capital is not the average of debt and equity, but rather a figure that was higher than both. Over 60 percent of those surveyed indicated that they performed risk analysis intuitively or subjectively, rather than by applying some objective quantitative calculus. Fifteen percent indicated that they didn't bother to make any adjustments for risk whatsoever.

Compared with American managers, the Japanese compute their cost of capital by more simplistic and sometimes incorrect methods with insufficient appreciation for the time value of money. While American corporations must pay considerable heed to credit ratings and attitudes of creditors in determining long-term debt levels, Japanese corporations generally have closer and more supportive relationships with banks, which are willing to extend credit despite high debt-equity ratios.

Similarly, Japanese corporate managers can count on fairly supportive stockholders, so long as the managers maintain the level and continuity of dividend payments. And Japanese stockholders, unlike those in the United States, seem more concerned with investing than trading.

The main financial concern for most Japanese managers is simply that investment projects break even, and soon after generate a positive cash flow. Implied in all this is that Japanese firms generally are leaner at the top than U.S. corporations.

Japanese management is more focused on the human elements of business success—the organization and motivation of people involved in research, development, production, and marketing—and less concerned with financial number crunching and paper pushing. While Japanese businesses do have some advantages over their American competitors because of cultural factors and because of structural and institutional differences that give them a lower cost of capital, their greatest strength lies not in finance, but in their superior management of human resources.

Mr. Powell is a fellow at the Hoover Institution, Stanford University.

IF THE JAPANESE BEAT YOU OUT,
DON'T CREDIT THEIR SALES FORCE

. . . .

by Robert White

J apanese companies' vaunted success at home and abroad can be attributed to a combination of factors (not the least of which is unduplicated marketing acumen), but stellar salesmanship is not among them. Despite claims presented by Western protectionists that the Japanese have mastered the art of salesmanship (fair and unfair), Japanese companies are not particularly skilled at selling. Up to now, they didn't need to be. The demand was so clamorous and the products so good that the use of professional sales techniques would have been gilding the lily.

Marketing and persistence are the cornerstones of Japanese success at moving merchandise in domestic and foreign markets alike. Japanese companies are famous for studying markets with infinite care, then tailoring products to slide into the gaps as smoothly as a well-sanded piece goes into a jigsaw puzzle. With advanced production technology delivering high quality at attractive prices, how can consumers resist those made-in-Japan labels? And when the rare product fiasco has occurred, the Japanese have been quick to adapt the offending product until it finds a comfortable market niche.

Luck has also played a role in Japan's successful export thrust. When the energy crisis first struck, Japanese automakers were fortunate to be based in a small, resource-poor country that had always demanded compact, fuel-efficient cars. It gave them an incredible head start.

There are other reasons it has been unnecessary for the Japanese to acquire fine-tuned selling skills. I recently spoke with a sales manager from Mitsui Electric Sales Company, which imports General Electric refrigerators. He is now nearing retirement, and remembers how different things were twenty years ago when he was a salesman.

In those boom years, customers wined and dined him for the privilege of buying a GE refrigerator. His problem was that he couldn't supply enough products to meet demand. Long-standing relationships with dealers guaranteed a hefty allocation of space on their sales floors. In fact, most deals in Japan were consummated through such personal relationships.

But times have changed. That young salesman has long since become a manager, as have many of his peers. Today they are confronted with a sales environment far different from the halcyon climate they enjoyed in the 1960s. GE refrigerators now face competition from Matsushita, Hitachi, and Toshiba—all of which have tailored their appliances to the specific demands of the Japanese market while providing superb service.

Japan's once-insatiable consumer society is pretty well sated by now. Today's products must fill the concrete needs of highly sophisticated and discriminating consumers, and it's the salesman's job to match one to the other. When the product is high-tech his difficulty is compounded. The competition very likely has the next appointment on the client's calendar.

Many Japanese sales managers, who never had to face such challenges themselves, simply can't cope. They're sending their sales force into the fray without appropriate tools and training. The neophytes don't know how to qualify prospects or even determine where they are in the sales cycle, both of which are critical factors.

Relationship selling, which aims at overwhelming customers with visits and personal attention—including lots of tea drinking and inconsequential chitchat—is an ineffective and very expensive way to sell the goods. The "feature, advantage, benefit" approach, on the other hand, a classic in most primers of American salesmanship, requires no more than an efficient call or two to make the sale. With this technique, which is little utilized in Japan, the salesman acts as a consultant. After ascertaining that the client really needs the product, he points out the product's features, demonstrates how these features are better than what the competition is offering, and shows how these features will solve the client's specific problems.

It's my experience that Japanese salesmen know everything there is to know about features—they can go on talking features, features, features forever. But they often fail to determine the needs that this product can satisfy. Consequently, they are unable to discuss the benefits that are so decisive in closing the deal.

When the product is a sofa bed, a tricycle, or a bar of soap, consumers have little trouble putting it to work. But when they're wandering through Japan's maze of options in computerized workstations, laser copiers, or facsimile machines, the salesman had darn well better know how these products can satisfy individual clients' needs.

Office equipment maker Ricoh is one Japanese company that has learned this lesson, and its skillful application of the famous "puppy dog close" put Ricoh equipment in my office. Here's how the "puppy dog close" works: The pet shop owner says: "Just take that puppy home for a few days and see how it goes; then, if you're not satisfied, we'll be happy to take him back." Hearts stony enough to resist a wagging tail are few indeed.

This approach traditionally is saved for small, portable products, but Ricoh gave it a new scale. One day there was a big commotion in our office because a Ricoh salesman was wheeling a huge copy machine through the door. Had we ordered it! No. This was a cold call! The Ricoh salesman had done his research and knew his machine would beat the one we already had. So here he was with a free tryout offer and a couple of panting delivery boys. It's hard to say no to that kind of deal. (By the way, our previous copy machine had been purchased on the basis of relationships.)

Unfortunately, Ricoh is still the exception. While most Japanese companies listen carefully to their domestic and international markets, they don't pay enough attention to individual customers. In Japan's highly competitive domestic market, the time has come for a better approach.

Sales skills don't come naturally. Acquiring them will call for a vastly stepped-up commitment—from the top down and the bottom up—and investment in training by Japanese companies. But the Japanese have proved, over and over again, to be remarkably quick learners.

Mr. White is president of ARC International, a Tokyo-based sales and management-training company.

JAPAN'S GROWING LABOR PAINS
. . . .
by Jay S. Siegel

A merican managers have long envied the relatively tranquil quality of Japanese labor relations. But that tranquility is in jeopardy if Japan's booming economy begins to shrink.

What both labor and management in Japan want to avoid is a return to the past militancy of labor-management relations. For the first twenty-five years after the end of World War II, the Japanese suffered the same basic kind of adversarial labor-management combat as found in America. But in the early 1970s they decided that another way had to be found if Japan was to compete in the global economy looming on the horizon of the Pacific Rim. Since then the system of cooperative labor relations, with the most favorable of economic backdrops, has been nourished by both management and labor, helping to sustain unprecedented prosperity.

However, because of the appreciation of the yen and the nation's huge trade surpluses, Japan may be pricing itself out of a labor market that sees competition from places such as

South China, South Korea, and Singapore. There, labor costs are less than a third of the $12.06-an-hour average rate paid by Japanese manufacturers. The higher prices this implies for Japanese-made goods are beginning to hurt overseas markets, even though the goods continue to be of the highest caliber.

Japanese employers consequently will find it hard to go to the bargaining table in the same spirit of cooperation that has marked earlier years of negotiation. The resultant pressures upon both management and labor must inevitably pervade the talks and could result in discord not seen in Japan for many years.

In years gone by, Japanese labor unions were content to accept relatively modest increases in wages and benefits. But the rising cost of living and the fear of inflation have pushed the new Japanese Private Sector Trade Union Confederation, or Rengo, to its first crucial test. Increasing economic pressure means that national unions are no longer willing to settle for the modest national wage increases obtained in previous labor offensives. Instead, Rengo leaders say they will press for substantially higher wages, despite the campaign by the Japan Federation of Employers' Associations to target inflation as "public enemy number one."

Created in 1987, the super union (actually a federation of the biggest enterprise unions) was designed to bolster the sagging fortunes of a trade-union movement whose membership had fallen to a record postwar low of just under 30 percent of the nation's work force. Right now it looks as though Rengo's only course will be to assume a more militant position.

This also comes at a time when the Japanese are quietly beginning to restructure their economy and press for higher domestic consumption to take up the slack of falling export sales. This, however, will require more money in the hands of consumers and will bring about demands for higher wages, increasing the cost of goods produced for domestic consumption. The average Japanese family, already hard-pressed to meet daily living expenses, has enthusiastically welcomed the

NIC stores throughout Japan, where foreign-made goods are being merchandised at 20 percent to 30 percent discounts.

Larger manufacturing enterprises are already cutting back in new hiring in anticipation of such developments, with the most substantial impact in those industries that are heavily unionized. In the face of extensive "downsizing," Rengo and its smaller and older counterpart, the General Council of Trade Unions of Japan (Sohyo), will seek both job-security protection and higher wage increases. Heightening the pressure will be the inevitable consolidation or shutdown of production facilities, particularly by companies that have shifted production overseas to reduce labor costs. Companies such as Fujitsu and Sanyo Electric have made substantial overseas investments in manufacturing facilities in places such as Spain, where labor is cheaper and where they have access to the Common Market.

The Japanese thus are also trying to avoid the mistake made by American industry in the 1960s—particularly in the auto and steel sectors—that priced the industry out of the market because of high domestic labor costs. With the substantial appreciation of the yen, many major Japanese manufacturers took full advantage of their currency position by investing in U.S. facilities: Nissan, Honda, Toyota, and Minolta have all, for example, built American plants to reduce their overall cost of selling to the U.S. market.

Nevertheless, this well-designed globalization of production facilities means less need for high-cost operations at home. Any resulting wave of plant closings will put more pressure on Rengo and Sohyo to protect their members and further jeopardize the underpinning of the harmony concept. In such circumstances it is unrealistic to expect that trade unions can continue to maintain a posture of benign bargaining if management is no longer able to afford the luxury of guaranteed high-wage employment.

Nevertheless, the Japanese may indeed come up with an alternative. What they fear most is the direction that labor unions have been taking in neighboring South Korea. There, a wave of union militancy has seen bitter strikes hit several of the nation's largest employers, such as Daewoo Shipbuilding and Heavy Machinery Company, which was forced to give a 19.1 percent general wage increase plus a cash bonus to obtain a strike settlement. Moreover, for almost six days in June 1988, the chairman and ten other plant executives of Hyundai's Precision facility in Ulsan were held "hostage" by workers. This spectacle was highly reminiscent of earlier times in Japan and was surely on the minds of Japanese business leaders.

The powerful Japanese economic machine has conquered many difficult obstacles before. A recent visit left me with the impression that the Japanese have a sense of purpose about their future and what it will take to meet the challenge. But the question of whether the country's business leaders and their trade-union counterparts can maintain a spirit of cooperation in the face of new economic pressures remains to be seen.

Mr. Siegel, a management attorney in Hartford, Connecticut, was national chairman of the American Bar Association's Section of Labor and Employment Law.

LEARNING TO SOAR ABOVE
JET LAG'S DEPTHS
. . . .
by E. S. Auerbach

J*et lag is* the executive's mystery. It has spawned a cottage industry of experts who proclaim often complicated and esoteric methods to meet, if not beat, jet lag and travel weariness. Some of these experts recommend involved diets and behavior-change programs designed to counteract the sleeplessness, moodiness, and confusion that are among the phenomenon's effects. But as good as these cures may be, the business traveler often doesn't have to use them, and should rely on simpler and more predictable ways to combat the problem.

In fact, there is no way to beat jet lag and the fatigue of hard travel. But there are a few steps that will minimize wear and tear:

Take with you only what you can carry on board the plane. This is easier than it seems, particularly since business travelers usually stay at hotels that offer same-day laundry service. Travelers pack more than they need. One approach is simple, and it works: Lay out on a bed all the things you think you need. Then, arbitrarily pack between one-third and one-half of them. Take the absolute minimum and no more, and then use a good hanging bag. There are advantages. You will never lose your bag, and you will often save a great deal of time at the end of your trip. I recall arriving one Sunday at Kennedy Airport on a full TWA 747 within fifteen minutes of the arrival of two other TWA 747s. I was already in Manhattan while passengers with checked baggage were probably still watching the carousels.

There's another tangible benefit to taking only hand-held luggage. Immigration and customs officials will spot you as a professional traveler. If your experience is similar to mine, these overworked people will process you faster and let you speed onward to your hotel and bed.

Dress comfortably. If you look at the first-class or business-class compartment of a Qantas 747 flying from Sydney to San Francisco, you will see the passengers attired in old pants, loafers, and sweaters. Dress as you do in your den on a Saturday afternoon. There is no one to impress.

Eat lightly. At thirty-seven thousand feet, the air in a plane is thin and dry and your body works much harder at each function than at sea level. Watch how the stewardesses eat. They eat moderately and they work hard on the planes. Passengers will be well served to eat salad, fish, chicken, or fruit and to avoid heavy meats, starches, and sweet deserts. If you take a night flight, eat before you fly, then avoid the meal served, put on the eyeshades, and simulate a normal bedtime routine on the plane. It usually works.

Drink a lot. But only water and juice. Again, because of the dry air, one dehydrates quickly. So drink a glass of liquid hourly when awake. You will thank yourself upon your arrival. Drink no booze. A jet-lag hangover is a distinct happening that is long remembered.

Sleep. Take eyeshades, take a nonprescription sleeping pill, and ask the flight crew to nudge you in eight hours (or whenever you want to awaken). Many people believe they cannot sleep. Eyeshades help. So do the airlines. They usually show such bland movies that they work almost as well as sleeping pills.

Exercise before and during your trip. If you are a jogger, run before you fly. When you arrive and have slept, jog again. Jogging clothes take little space. If you are a swimmer, swim. Business hotels often have pools and gym facilities. Use them. Travelers who are fit have more endurance than those who are not.

Everything in moderation. At thirteen-course Oriental banquets I eat from each course, but only one or two chopsticks full of anything. I always drink the proffered sake, but only one thimbleful. Once the evening's social event is formally over, go to bed. Your hosts will know you have a full schedule and will be sympathetic. Sleep well and be rested for the next day's labors.

Don't make important decisions soon after your arrival. Plan your schedule to avoid heavy negotiations or serious decision making on the day of arrival and even the next day. This may mean traveling on weekends. But it's worth doing when you think of sitting across the table after jumping eleven time zones to face your well-rested opponent. President Reagan arrived in Geneva two days early for his meeting with Soviet General Secretary Mikhail Gorbachev in order to overcome jet lag. This is the rule in the U.S. State Department and could profitably be adopted by private industry.

Upon return to home base, be prudent. Spend the first day back with your family—it's worth it.

I have learned these techniques from experience and, by following them, found I can make a three-stop, round-the-world trip in ten days and not be dead on my feet the day after the trip's completion. These are easy steps that every traveler can follow. So let the ice cream topped with chocolate sauce and whipped cream pass you by and take another swig of Perrier. There will be lots of fish heads and white fungus soup to tempt you when you arrive at that big banquet on the other side of the world.

Mr. Auerbach is president of New York Life Worldwide Holding Company.